Long-Range Public Investment

Social Problems and Social Issues
Leon Ginsberg, Series Editor

Long-Range Public Investment

· THE FORGOTTEN LEGACY OF THE NEW DEAL ·

Robert D. Leighninger Jr.

THE UNIVERSITY OF SOUTH CAROLINA PRESS

© 2007 University of South Carolina

Published by the University of South Carolina Press
Columbia, South Carolina 29208

www.sc.edu/uscpress

Manufactured in the United States of America

15 14 13 12 11 10 09 08 07 06   10 9 8 7 6 5 4 3 2 1

Library of Congress Cataloging-in-Publication Data

Leighninger, Robert D., 1941–
    Long-range public investment : the forgotten legacy of the New Deal / Robert D.
  Leighninger Jr.
      p. cm.
    Includes bibliographical references and index.
    ISBN-13: 978-1-57003-663-7 (pbk : alk. paper)
    ISBN-10: 1-57003-663-2 (pbk : alk. paper)
    1. Public works—United States—History—20th century. 2. New Deal, 1933–1939.
  3. United States—Economic conditions—1918–1945. I. Title.
    HD3885.L45 2007
    332.67'252097309043—dc22
                                            2006026456

To Hal Swan (1960–2006)
of H. Anderson Photography

Contents

Illustrations

Figures

Tables

Series Editor's Preface

Modern social work, especially modern American social work, began with President Franklin Delano Roosevelt's Depression-era New Deal of the 1930s. Until that time social work programs, and social workers themselves, were employed by local and sometimes state social welfare programs, many of them voluntary and dependent on charitable contributions.

Those of us who teach and write about social work attribute much of what we now see as social welfare programs to that era in American government. Many of the services available to Americans are part of the 1935 Social Security Act, which, with its periodic amendments, administers and finances such fundamental programs as Old Age, Survivors, and Disability Insurance; Temporary Assistance for Needy Families (the replacement for Aid to Families with Dependent Children); Medicare; Medicaid; Supplemental Security Income; and many other services for children, families, and older adults.

Today the mass of employees who are social workers or who work in social welfare agencies are paid, in one way or another, by Social Security Act programs. The state human services are largely funded through the various titles of that act. And, through contracts and purchases of services, many private or voluntary agencies receive large portions of their support from Social Security Act funding. Children's homes, long-term care facilities for people with disabilities, and hospitals—listings of all these would be extensive—function with the support of the various programs of the Social Security Act and the organizations that implement its provisions.

As Robert D. Leighninger Jr. points out, books about the social services and economics of the New Deal are extensive. However, relatively little has been written about the long-term, physical contributions of that era. As Leighninger notes, many of the nation's auditoriums, schools, courthouses, prisons, zoos, parks, and myriad other facilities and buildings were built as part of the New Deal's relief efforts. I knew as a youth in San Antonio that the appropriately named Alamo Stadium, which was so much a part of our lives, was a New Deal project. For another example the Blue Ridge Parkway, which runs just a few miles from where I am writing this preface, covers six hundred scenic miles in North Carolina and Virginia and was a project of the Public Works Administration and the Civilian Conservation Corps. My office building is a converted school that was built by the WPA, along with the old post office and courthouse in Boone, North Carolina.

One local resident, having lived here longer than I, notes that repairs and restorations of those buildings are difficult because no one currently working understands the materials and construction techniques that were used to create them. Most of us do not give much thought to the long-ago contributions of the New Deal to the physical realities of our own communities, but they are profound.

These efforts were a combination of what the economist John Maynard Keynes might have called the "multiplier" and "leverage" effects—the "trickle up" and "trickle down" processes of stimulating the economy. They worked through the injection of public funds into the hands of people who had little or no money, having been impoverished by the Depression, and into the construction of public facilities, often through the labor of those same people.

Despite the extensive efforts and investments, little is known or written about the actual results of these efforts. This author points out that only one New Deal public works agency lasted more than ten years, and the actual building efforts took about six years. But the achievements of the New Deal construction projects then were and still are enormous.

Leighninger pursued this project for many years. Not only does he provide extensive and detailed notes on the public projects, he traveled the nation as a photographer and documented many of the projects, some having lasted for some seventy years since they were constructed.

The author not only describes what was done and what remains, he also places the investments of the New Deal in historic context with discussions of the ways in which American public buildings and infrastructure were and continue to be financed. In addition he discusses the relevant social policies that are associated with such investments. For a variety of complex social and economic reasons, these kinds of projects are no longer part of the conscious social assistance systems, although they may still function as such. For example, communities devastated by natural disasters, such as Charleston, South Carolina, by Hurricane Hugo in 1989, often become much more economically viable, in part because of public as well as private investment in recovery. In other words, as the title of this book suggests, these New Deal initiatives were not simply relief and recovery ventures but represent long-term investments in the United States.

Leighninger's book represents a major preservation of the physical investments of the New Deal. It makes information about some of the ways the Depression was addressed available to generations that know little about them. And with its excellent text, detailed timeline, and photographs, it provides a record that did not exist before it was written. We are proud to add this fine work to the Social Problems and Social Issues series of the University of South Carolina Press.

LEON GINSBERG

Preface

Long-range public investment is rarely discussed in public affairs. When it is, it is with skepticism or derision. Public works are defended in terms of immediate job opportunities. They are attacked as wasteful, pork-barrel spending. The fact that they might last seventy years as community assets is not part of the calculation. Yet examples of such investment surround us. They are products of the many public building programs begun in 1933 in the administration of Franklin Roosevelt. They may not have been conceived as long-range public investment, but it was soon apparent that they were. Therefore, contemporary thinking about public investment does not require speculation or conjecture. There are examples to inspect, a track record to examine. Long-range public investment is a reality.

The first purpose of this book, addressed in part 1, is simply to uncover this reality for inspection. Only one of the New Deal public works agencies lasted longer than ten years (see timeline, page xix). Their period of active building was closer to six years. Yet in this brief time they produced thousands of enduring contributions to community life. Schools and university buildings, courthouses and prisons, hospitals and clinics, waterworks and incinerators, parks and zoos, golf courses and tennis courts, stadiums and auditoriums, botanical gardens and museums, fairgrounds and farmers' markets, city halls and fire stations appeared almost magically. Few people, even historians, are aware of just how much was built and how much is still in use.

The second purpose is to begin a reappraisal of this investment. This is pursued in part 2. What can be learned that might be useful to current planning for public investment? None of the many New Deal building agencies was quite the same as another. They were designed for different purposes. Some worked better than others. Most were popular with some segments of the population, some wildly so. All had their critics, then and now. It is time for a new perspective on their successes and failures.

There are many books about the New Deal's economic philosophy (or lack thereof), about Roosevelt's political leadership and organizational style, about whether the New Deal helped end the Great Depression or made it worse, and about the political coalition that made the New Deal possible and has now all but vanished. In the midst of these arguments are the silent and largely forgotten physical accomplishments of the New Deal. They were vast in number. They were useful. Many of them are still being used. They must be reckoned with.

Analyses of the political organization and disorganization of the New Deal will henceforth have to include the fact that these peculiar programs, often held together with little more than twine and baling wire, produced concrete results that have outlived their birth struggles by seventy years and are continuing to function. Economic assessments of these programs can no longer end with what they cost at the time and what they did to accelerate or retard recovery from the Depression but will have to add calculations of their contributions to the health, education, recreation, civic administration, and cultural life of the country during three-quarters of a century.

There are also specific questions of public policy that the experience of New Deal public works can speak to. Can public works stimulate the economy more effectively than tax cuts? Is there a place for public jobs in the expansion and contraction of national employment? Who should build our civic infrastructure, and how should it be paid for? How do we distinguish useful, locally supported public projects from wasteful pork? New Deal public works programs gave us a legacy of not only useful structures but also useful ideas about how to construct them.

Acknowledgments

This project has covered many years and miles, and I've rarely lacked companionship. Foremost among my fellow travelers is my family. They have helped locate projects in the field and driven me to see them, proofread chapters and consulted on language, identified sources and checked facts, sat through endless slide shows, and rarely questioned my sanity. My children, Matt Leighninger and Maggie Hopkins, and their spouses, Pamela Swett and Ben Hopkins, my brothers, Dick and Jim, and their spouses, Sally and June, my sister-in-law Toni Hartrich, and my wife, Leslie, were unceasingly supportive even though they all have busy careers of their own and, in some cases, their own books to write.

Jeff Chapman and Larry Mankin of the Arizona State University Department of Public Affairs and Jason Scott Smith of the Harvard Business School read individual policy chapters. Emerson Baker, a Civilian Conservation Corps (CCC) veteran, edited not only the CCC chapter but several more. Michael Pagano of the University of Illinois–Chicago contributed expertise on municipal bonds. Linda McClelland of the National Park Service advised me on the CCC design process, and Paul Lusignan of the National Register stimulated my reappraisal of the U.S. Housing Authority. Park ranger Reed Engle shared his enthusiasm and research on the CCC in Shenandoah. The many hours I spent in the National Archives with the Public Works Administration (PWA) microfilm collection were made much easier and more enjoyable by archivists Bill Creech (downtown) and Gene Morris (College Park).

In addition to family members, other people have accompanied me chasing buildings: Judy Garrels in Charleston, Suzanne Levison and Bob Diller in Pasadena, and Jim Wolk in Philadelphia. I had many serendipitous encounters in the field with people who took time out to show me around: Eddie Heuston at Fair Park in Dallas; Cadet Garratt Jackson of the Citadel; Claudia Mathes and Kristi Gore at the Albuquerque Little Theater; Kris Staub of the Phoenix Homesteads Neighborhood Association; Beverly Jackson, Freeborn County historian, who grew up in Albert Lea Homesteads; Opal Jones and Sheila Durens of the Atlanta Housing Authority; Verna Mobley, community organizer, and Mrs. Elizabeth Webb, an original resident of University Homes, Atlanta; and a woman in a pickup truck at Bosque Farms who directed me to Richard Melzer, University of New Mexico historian, who put me in touch with Joan Arvizu, whose home is pictured in chapter 9.

There are others whose names I failed to record but who are no less appreciated. Fieldwork is full of delightful surprises.

One of the stories that did not fit into this book was the pursuit of CCC architect David Fried, the mysterious modernist of Crystal Lake State Park. My cousin, Dr. Alice Wright; Sally Pollak of the *Burlington Free Press,* Emerson Baker, Ed O'Leary of the Vermont Department of Forests, Parks, and Recreation, and Brian Lindner, who likes to tell people he was conceived in the Mount Mansfield base lodge, another CCC project designed by Fried, all shared my enthusiasm for the mystery and my appreciation of Fried's architecture.

Bill Barnes of the National League of Cities and Gail Radford of the State University of New York–Buffalo, in addition to reading chapters, were indefatigable sounding boards and unflagging morale boosters.

Leon Ginsberg improved my writing style and toned down my rhetoric. Paul Stuart made many useful contributions to the entire manuscript. Hal Swan of H. Anderson Photography helped me select slides. Barry Blose of University of South Carolina Press has been much more than an editor. His contributions to the book can be found on or behind almost every page. I deeply appreciate his long-range investment.

Mike Desmond, Louisiana State University School of Architecture; Charlie Grenier, retired sociologist turned apprentice New Deal mural restorer; Karen Kingsley, Tulane School of Architecture; John Stuart, Florida International University School of Architecture; and Yolanda Burwell, East Carolina University School of Social Work were very early supporters of this work.

None of these people can be blamed for the likely defects in this project. But if necessary, I'll find someone.

New Deal Timeline

Civilian Conservation Corps: 3/31/33–7/1/42

Federal Emergency Relief Administration: 5/12/33–12/35

Tennessee Valley Authority: 5/18/33–present

Public Works Administration: 6/16/33–6/30/42

Civil Works Administration: 11/9/33–3/30/34

Federal Housing Administration: 6/27/34–present

Resettlement Administration: 4/30/35–9/1/37

Works Progress Administration: 5/6/35–6/30/43

Farm Security Administration: 9/1/37–8/14/46

U.S. Housing Authority: 9/1/37–1/5/42

Federal Works Agency: 7/1/39–47

| 1933 | 1934 | 1935 | 1936 | 1937 | 1938 | 1939 | 1940 | 1941 | 1942 | 1943 | 1944 . . . . . 1946 | 1947 |

Part One
PROGRAMS

Chapter 1

▪ PUBLIC WORKS IN AMERICAN HISTORY ▪

The idea that public works could be used to combat an economic depression was not born in the New Deal. It was part of what one historian has called a "drawn-out process by which industrial society sought and seeks to come to terms with the conditions that produced it."[1] The idea developed through three historical eras involving three levels of government and an equal number of phases in economic theory. Public works were used first to promote the commercial economy by the states in the early part of the nineteenth century, second to solve social problems of cities in the second half of the century, and finally to allay unemployment at the federal level in the twentieth century. Paralleling the changes in attitudes toward public works were changes in attitudes toward business cycles, which were first seen as inevitable, then as amenable to tinkering, and finally as requiring frontal assault.

The use of public works to strengthen the nation is almost as old as the nation itself. John Quincy Adams and other early leaders saw "internal improvements" such as roads, canals, harbors, and lighthouses as a means of aiding commerce and uniting the widely separated colonies. If these efforts were paid for by taxes, they were also symbolic of this unity: the contributions of the many to support the whole. If they were paid for by deficit spending, according to Alexander Hamilton, this had other benefits. Those who financed the debt now had a stake in the well-being of the government. Also the government had an opportunity to establish strong credit by paying off the debt. The nation would then know that it could command resources if and when it needed to borrow.[2]

Canals, turnpikes, and railroads were large undertakings, and private investors were scarce, so if such things were to be built, the government had to do it. Even if investment capital had been more plentiful, the risks involved in such projects would have made those who held it unlikely underwriters. The distances were vast, the forests dense, the rivers wild, and the indigenous occupants did not welcome the encroachment. A further risk attended the fact that these routes were pushing into places with no preexisting economic development. Government was the most likely candidate to take such risks.[3]

The federal government might seem the likely agent to begin linking the outposts of the new nation with dependable roadways and canals, but it did not happen that way. Founding fathers like George Washington and Alexander Hamilton favored national public works projects, but later political leaders like Andrew Jackson opposed them. Jackson believed that such projects would increase the influence of his enemies, the wealthy business interests. Southern states were afraid to do anything to strengthen the central government, because the power might be used eventually to deprive them of their "peculiar institution," slavery. But mostly the fear of the central direction of public works projects was grounded in regional jealousies.[4]

Thus the federal government was regularly blocked from financing public works. It did, however, create a very useful tool for it and other governmental units to use: the right of eminent domain. This allows the taking of private land for public purposes. Lodged in the Fifth Amendment and upheld by the Supreme Court in 1795, this cleared the way for public building at all governmental levels.[5] It is interesting that such a powerful instrument was used so early in the nation's history when suspicions of a strong central government were still widespread and, in fact, many people doubted the wisdom of having a federal government at all.

The states had fewer doubts about their own interests, so they began the first great era of public works with enthusiasm. Canals, turnpikes, and infant railroads proliferated. The Erie Canal was an international marvel. The economic benefits through reduced shipping costs were considerable. Even fiscal conservatives like George F. Will acknowledge that "infrastructure spending midwived modern America."[6]

Because state legislatures did not want to raise taxes to support these ventures, they sold bonds instead. They often went heavily into debt without the customary securities to back their bonds. The panic of 1837 brought this breathless expansion to a gasping halt. States stared at impending ruin, and their legislators soon insisted on constitutional limits to state borrowing power.[7]

But the need for public building remained. The action shifted to the cities, where industrialization and population growth were creating new problems. Cities, too, chose to borrow rather than tax. But they were borrowing for different reasons. In addition to trying to encourage business, they also had to provide the water, sewers, parks, schools, health facilities, and other public buildings needed by their growing populations, including many immigrants. The arena of public works now broadened considerably to address social as well as economic problems. Epidemics and devastating fires were only the most dramatic of many threats that cities now posed to all who lived in them. Health and safety required clean water, sanitation, and fire protection. Education and police protection were also essential.[8]

Cities built, incurred more debt, and in turn ran up against another national economic crisis. The depression of 1870 forced many of them to default on their loans. This brought the same response that the states experienced a generation earlier: debt ceilings.[9]

Thus both state and local governments entered the Depression of the 1930s with limited ability to borrow. Fiscal conservatives would say that their prior behavior had earned them these fetters. One can argue the early state investment in railroads was excessive. The problems of the cities were different. It is harder to see what cities should have done to avoid debt other than raise taxes or ignore their problems until fire, pestilence, or riot wiped them out. One might also ask whether those railroad investments might not have paid off well but for the intervention of a depression. When debt mounts, one solution is to forbid borrowing. But it is not clear that caps on borrowing were a true solution to a state's or city's problems.

The infrastructure needs of growing cities, of course, did not go away with the imposition of debt limits. So cities sought and found two ways around these restraints. This could be seen as further evidence of the perfidy of politicians or as recognition that some things needed to be done and ways had to be found to do them. One invention was the revenue bond; the other was the public "authority." The collateral for a revenue bond was income from the project being financed, such as a waterworks or a subway, and not the general tax revenues of the city. As such, the debt was not counted against the limit placed on the city's ability to borrow. The revenue bond was first used in the United States in 1895 but was not generally accepted until the late 1920s. The special "authority" was a quasi-governmental unit created to administer a particular facility, like New York's Triborough Bridge. It could issue bonds on its own.[10]

These devices provided a safety valve for the cities but could not meet all their needs. Education, police and fire protection, parks, libraries, and other services that did not generate revenue could not be funded this way. However, when the New Deal began and its agencies were frantically trying to get federal money put to work through state and local auspices, they found authorities handy.

The economic crises that first brought states and then cities to grief were manifestations of what were known to economists as business cycles, the ups and downs of economic activity. Orthodox economics at the turn of the twentieth century regarded these as inevitable facts of life. They should be expected even if they could not be predicted. Bust followed boom and was followed by another boom. Some people were hurt, some even wiped out, but nothing could be done about it. Trying to do something might disturb the natural order of things and cause more problems than it solved.[11]

But as the new century advanced, some economists and public administrators were beginning to question the orthodoxy of the business cycle theory. One of them was Herbert Hoover. As U.S. food administrator during World War I, he had managed a large governmental enterprise. As president of the Federated American Engineers' Society, he had conducted an investigation into waste in industry. He developed a certain skepticism of orthodoxy. Business cycles, he and others concluded, were not intractable. One of the tools that might be used to smooth them out was strategic timing of public works projects.[12]

Government intervention to provide infrastructure for commerce or health and safety was sometimes popular and often necessary but always controversial. Intervention in business cycles was also controversial, though untried. Government intervention in the economy in times of emergency, however, has a long history and wide acceptance. Wars and natural disasters usually produce demands for action without a lot of discussion of how the action will be paid for. They also offer periodic reminders of what can and cannot be accomplished by governments. The experience of the First World War was particularly influential in demonstrating that government could increase the productive capacity of the economy considerably. Cooperation between public and private sectors could achieve results that had not been thought possible before. More important, Hoover and others came to believe that well-planned government intervention *before* the emergency might soften the emergency when it inevitably arrived. This integrated the experience of wartime economy with the new approach to business cycles.[13]

The acceptance of government attention to unemployment is more recent than government investment in infrastructure, though not as recent as we might think. In a culture that stresses individual responsibility so strongly, it is understandable that it would take a while to realize that unemployment might be beyond an individual's control. In an agricultural society with land available for the claiming, what reason could there be for a healthy man or woman to be idle? Laziness was the logical explanation. Industrialism transformed the employment picture radically, but it was a while before logic caught up.

It took two depressions, one in 1870 and another in 1893, to convince people that one could be unemployed for reasons other than one's own failings. The eccentric but widely read economist Henry George wrote in 1879 about "enforced idleness." The founder of the Charity Organization Society (COS), Josephine Shaw Lowell, changed the focus of her organization from preventing the abuse of relief to providing new work-relief assistance. Edward T. Devine, another COS leader, argued that the causes of modern misery were economic, not moral. Throughout the Progressive era, according to Udo Sautter, ran a nagging fear that all was not right with industrial capitalism. Casualties of the system were increasing and along with them the conviction that something would have to be done, for the good of the system as a whole, to keep the victims functioning.[14]

Using public works to relieve unemployment was also not unknown prior to the Hoover administration. Various cities met the economic downturns of the late nineteenth century with work projects. The president of the American Federation of Labor, Samuel Gompers, asserted the right of guaranteed employment in 1893. The following year, Jacob Coxey's "army" of unemployed industrial workers marched on Washington with a similar demand. Washington Gladden, one of the founders of the social gospel movement that was to become an important influence on young Harry Hopkins, called for state-organized jobs.[15]

Their pleas were rejected but not because the potential importance of public works was being ignored. A presidential conference, organized and chaired by Hoover in 1921 while he was secretary of commerce, discussed the ability of public works to stimulate both production and consumption. Participants even drew charts of the multiplier effects. However, they were adamant that such projects had to be for "commercial" rather than relief purposes. They were equally convinced that this kind of activity properly belonged at the state and local level. The federal government accounted at best for only 10 percent of all public construction. Anything more would be an assault on the "ideals of American federalism."[16]

The stock market crash of October 1929 brought these ideas back to prominence. Unemployment had been rising throughout the late 1920s. The crash brought misery to the top as well as the bottom of the economic hierarchy. Those who could dismiss "tramps" could not ignore business and bank failures. The image of ruined brokers hurling themselves out of windows up and down Wall Street was a myth, but the vaporization of $115 million worth of deposits in 346 banks across the country was a reality that wiped out the life savings of many depositors, small and large.[17]

The floodwaters of unemployment rose, swamping first the private charities, then the county and city boards who were the government bodies traditionally responsible for relief. Soon the states were bailing furiously. Some denied any responsibility. Some responded by relaxing the restrictions on borrowing they had earlier imposed on local governments. This bought them little time. Some states, particularly in the industrial East, began spending their own money, even raising state taxes to do it. It was not nearly enough. They quickly found themselves treading water, with only the federal government left to throw them a lifeline.

Herbert Hoover, who had served as secretary of commerce under both Warren G. Harding and Calvin Coolidge, had been elected president in 1928 to maintain the prosperity of the Coolidge years. That, however, was not going to be easy. Hoover had seen the developing Depression even before the crash, and he responded both to the growing calls for federal intervention and to the increasing perception that public works might be part of that intervention. It was time to put ideas about influencing business cycles into effect. He suggested the creation of a three-billion-dollar reserve fund for public works. This was a nice gesture and had the additional advantage of costing nothing. The money was to come from deferring public projects during prosperous times, as the new theory advocated, until they were needed later. But since prosperous times were now history and the need was current, it was an inspiration of "manifest impracticality."[18]

Public works proposals with more substance were introduced in Congress during the next three years. Inside the administration, a report was issued exploring the possible uses of public works for economic stabilization. Hoover resisted. He declared in 1930 that "to increase taxation for purposes of construction work defeats its own purpose." The best he would do was allow modest increases in federal road, river, and harbor projects and permit the Treasury Department to speed up its program for building new post offices.[19]

Hoover firmly believed that his role was to advocate rather than coerce. He tried earnestly to persuade businessmen to maintain their workforces and their investment plans. He hoped that public relations campaigns would substitute for spending real money. One project had billboards erected across the country exhorting businesses to "GIVE A JOB" or "SPRUCE UP." Such efforts were described as "roughly analogous to that of a 'booster engine' . . . which is hitched to a train temporarily to supplement the regular motive power in getting the train up a particularly stiff grade." One analyst at the time found the simile "rather strained." Since the committees behind these projects gave local governments no real resources, it was, she said, not a booster engine but more like "cheering beside the tracks."[20]

Hoover moved gradually toward putting federal dollars to work in larger amounts. He was also running for reelection. Just prior to the Republican National Convention he vetoed a one-billion-dollar public works bill that had passed both House and Senate by large margins. After the convention had nominated him for a second term, he signed a quite similar bill, the Emergency Relief and Construction Act (ERCA). Title 1 of the act provided loans to the states for unemployment relief. This was significant because it represented the abandonment of the position that relief was solely a local or state problem. Title 3 offered more highway and road money, but more than half of it could not be spent unless the Treasury Department approved. This was a concession to the growing importance of federal construction. But Title 2 had greater implications. It allowed loans to state and local governments for public works of their own.[21]

The grants were to be made under the supervision of the Reconstruction Finance Corporation (RFC), a body created earlier in the year to make loans to private corporations, railroads, and banks. The ERCA now allowed it to include public bodies. Any building projects, however, had to be "self-liquidating." That meant they had to produce enough income to repay the cost of their construction. A toll bridge is a good example. Any project that was not self-liquidating, or "bankable," was "non-productive." Highways, schools, and fire stations were all non-productive by this definition.[22]

Still, this could work for some badly needed community services such as water mains and treatment plants. Users of water could be charged according to what they used. Factories that used a lot of water would pay proportionately more than households. However, there was a rub. It was not enough that the project generated revenue, which sufficed for the issuance of revenue bonds; the income had to meet all operating and maintenance costs, *and* it had to be paid off in ten years. The problem was that most water systems were part of the city fire-protection system. If the charges for fire protection, which ought to be borne out of general tax revenues, were added to charges for water, heavy users would be paying a disproportionate share of the city's fire-protection costs. Nonusers, citizens with wells, would be paying nothing. So a water project could not be both self-liquidating, under the definition of the legislation, and fair to all citizens. Extensions to an existing water and sewer system already supported by general taxation would not qualify either. Any project, it seemed, that was jointly supported by both taxes and fees was ineligible.[23]

Another obstacle between the RFC and its intended goals was interest rates, which were set at 5.5 percent, well above market rates, to avoid competition with private lenders. It did not matter that private lenders had no interest in such investments. Sen. Robert Wagner and former New York governor and presidential candidate Al Smith sought RFC approval for a low-income housing project and asked for a lower interest rate. They were denied. They protested that there were no banks at all interested in the project. The answer was still no.[24]

"Municipalities . . . soon discovered . . . that 'self-liquidating' public works projects, as defined by the act, were practically non-existent." The vast majority of proposals were rejected. By the end of the year, only $147 million of the $1.6 billion in Title 2 had been authorized and only $15.7 million spent. When Franklin Roosevelt took office two months later, RFC still had only spent $20 million. The loans were "on the whole, ineffective, because of the requirement that projects be self-liquidating without recourse to special or regular taxation or assessment, and of the high interest rates charged by the RFC."[25]

Roosevelt benefited from important changes that had taken place during the preceding decade in both academic and popular attitudes toward a variety of issues related to what the federal government might do to combat the Depression. There was now widespread appreciation that unemployment was a result of structural problems in the economy, not the fault of individuals. There was the growing belief that those problems could be mitigated by government intervention. There was general agreement that public works had an important role to play in that intervention. New relationships allowing the federal government to assist state and local authorities in undertaking public works had been explored.

Some public works projects had even been started. Despite the difficulty of meeting the RFC's definition of self-liquidation, some very important proposals passed the test. New York City's Triborough Bridge; the San Francisco Bay Bridge; a bridge over the Mississippi River at New Orleans, later named for Huey P. Long;

Fig. 1.1. Carl Mackley Houses, designed by Oscar Storonov and Alfred Kastner, incorporated both the aesthetics and amenities of European "social housing": a nursery school, a co-op grocery, rooftop laundries, and a swimming pool. Photograph by R. D. Leighninger

the Hayden Planetarium in New York City; a stadium at the University of South Carolina; a power project in Los Angeles; a sewer project in Bowling Green, Kentucky; and waterworks in Chicago, Seattle, Corpus Christi, San Juan, and other places were approved for RFC loans.[26] They could be taken over immediately when Roosevelt created the Public Works Administration in July 1933.

Herbert Hoover had done his best, but it was not enough. In 1920 Roosevelt, then assistant secretary of the navy, said of Hoover: "He is certainly a wonder, and I wish we could make him President of the United States. There could not be a better one."[27] Hoover's experience in engineering, business, diplomacy, and administration made a powerful resume. But the power and complexity of the Great Depression were greater. Hoover was deficient in too many important ways: willingness to act instead of just trying to persuade, to reject orthodoxy firmly rather than merely questioning it, to see things built and not just planned, and to change his rhetoric of "rugged individualism" to match his changing perceptions of common cause. Roosevelt had a strong resume too. He also subscribed to economic orthodoxy, but his convictions about how an economy should be run were not as deep as Hoover's. This deficit proved to be a great advantage when he was elected president and began to forge tools to fight the Depression.

Chapter 2

• THE CIVILIAN CONSERVATION CORPS •
1933–42

The Civilian Conservation Corps (CCC) was the first of the New Deal building programs. It was an original and very personal creation by the new president, Franklin Delano Roosevelt,[1] and became one of the most, if not *the* most, popular of all New Deal programs. This popularity was expressed both in politics and in national opinion polls. It has also been confirmed over the succeeding seven decades by the activities of its veterans. It is the only New Deal agency to have its own alumni association. It has inspired scores of books written by corps alumni, an unlikely group of prospective authors. Some are scholarly works; others are simple stream-of-consciousness memoirs.[2] Many are published at the authors' expense. All pay convincingly heartfelt testimony to the life-changing experience of enrollment in the CCC. Whatever the accomplishments of the other New Deal programs, none has inspired such lifelong loyalty or such passionate authorship.

The CCC was a response to two grave problems facing the country—one human, one natural. By the time the new president took office, the ravages of the Depression had so uprooted the population that "almost two million men and women had abandoned all pretense of settled existence and had simply taken to the road."[3] A quarter million of them were young people. More than half of youth ages fifteen to twenty-five had only part-time employment or none at all. Our physical landscape had been similarly uprooted. Of the eight hundred million acres of forest that had once covered the country, only one hundred million acres of virgin forest survived. A sixth of our 610 million acres of tillable soil was ruined by 1934. Much of that soil was transported hundreds of miles into the Atlantic Ocean by the fierce dust storms of the early 1930s. In 1934 the snow in Vermont was tinted brown.[4]

Thus, says John Salmond, Roosevelt "brought together two wasted resources, the young men and the land, in an attempt to save both."[5] It was a brilliant idea. This dual purpose was both the cause of the program's widespread popularity and the seed of its demise. The balance of conservation and relief was more delicate than Roosevelt understood. Underneath the compelling synthesis were several issues that posed threats of cleavage: education, class, and military control. They could be ignored in the early years, but as Roosevelt shifted his ground to defend the program in the later years, they cracked open beneath him. It was a small-scale Greek tragedy wherein a noble idea was undone by a fatal flaw.

Roosevelt's passion for conservation was deep and long-standing. He had devoted much energy to the stewardship of his family estate, Hyde Park, and done pioneering conservation work for his home state as a New York state senator and governor. It is likely that the CCC became one of his first initiatives because he already knew a lot about the issues involved.[6]

If the idea was divinely simple—putting unemployed youth to work saving the nation's natural resources—its execution was devilishly complex. Those who have studied it most thoroughly believe it would not have been possible without Roosevelt's intense personal involvement. He made it happen through "sheer force and drive." The extent of his personal involvement may also have fatally weakened it when it got caught up in fights that Democratic legislators were having with their president over other issues.[7]

A bill was drafted in five hours by a team including four cabinet heads and sent to Congress. It was passed and signed in ten days. The official title of the program was Emergency Conservation Work; but Roosevelt had used the name Civilian Conservation Corps in a speech a month earlier, and the public liked his term better. The name became official in an act of Congress adopted June 28, 1937.[8] This would not be the last New Deal agency to be christened with one name but grow up using another.

Perhaps it was the sense of purpose and camaraderie embodied in the word "corps" that people found preferable to the more mundane "work." If so, it was a prescient intuition. The nation was desperate for a sense of common purpose, and the young CCC enrollees were soon to demonstrate what such purpose could accomplish.

The targets of the new program were to be 250,000 young men between eighteen and twenty-five years of age, single, and on relief. Despite the fact that this range extends well into adulthood, the members of the CCC were referred to almost universally as "CCC boys." The corps members adopted that label themselves, and their octogenarian survivors still use it.

The structure that emerged to implement the CCC was most unusual. It involved four cabinet departments. The Department of Labor would select the enrollees, often working through county relief offices. The Departments of Agriculture and Interior, through their respective Forest Service and National Park Service (NPS), would choose and direct the work projects. The army would assemble the enrollees in companies of two hundred, put them through two weeks of

Fig. 2.1. Reunion of CCC "boys" at Shenandoah National Park, 1998, when Skyline Drive was placed on the National Register of Historic Places. Photograph by R. D. Leighninger

conditioning, pack them a lunch, and deliver them to camps. It is not too much of an exaggeration to label this an "organizational freak."[9]

It soon became clear that the army's role would not stop with the arrival of the enrollees at the camp gate. The camps first had to be built. The Forest Service quickly realized that the army was the only organization with sufficient experience to set up and manage the camps, so it was given that job as well.[10] The army brass was not too happy about it, but they pitched in. They fulfilled the task with impressive efficiency. It was the largest peacetime mobilization in U.S. history. In the first three months of the Great War, 181,000 men were enrolled; in a similar period the CCC produced 275,000.[11]

The men who found themselves in charge of the CCC camps were for the most part Army Reserve officers, often themselves unemployed. Contact with the ravages of the Depression may have made them more sympathetic to their charges than the regulars might have been. As reservists, they were also less rigid in interpreting army rules and regulations.[12] This flexibility probably gave the experiment time to get under way.

The army's role in running the camps inspired immediate criticism from isolationists who feared this might be a part of American preparation for war. Perhaps for this reason, military traditions were kept to a minimum. Interestingly, they were explained to the boys in the CCC handbook as matters of efficiency and courtesy. Standing formations provided orderly movement, and saying "yes, sir" was just good manners.[13]

A more serious challenge came from labor leaders who objected to the rate of pay established for CCC enrollees. They were to get thirty dollars a month, twenty-five dollars of which was to be sent home to their families. The American Federation of Labor (AFL) and other groups could quite easily envision this becoming the new standard wage. Secretary of Labor Frances Perkins pointed out that the enrollees got room, board, and clothes in addition to their dollar a day. Congress avoided debate by giving considerable authority to the president to set up the program as he saw fit. They were willing to get something going and worry about details later.[14]

To direct the corps, Roosevelt picked Robert Fechner, an official in the International Association of Machinists and vice president of the AFL. Plucking Fechner from the heart of the opposition was an obvious move to placate labor, but there were other qualities to recommend the Georgia mechanic. He was an experienced mediator and had lectured at Ivy League universities on labor relations. He was modest and self-deprecating, fond of pointing out that his staff had more formal education than he did. As a New Dealer, he described himself as "a potato bug among dragon flies." These qualities helped make this organizational anomaly a going concern.[15]

Fechner was given an advisory council with representatives from the four cabinet departments. For the most part, he respected their advice. He deferred to the army on most issues. He traveled a lot and gained a good working knowledge of the camps. Being a southerner and not a city lawyer like many New Deal officials probably helped his relations with Congress considerably. Under Fechner's unobtrusive guidance, interagency cooperation blossomed. Only toward the end of his administration did he stop consulting the council and begin trying to gain more personal control.[16] This, probably not coincidentally, marked the beginning of the collapse of the CCC.

As the recruitment of the boys began, several groups of older citizens stepped forward. The first were World War I veterans. During the Hoover administration they had come to Washington and camped outside the city, waiting payment of a promised bonus for their service. Gen. Douglas MacArthur was in charge of protecting the Capitol. Without Hoover's authority, he dispersed the bonus marchers with tear gas and burned their camps. When a similar encampment sprung up to present their claim to the new president, Roosevelt sent his wife to lead them in a sing-along and offered them enlistment in the new "Tree Army."[17]

A second group of older recruits were inhabitants of the forests and fields that the CCC boys were soon to begin work in. Foresters, lumbermen, farmers, carpenters, masons, and surveyors, many of them also unemployed, heard about the government's plan to hire thousands of kids to work in their backyards. Forest Service personnel were well aware that they could not possibly supervise hundreds of thousands of enrollees with the staff available, and turning a bunch of boys loose in the woods with sharp tools was asking for trouble. They were aware also that there would be considerable resentment among the locals if *their* unemployment problem was ignored. To solve both problems, they recommended hiring these men to teach the boys their skills. They became officially known as Local Experienced Men (LEMs). Quickly, 24,375 LEMs were taken on and were customarily assigned in groups of eight to twelve to each company.[18]

A third group, this one including boys but also older men, were Native Americans in the West, living on land devastated by drought and erosion. They had fewer job opportunities than most other citizens during the Depression, so the decision to include them in the CCC was welcome. At one Navajo site, twelve hundred men were enrolled in four days. Some were married. This, and the fact that the work was close at hand, meant that most were not organized into camps but allowed to go home at night. Tribal councils participated in administering the program and choosing the projects. Thirty-three reservations were involved in CCC operations.[19]

The legislation establishing the CCC included a policy of nondiscrimination. This was generally overlooked in the South. Frank Persons, the head of the U.S. Employment Service branch in charge of CCC enrollment, began making inquiries as he noticed the pattern. Various excuses were offered, but no action was

Fig. 2.2. Mountain Theater, Mount Tamalpais, a popular theater and music venue for the San Francisco Bay Area, with seating for six thousand. These massive stones were put in place by companies of World War I veterans using hand tools. Photograph by R. D. Leighninger

taken until Persons threatened to stop enrollment in the resisting states. Then token numbers of African Americans appeared on the rolls.[20]

Most African Americans were organized into separate camps. Interestingly, there were widespread exceptions to this policy at first. In regions outside the South, blacks were sent to white companies when there were not enough to form a separate unit. In New England, 250 blacks were distributed among sixty-eight mainly white companies. The army, though a segregated institution itself, was not particularly bothered by the practice. It was the most efficient way of getting the camps filled and running. Hispanics and Asians received no special attention.[21]

At some of the integrated camps, however, the army found a way of maintaining an internal form of segregation. African Americans tended to get kitchen duty more often than whites. This meant they ate at separate times. Often they slept in separate tents. Sometimes their commanding officers subjected them to racial insults. But many others accorded them equal treatment. In one instance, an overtly racist CO was removed after enrollees complained.[22]

From interviews with California CCC veterans, Olen Cole concluded that, "in general, [African Americans] were well-treated by other corpsmen." Scattered interviews from other states support this. A common refrain in the alumni memoirs is that the corps taught its members to get along with all kinds of people. Sometimes this cooperation is stated just in terms of urban and rural origins, but sometimes ethnicity, race, and religion are mentioned specifically. One Vermonter reported: "We had blacks in our camp. . . . I got to know these boys in work and play and realized that discrimination had no place in our world."[23]

Fechner, however, shared the prejudice of his southern roots. In September 1934, Fechner ordered all CCC camps segregated. He justified this by the need to prevent racial violence in the camps, even though this was a minor problem. In fact, some of the blacks he removed from the white camps were "among the most popular enrollees there." In one instance, the white enrollees wrote a formal protest. "We would like action taken regarding transfer of six colored members of this camp. These men came west with us and have been in camp sufficient time to merit better treatment than that to which they have been subjected. . . . 190 Bay State men shall demand to be returned to Massachusetts if these men are sent back home because of racial prejudice." Assistant director James McEntee disregarded the protest. It seems the threatened mutiny did not take place, but the fact it was threatened is in itself significant.[24]

The direct result of this policy was that more black camps had to be established. But Fechner was already convinced that there were few places this could be done. Interestingly, one of the few regions that cheerfully accommodated and even welcomed black camps was the South. A congressman in Prairie View, Texas, and a chamber of commerce head in Laurens County, Georgia, were among those requesting "a Negro camp."[25]

Outside the South, there were indeed protests from communities when they learned that a black camp was to be established nearby. Fechner claimed that there was a "flood" of such complaints. Therefore, having cut off the possibility of integrated camps and being unwilling to locate new black companies, the only solution he saw was to limit black enrollment, which he ordered in July 1935. Frank Persons balked, but the president backed Fechner.[26]

The alleged "flood" of protests against black camps that Fechner had used to justify the enrollment limitation was largely in his own mind. The CCC over the course of its existence received something like 1,700 letters of all kinds from local communities. A 12 percent sample (202) of these found only 13.4 percent (17) in any way negative. The same study also reviewed 558 letters that had been filed under such labels as "complaints," "dissatisfaction," and "protest." Only 16 (6.8 percent) were in opposition to black camps. In a rank order of problems, it was sixth out of seven.[27]

In fact, anxiety about the coming of CCC camps was hardly confined to racial prejudices. People in rural areas were worried about city youth "of the roughest kind" traveling their roads and visiting their towns. "Outsiders" of any kind, even from the next county, were threatening. One Utah resident reported that "at first they were welcomed like an epidemic of smallpox."[28] But such fears quickly disappeared after the camps were established. The work projects started taking shape; the boys became known as individuals; and, perhaps most important, the camp supply sergeants, officers, and boys began spending money in town. For many communities, the money was a godsend, well worth the cost of reconsidering some of their prejudices. Even opposition to black camps, according to one army report, dissolved as the work proceeded and the local economy revived.[29]

Fears and protests notwithstanding, the camps were sited, built, staffed, and filled with willing if uncertain boys. They were no angels. They fought a lot, which was not regarded as unusual. They sometimes stole things or tried to sell CCC equipment to the locals. However, the conduct was on the whole endearing to their host communities. They were invited to local social functions and drew enthusiastic crowds of locals to the talent shows, boxing matches, baseball games, and dances in their camps. They were even invited into homes for Sunday dinner. As the anxieties of parents were overcome, they dated local girls and often returned after their CCC and military service to marry them.[30]

Girls might have played a larger role than that of dance partner and potential wife of a CCC boy. Eleanor Roosevelt and Labor Secretary Frances Perkins conceived of residential summer camps for girls patterned after the CCC. Journalists immediately named it the "she, she, she corps." It was, however, never part of the CCC. It was run by the Federal Emergency Relief Administration (FERA) and later the National Youth Administration. It enrolled single women ages twenty to forty-five with no source of income. They spent most of their time on education and handicrafts. But it was not all poetry and potholders. One camp in Texas had the girls building vacation cottages. By May 1936, sixty-four hundred women from thirty-three states at eighty-six camps had participated. There was also at least one attempt to start a women's CCC at the state level.[31]

In addition to its infrastructure investment, the CCC also invested in people. Though the same might be said of the other programs, the CCC's investment seems more dramatic because of the youth of the participants. Most of the workers in the other works programs were already set on their paths of life. They were usually married and had families. The CCC boys, even if not literally boys, were just beginning. Most had never had full-time jobs. Most had dropped out of school. Few had any idea of a future for themselves. Many freely acknowledged that they were headed for criminal activity. They had little sense of their own abilities, much less confidence in them. The CCC gave them purposeful lives. This is the reason for all those testimonial letters and self-published memoirs.

Thus the program invested in them, and they invested for their country. Their work projects were varied. Perry Merrill, who as Vermont's state forester was in charge of all CCC projects in the state and who wrote a book attempting a state-by-state inventory of CCC accomplishments, estimates that there were at least three hundred different types of projects, which he divides into ten categories:

Structural Improvement, including bridges, fire towers, park buildings and museums;
Transportation, including roads, trails, and even airport landing strips;
Erosion Control, including check dams, terracing, and planting;
Flood Control, including irrigation and drainage, dams, ditches, channels, and riprap;
Forest Culture, including tree and shrub planting, timber stand improvement, seed collection, and nursery work;
Forest Protection, including firefighting, fire prevention, and insect control;
Landscape and Recreation, including development of camp and picnic grounds and clearing of lake and pond sites;
Range Improvement, including improvement of grazing lands and elimination of predators;
Wildlife Care, including stocking fish, improving streams, and providing forest animals with cover and food; and
Miscellaneous, which covers an even wider range of activities such as mosquito control, surveying, search and rescue operations, and other responses to local emergencies.[32]

One of the first projects to get under way and one of the largest was an effort to control floods in north central Vermont. Recent floods on the Winooski River had killed eighty-four people and cost thirty million dollars in property damage, including twelve hundred highway bridges. The Army Corps of Engineers devised a plan to prevent future carnage by constructing four dams, three of which were to be earth fill. The CCC was assigned to build them.

The first to arrive was a company of black World War I veterans. With only picks, shovels, and wheelbarrows, they built dams at East Barre, Wrightsville, and Waterbury. The last is two thousand feet long and faced with granite. The blocks were laid end on and are still there. It is among the largest earthen dams in New England. Junior companies joined the veterans; as many as three thousand worked at Waterbury.[33]

Another early project sent five companies into Shenandoah National Park to clear the way for the Skyline Drive. In August 1933 the president drove out to inspect the camps. In addition to Interior secretary Ickes and director Fechner, he brought along William Green of the AFL. Green's early criticism of the program was widely publicized. The party inspected the five camps and at the Big Meadows camp had a lunch of steak, mashed potatoes, green beans, and salad. There was apple pie for dessert, though the cooks may have been improvising, because Ickes referred to it in his diary as "so-called apple pie." Ickes was told by the general in charge that it was a typical meal and that the average boy had gained fifteen pounds since the corps arrived in the Shenandoah three months earlier. Green had a great time and became an ardent convert; organized labor supported the CCC to its final days.[34]

On this same trip, the commanding officer told the visitors that, in addition to the work projects, the army was doing a great job of educating the boys. "There won't none of these boys leave these camps illiterate," he told the visitors. Ickes thought this was funny, both because the officer was hardly a role model of literacy, but mostly because the educational program that had recently been adopted had been strongly opposed by the army.[35] In fact, education was going to be an ongoing battleground for the corps.

One could easily argue that the CCC, in exposing the boys to nature and teaching them to work together, was already "education in the large."[36] But how far should one go beyond that? Should the three Rs be added to the three Cs? Should vocational education be undertaken? Many of the boys were indeed illiterate, and most had not finished high school. Should the CCC not only employ them now but also prepare them to enter the private labor force as the economy improved?

Whether formal education was begun by the army, was forced upon it by outsider groups, or arose spontaneously within the camps is a subject of debate, but by May 1933, it was under way.[37] It required delicate negotiation, however. Early in the life of the corps, there were already night classes in forestry held by the NPS and U.S. Forest Service (USFS) supervisors and some other classes offered by the officers. But bringing in an "educational advisor," presumably a teacher or college professor, was a different matter entirely. Fechner was reluctant to dilute the effort being expended on the work projects. The army was even more skeptical. Col. Duncan Major wanted no part of the "long-haired men and short-haired women" who might bring radical ideas into his camps. The army already had to share control of the camps during the day with two other branches of government. To share it at night with a third might be the last straw that could bring down the shaky edifice of multiagency cooperation.

The federal commissioner of education, however, along with most educational and professional organizations in the country, thought it was a fine idea. Washington came to agree, but with an important and probably lifesaving reservation. The plan for one educational advisor per camp was approved, but the advisor was to be responsible to the Army Corps Area commander, and participation was to be voluntary. In a summation tinged with irony, F. E. Hill describes the army as "cordially accepting the Office of Education as a branch of its own service." Roosevelt was interested in saving both trees and men, writes James Russell Woods, "but when the struggle was over, the balsams got the nod over the books."[38]

The outcome of CCC education efforts was impressive nonetheless. The camp commanders gave the education advisors, regardless of hair length, enough support to deliver a respectable program. Some not only cooperated with the advisors but actually helped them build schoolhouses. Army regulations forbade this, and the CCC provided no funding for it. But schools went up, from scrap and scrounged materials, with community donations, and with the boys working after hours. "Who gave you permission to build a schoolhouse?" Hill asked one camp commanding officer. "'Nobody,' he grinned. 'I just did it.'"[39]

Conducting even semiformal education under these circumstances was a challenge even with army support. The boys had done a hard day's work and looked forward to rest and relaxation in the evenings. For many farm boys and immigrant city kids, formal schooling had been more humiliation than opportunity. Yet by June 1937, thirty-five hundred young men had learned to read, over one thousand had earned high school diplomas, and thirty-nine emerged with college degrees.[40]

African Americans shared in the benefits. Though some were steered to "serving" and cooking courses, others took college work. The education program also presented an opportunity for black professionals. Though the army was reluctant to see blacks in positions of authority, after some pressure from Ickes almost all of the black camps received black advisors.[41]

The education program was the first challenge to the delicate balance of relief versus conservation. Insofar as the CCC was a relief program, education might be seen as the best way to make sure the boys would never again be on relief. But Roosevelt and Fechner kept the focus of the working day on conservation and relegated education to the evenings. Thus they got the best of both worlds. The boys were on the job during the day for all in the vicinity to see, and the tangible products of the conservation effort continued to mount. They derived considerable benefit from the evening classes as well. The corps was not so fortunate in later challenges.

By January 1934, the program was humming. It was initially financed by unobligated funds left from Hoover's Reconstruction Finance Corporation. Roosevelt now got $275 million from Congress to continue it until April 1935. Enrollees were permitted to reenlist for an additional six-month hitch. Erosion control and timber-stand improvement were proceeding energetically, and damage from forest fires had decreased "spectacularly" thanks to the ability of the boys to drop whatever they were doing to fight fires. The boys had gained noticeable weight and strength, and their families were being sustained by $72,500,000 that had so far been issued in their paychecks. That money, plus what the boys and their supply sergeants were spending, was making many a retailer happy across the country.[42]

In June 1934, Roosevelt persuaded Congress to allot fifty million dollars to put fifty thousand more boys and five thousand more veterans to work. The corps was now 353,000 strong and operating from 1,625 camps.[43] As the April 1935 expiration date approached, Roosevelt planned further expansion. However, he was now engaged on a much larger battlefront against unemployment. The Public Works Administration (PWA) was in operation, and the more broadly based Civil Works Administration had been created and disbanded. It was now clear that some kind of integrated public works and work relief program was needed. But how to integrate it was a thorny problem.

A comprehensive public works bill was enacted, creating yet another building agency, the Works Progress Administration (WPA). The popularity of the CCC was probably instrumental in the passage of the entire package. The outcome was settled on April 8, 1935, and gave the CCC two more years of life and six hundred million dollars to operate for the first year. The corps doubled its original strength. By September there were 502,000 men in 2,514 camps. But this flush of hot summer activity ran into an autumn chill. Reelection was approaching, and the president began again to entertain thoughts of a balanced budget. This led to plans for closing some camps, which led to unexpected trouble.[44]

In a way it was the kind of trouble all presidents would like to have. People from across the country, from both major parties, were telling him that he had done something right. "Please, please, don't close our camp! Send us another one!" Why would a president want to do anything but bask in this outpouring of praise? Roosevelt, however, was at heart a believer in economic orthodoxy. He was flexible, willing to experiment, open to new ideas. But at regular intervals in his wide-ranging excursions into new economic territory, his compass needle would point toward the lodestone of traditionalism, the balanced budget. He had campaigned on it, and despite a tolerance for heresy that sent most conservatives into apoplexy, he still believed in it. That meant cutbacks.

In January 1936, 489 camps closed and the preparation for opening other sites was abandoned. The president wanted further reductions, down to 1,456 by June. Secretary of Agriculture Henry Wallace and others within the administration warned him that this was going to have major repercussions across the land, but Roosevelt held firm.[45]

On March 14, 1936, the repercussions landed on the president's desk. The Speaker of the House presented a petition signed by 233 members, including a lot of Republicans, calling for suspension of camp closings. Even this was not strong enough to counteract the lure of the balanced budget. Roosevelt refused to budge. Four days later he found his party in open rebellion. House Democrats held a meeting. Leaders reminded their colleagues that, whether they had a camp in their districts or not, each would soon be facing approximately three hundred families who had just lost their breadwinners. They got the point and threatened to block the administration's whole legislation program unless CCC was continued. Faced with such determination, Roosevelt folded. He agreed that all existing camps would continue until their projects were completed; $6.8 million would be committed to cover them. Newspapers across the country, even those with little use for the New Deal, applauded the decision.[46]

The election of 1936 was a Roosevelt landslide. Despite deficits caused by the CCC and other New Deal programs, he was still able to tell voters that a balanced budget was "on the way."[47] There were no exit pollsters to tell us whether such a pledge helped him in the election more than the continuation of the CCC. In any case he began his second term with what seemed like a mandate to accomplish several things that he had wanted to do. One was to insulate his legislation from the septuagenarian majority of the Supreme Court, whose constitutional philosophy allowed little role for government in the economy. Another was to make the CCC a permanent agency, which he had proposed during the campaign. One got in the way of the other.

There were no critical voices whatsoever raised against the CCC when hearings were conducted on the plan for making it permanent. The labor committees of both houses of Congress favorably reported out permanency bills. When the House bill reached the floor, however, there was a swell of argument for another two-year extension rather than permanency. No one questioned the value of the corps; with a recent national poll giving it an 87 percent approval rating, they would have been inviting trouble to do so. Instead, they said merely that the matter should be decided only after further investigation. There was no rush.[48]

One explanation for the surprise derailment of the CCC from what seemed to be a clear track to permanence was a backlash against the court-packing effort. The proposal to add new justices on the court if sitting justices did not retire at age seventy was generally unpopular with both parties even though it was put forth as an effort to increase court efficiency. The bill was defeated but not before causing considerable dissension within the president's own party. Conservatives becoming more uneasy with Roosevelt's economic policies now had a higher-minded reason for breaking ranks. Others who still supported the party's main policies wanted a way to show their displeasure at being pushed into this dubious legal adventure. Blocking permanency for the corps while still keeping it in operation was one way to do this.[49]

Another, and perhaps more important, crack in corps support was widening during the permanency debate. One argument voiced by those resisting a commitment to make the corps a part of the federal establishment was that it would represent an admission that the country could never again provide full employment for its young men without resorting to public jobs. The CCC was an emergency effort, and someday the emergency would be over. This position labeled the corps a measure whose primary purpose, if not its sole purpose, was relief of unemployment. No one seemed to notice that an important act of redefinition was taking place.

Because no one noticed, it did not occur to anyone to counter this redefinition. No one pointed out that the conservation work the corps had been engaging in desperately needed doing and was not a "make-work" project invented just to give young men something to do instead of riding boxcars. Conservation, thanks to decades of indifference, was also an emergency effort. But even after a decade of reforestation, erosion and flood control, and park development, there would still be much to do. There would always be forest fires, and the dams, waterways, parks, and recreation facilities would always need maintaining. In fact the need for this maintenance became apparent almost as soon as the corps left the scene.[50] The country would not always need five hundred thousand people to do this work, but it could always use a mobile, flexible, rapidly deployable group to see to the regular chores and the irregular emergencies on the public landscape. Yet no one rose to defend the corps in this way.

Redefining the CCC as purely a conservation program was not necessary. It would retain an economic function as well. Unemployment could be expected to continue to vary with business cycles. Having conservation work for young people would help smooth the economic upturns and downturns, expanding and contracting as needed and not requiring reinvention during each cycle. Apparently no one saw this.

The president did not seem overly concerned with the ambush of his carefully nurtured program. It would continue another two years and could be made permanent at a later date. It was still very popular with the nation and in Congress. Unfortunately, he learned nothing from the experience that would help him perpetuate that popularity.

As the first battle for CCC permanency was getting under way, Roosevelt took a step that would soon lead to a reenactment of the previous fall's battle over camp closing. On April 20, 1937, believing that recovery was really now on the way, his economic compass pointed once again toward the balanced budget, and he announced cuts in all the work programs. The result was a roaring recession that by fall was being compared to the crash of 1929. The CCC took its share of cuts despite renewed congressional protests. Only after a year of continuing recession was Roosevelt convinced that the work programs had to be revived. On April 14, 1938, he asked Congress to put the PWA and WPA back to work. He gave the CCC fifty million dollars. Only six members of the House opposed the appropriation.[51]

In 1939 another extension of the CCC came due and another attempt at permanency was made. Again only a limited extension was achieved, this time until July 1943. During the debate, however, another issue emerged: military training for the boys. This was a divisive issue. The Second World War had begun, and many saw America's entry a necessity. Vocal isolationists opposed it. Getting embroiled in this could not help the CCC. After some debate the program was left unchanged, but the issue of military involvement was far from settled.[52]

There was another development in 1939, one that was probably worse for the long-term future of the CCC than the debate on military training. Roosevelt's Reorganization Act regrouped federal agencies according to function under a few broad categories, presumably to simplify administration and save money. The Federal Works Agency took in the PWA and the WPA. The CCC, however, did not join them. It was placed under the Federal Security Agency, along with the Office of Education, the Public Health Service, the U.S. Employment Agency, and the Social Security Board. This completed the redefinition of the program as a "relief" agency, part of the "welfare group."[53]

It would have made equal sense to place CCC in the "works group." Construction occupied most of its time and energy. The many buildings it put up in the state and national parks were no different in size and function from a lot of what WPA was doing. Fechner, while always more interested in work than relief, did not make this argument. He was instead trying to keep the CCC independent of either of the two megastructures. The fate of the CCC might not have been any different had it been included in the Federal Works Agency, but becoming a welfare agency foreshadowed its doom.

To make matters worse, the "freakish" organizational structure of the CCC was finally coming apart. Having balanced four cabinet departments, including the usually intractable U.S. Army, with respectful diplomacy and minimal display of ego for over six years, Fechner decided he wanted more control. He stopped convening the advisory council and began centralizing his administration. He was soon at war with all of the cooperating agencies and demanding that the president confirm that he had the final authority over all matters concerning the CCC. Fechner won some battles and lost some, and the war ended only when he died of a heart attack in December 1939. Unfortunately, his successor, James McEntee, continued the push for centralization in an even more heavy-handed manner. He also undermined community support by cutting back on local purchases of supplies. Soon the cooperating agencies had lost any enthusiasm for cooperating.[54]

Other factors, outside the control of the CCC administration, were undermining its fragile constitution. The army had finally realized that the experience of administrating the camps had given its officers excellent opportunities to improve their leadership skills. Because they did not have the full apparatus of military punishment behind them, officers had to lead by persuasion and example, separating the true leaders from the martinets. The army wanted to move these men into the regular ranks and bring a new crop into the CCC for seasoning. Fechner fought this off, but there was no denying the growing need to call reserve officers into the regular army as war preparations grew.[55]

The line between the CCC and the army was blurring. Some CCC projects were now located on army bases, and others were doing work that freed service personnel for war-related duties. An editorial in the *New York Times* proposed that CCC boys be sent into aircraft factories. Military training was finally approved for all camps. Roosevelt's last attempts to prolong the life of the organization were based on its importance to "war work."[56]

Whether or not the last-ditch defense of the CCC solely as a means of preparation for war was a mistake, the corps did in fact aid greatly in that preparation. The leadership experience given to reserve and regular army officers and the introduction to discipline and collective effort given to three million young men certainly improved the performance of the armed forces in the early years of World War II. The eighty camps devoted to building barracks, airfields, rifle ranges, and other facilities on army posts were also important to the mobilization and training of millions of other young people. Increased instruction in motor repair, radio operation, cooking, mapping, and other skills related to military operation that the corps offered made the CCC enlistees doubly useful. Many of the vets attribute their advancement in the armed forces to their CCC experience. Two even credit it with their survival of the Bataan death march in 1942.[57]

A final fissure opened underneath the CCC's shaky ground in 1940 when the Department of Agriculture proposed creation of a CCC "staff college." Many of the reserve officers running the camps had been called up. New leadership would be needed. A group of recent Dartmouth and Harvard graduates, with the support of Mrs. Roosevelt and newspaper columnist Dorothy Thompson, obtained approval for a camp in Vermont to aid local farmers and train future CCC camp administrators. Because some of the participants were "pampered sons of rich families usurping a form of relief meant only for the nation's underprivileged," the project was widely ridiculed.[58]

The appearance of class as an issue is interesting, because it underlines the redefinition of the corps as a welfare agency. When Vermont senator George Aiken, a Republican, came to the defense of the camp, he did so on the grounds that all boys, rich or poor, should have a chance to work in the forests.[59] Had the CCC maintained its stature as a conservation agency, that argument would have carried some weight. But as it was now seen as something reserved for the "underprivileged," opening it to Ivy Leaguers was a lost cause. In itself the staff college was just another ill-fated experiment in an era when experimentation was a necessary thing. It came, however, when the CCC was already being pulled apart by forces inside and outside. It was not built to withstand further shocks.

The collapse came in the debate over appropriations for 1941–42. A joint committee, dominated by anti–New Deal conservatives, had been formed to review all federal agencies. Slanderous allegations were made against the CCC with little protest. McEntee, the Forest Service, and the president defended the CCC only as part of the war effort.[60] As Congress pondered, the Japanese bombed Pearl Harbor and America entered the war. In this new environment, the fate of the CCC seemed unimportant. Popularity remained strong, but even among its supporters a consensus developed that its time had passed. On June 30, 1942, Congress agreed on eight million dollars for its liquidation.

The CCC's peculiar organization might be blamed for its failure to survive. It was ingeniously pieced together out of ill-fitting parts. "Its structure," concludes John A. Salmond, "never lost its temporary look, and its machinery, though for a long time surprisingly efficient, was essentially makeshift, loose, and diffuse." Woods agrees but adds that "any organization [might] have folded under the impact of war." He also believes that a key to the downfall of the CCC was the president's inability to give it the personal attention he had lavished on it in its first years. "In his highly individualistic manner of conducting the affairs of government he had created and nurtured a one-man institution in the CCC, and when he was no longer able to attend to its details it fell easy prey to the vagaries of officialdom."[61] Perhaps. Had Roosevelt stayed more involved, he might have been able to continue to articulate his original vision of a program conserving both young men and trees and not let it be redefined as a relief program only. But he may also have never fully appreciated its need to be a program for *both* people and the land. His uses and defenses of it after it got going show no sign of this awareness. That lack may deny the story the quality of Greek tragedy, but the fall of the CCC is a cause for sorrow that is still felt.

A review of the accomplishments of other New Deal programs will be filled with large and often well-known examples. The CCC did complete some large and impressive projects, but its particular glory lies in its many small ones. The picnic pavilions that shelter family reunions and office parties, the vacation cabins where families can spend a week in the woods near a lake for a small fee, even the simple barbeque grills that make it easy to cook hot dogs and toast marshmallows on a summer evening have had an impact on millions of ordinary people. Simple pleasures multiplied over the decades can add up to a high improvement in the quality of American life.

Yet these modest amenities are taken for granted, because they seem as if they have always been there. Few now remember when they were not. However, like the products of the other programs, they did not accumulate slowly as state and local governments gradually decided in their own good time to provide them. They were bequeathed to us in just nine years. Because of their modest sizes and peripheral locations, they may not have been noticed by many even at the time. But together they form a mighty background chorus behind the solo and ensemble performances of the other agencies (see table 2.1).

When one looks for them, however, recognizing the thousands of CCC projects around the country is easier than identifying the products of the other New Deal agencies. Unlike the Public Works Administration and the Works Progress Administration, whose projects were designed by local architects and engineers with no attempt by the agencies to control how they should look, CCC buildings

Table 2.1 Accomplishments of the Civilian Conservation Corps

Bridges	46,854
Lodges and museums	204
Historic structures restored	3,980
Drinking fountains	1,865
Fire lookout towers	3,116
Wells and pump houses	8,065
Forest roads	2,500 miles
Roads and truck trails*	7,442 miles
Cabins*	1,477
Bathhouses*	165
Large dams *	197
Water supply lines	5,000 miles
Fences	27,191 miles
Fish-rearing ponds	4,622
Beaches improved	3,462
Trees planted	3 billion
Fires fought	6.5 million days
Lives lost fighting fires	47

* National and state parks only.

Sources: National Association of Civilian Conservation Corps Alumni, "Did You Know?" (Jefferson Barracks, Mo.: NACCCA, n.d.); Alison T. Otis, William D. Honey, Thomas C. Hogg, and Kimberly K. Larkin, *The Forest Service and the Civilian Conservation Corps* (Washington, D.C.: U.S. Department of Agriculture, 1986), 19; Conrad Wirth, *Parks, Politics, and People* (Norman: University of Oklahoma Press, 1980), 145.

were usually constructed following pattern books or style guidelines. Both the National Park Service and the U.S. Forest Service published books showing the proper style for a ranger station or a picnic shelter. *Park and Recreation Structures* by NPS architect Albert H. Good, published in 1935 with CCC funds, was expanded to three volumes in 1938. The Forest Service's version, also published in 1938 but incorporating earlier published guidelines, was called *Acceptable Building Plans,* which provides a clue to the strength of conviction behind it.[62]

The philosophy of both the NPS and USFS was that a building should intrude as little as possible on nature. It should give "the feeling of having been executed by pioneer craftsmen with limited hand tools." This pioneer aesthetic fit CCC reality nicely: limited hand tools were pretty much what the boys and the LEMs had to work with. Thus wood and stone were the materials of choice; brick, concrete, and steel should be used as little as possible. Stone should be left rough and laid horizontally in uneven sizes to look like natural ledges or pioneer fences. The style became known as "Government Rustic."[63]

Some truly magnificent buildings, such as the lodge at Pere Marquette State Park in Illinois, resulted from the guiding aesthetic of government rustic as well as thousands of more humble structures at campgrounds, picnic areas, recreation facilities, and ranger stations. Since the Park and Forest Services moved away from government rustic in the postwar period, the CCC buildings are usually recognized easily. Even the "rustic" park signs may be the original CCC work.

Though the first mission of the CCC was to preserve our forests, grasslands, and other natural resources, its second became devising ways to allow people to experience and learn more about the beauty and excitement of nature. Campgrounds and picnic areas were one way of accomplishing this. Another was scenic vistas. As they built roads and trails through parks, CCC crews also embellished certain points with shelters where a traveler could pause and enjoy an extended view of the landscape. The lookout on Harney Peak surveys the Black Hills of South Dakota. Sourdough Lookout in North Cascades National Park and Vista House on Mount Spokane provide breathtaking views of Washington State. Massai Point in Chiricahua National Monument shows one what Arizona looked like to the Apache chief Cochise. Bunker Hill Lookout in California's Eldorado National Forest provides a view from 7,524 feet above sea level. One of the most unusual views to be had from a CCC-engineered viewpoint is Dobbins Lookout on South Mountain, twelve hundred feet above Phoenix, Arizona. It combines both natural and human wonders. It is also an opportunity to contemplate how one not only complements but also threatens the other.

The corps hit the low spots as well as the high ones. Mammoth Cave in Kentucky got electric lights inside and tourist cabins and a 350–seat amphitheater outside. Colossal Cave in Arizona was made accessible with lights and roads and administration buildings behind a massive stone retaining wall. Carlsbad Caverns

Fig. 2.3. Dobbins Point Lookout on South Mountain above Phoenix. The CCC built numerous lookouts, picnicking ramadas, restrooms, and offices in this large city park. Photograph by H. Anderson Photography

Fig. 2.4. Colossal Cave near Tucson, Arizona. Behind this massive stone retaining wall are offices, a gift shop, and the entrance to the cave, which the CCC made accessible with lights, stairs, and walkways. Photograph by H. Anderson Photography

in New Mexico received water system improvements and a concrete floor for its underground lunchroom. Wind Cave in South Dakota also got CCC attention. In Missouri there is a system of parks where natural springs gush out of the limestone bedrock. The CCC did work in most of them, including the construction of the lodge at Big Springs.

The forests and parks already in existence were obvious places to put the first CCC camps. But developing parks where none had existed prior to the New Deal soon became an important assignment. In 1921 only nineteen states had any state parks. By 1928 all states had begun plans for them but were not very far along when the Depression came. The CCC took over. When the boys went home, they left behind eight hundred state parks that had been created whole or greatly improved by their energies.[64]

The corps was also a major contributor to the creation of forty-six recreation demonstration areas (RDAs). The government acquired "submarginal" land, acreage agriculturally exhausted or unfit for farming in the first place, and built outdoor recreation complexes for poor city dwellers (see table 2.2). Since these were not places of great natural beauty to begin with, the usual NPS qualms about being unobtrusive were no obstacle to digging new lakes and building baseball diamonds. Large "organization camps," including cabins, dining halls, and administration buildings, were regular features of RDAs. School classes, Girl Scout troops, and other groups could have access to the great outdoors. Most RDAs became state parks; others merged into existing national parks and monuments.[65]

While preserving our natural resources was the CCC's first order of business, it also preserved our history. It cleaned up, landscaped, improved access to, and added tourist facilities to historical sites across the country. The boys were particularly busy at Civil War sites, including Shiloh, Fredericksburg, Spotsylvania, Petersburg, Chattanooga, and Chickamauga. They worked on the Gettysburg battlefield, where the tide of the Civil War turned; Fort Pulaski, a Georgia battle site where rifled artillery was first used; and Appomattox, where the carnage finally ended. They labored at the infamous Confederate prison at Andersonville.

The CCC has provided Americans with further acquaintance with their great presidents. They restored Fort Necessity, Pennsylvania, where a young officer named George Washington helped regroup Braddock's defeated army during the French and Indian War. They restored Wick House in Morristown, New Jersey, the site of Washington's winter encampment of 1779–80. They also did work on Yorktown Battlefield, where he successfully concluded the Revolutionary War. The village of New Salem, Illinois, which includes the primitive cabin where Abraham Lincoln spent six years of his youth, was reconstructed by CCC companies. They cleaned up the mountain from which the visages of Washington, Lincoln, and two other presidents gaze down—Mount Rushmore. Their camp at Catoctin Mountain in Maryland, part of an RDA, also provided the basis of the presidential retreat that became Camp David.

Table 2.2 Recreation demonstration areas

State	Name	In the vicinity of . . .
Alabama	Oak Mountain	Birmingham
California	Mendocino Woodlands	Mendocino
Georgia	Alex H. Stephens	Crawfordville
	Hard Labor Creek	Rutledge
	Pine Mountain	Pine Mountain
Illinois	Pere Marquette	Grafton
Indiana	Versailles	Versailles
	Winamac	Winamac
Kentucky	Otter Creek	West Point
Maine	Camden Hills	Camden
Maryland	Catoctin (Camp David)	Thurmond
Michigan	Waterloo	Chelsea
Minnesota	St. Croix	Hinkley
Missouri	Cuivre River	Troy
	Lake of the Ozarks	Kaiser
	Montserrat	Knob Noster
Oklahoma	Lake Murray	Ardmore
Oregon	Silver Creek	Sublimity
Pennsylvania	Blue Knob	Bedford
	French Creek	Birdsboro
	Hickory Run	Hickory Run
	Laurel Hill	Rockwood
	Raccoon Creek	Beaver
Rhode Island	Beach Pond	West Greenwich
South Carolina	Kings Mountain	York
	Cheraw	Cheraw
Tennessee	Fall Creek Falls	Pikeville
	Montgomery Bell	Burns
	Shelby Forest	Millington
Virginia	Chopawamsic	Quantico
	Swift Creek	Chester

Source: Phoebe Cutler, *The Public Landscape of the New Deal* (New Haven, Conn.: Yale University Press, 1985), 157.

Monuments of our Spanish colonial heritage were returned to our notice by the CCC. La Purisima Mission near Lompoc, California, was lovingly rebuilt brick by brick using original adobe construction. Members of the company, "a bunch of Brooklyn toughs," cried when they left it.[66] Another mission in Texas, Nuestra Señora del Espiritu Santo de Zuñiga, was not only restored but equipped with CCC-built furniture and metal work. The boys got a lot of experience with adobe, in new construction as well as restoration. Many of the park structures in the Southwest, both modest and monumental, were erected with this inexpensive material. The National Park Service headquarters in Santa Fe, New Mexico, is the largest adobe office building in the country.

Still earlier parts of our history were made available to us by the CCC at Mesa Verde, Colorado. The boys built walks, walls, dams, campgrounds, and cabins; helped stabilize the Cliff Palace ruin; and constructed five dioramas depicting life in the cliff-dwelling era. At Bandelier National Monument in New Mexico, ruins were stabilized and thirty-one structures built, including a visitors' center and lodge.

Though Native companies in the Southwest spent most of their time on erosion control, rehabilitation of grazing lands, and road building, some major construction was undertaken. Navajo CCC members built a thirty-five-hundred-seat stadium, stock barns, exhibit and concession buildings, campgrounds, and a race track for a fairgrounds near Window Rock, the tribal headquarters. They also stabilized the pueblos and cliff dwellings of Chaco Canyon, Montezuma's Castle, and other archeological sites.[67]

Another Native company restored Tlingit and Haida totem poles and village houses in Alaska, including the Tlingit Clan House in Ketchikan. In the process 110 totem poles were recovered and saved from decay. The art and history of these tribes had been "all but lost even among the older Indians." Photographic records

Fig. 2.5. Bandelier National Monument, New Mexico. The CCC worked for seven years making the monument accessible to tourists and building all its basic facilities. Photograph by H. Anderson Photography

Fig. 2.6. Stone Hut, Mount Mansfield, Vermont, near the top of the CCC ski trails that made Stowe, Vermont, a national skiing center. Photograph by R. D. Leighninger

were made of the totems, and ethnographic data from libraries on the West Coast and in Washington, D.C., were used to aid their restoration. Under the supervision of elders, enrollees also learned to carve new poles and totem screens.[68]

The parks and forests that the CCC built or improved have provided for decades the benefits of outdoor recreation, most of which, despite their undeniable importance, are immeasurable. But some of the effects of CCC toil and sweat can be measured. Stowe, Vermont, was already a summer resort area when the boys cut the first ski trails on the slopes of Mount Mansfield and built the base lodge from which ski tows would soon embark. Their efforts turned Stowe into a year-round tourist magnet. Now, a million people visit Stowe each year and in 2000 spent an estimated $61.5 million on food, drink, and lodging, a tidy return on this investment. The ski industry was spurred in other states as well, including New Hampshire and Colorado, as well as many of the western national parks and forests.[69]

Another project that has made millions of dollars over the decades is the spectacular amphitheater outside Denver called Red Rocks. Its acoustics had been long appreciated, and it was a popular site for picnics as well as concerts. The City of Denver acquired the property and developed plans for a theater but had to bring in the CCC to get it done. It has since hosted concerts of all kinds. The Beatles played there.

On some projects, CCC boys worked in concert with other New Deal programs. Together with the WPA, they built Timberline Lodge on Oregon's Mount Hood. With the PWA they built the Skyline Drive and the Blue Ridge Parkway extending almost six hundred miles through Virginia and North Carolina. The PWA also collaborated with the corps on the Painted Desert Inn and the NPS headquarters building in Santa Fe.[70]

The ranks of the Civilian Conservation Corps Alumni Association grow smaller every year. Their monthly newspaper, the *NACCCA Journal,* records their passing in the Chapter Eternal section of each issue. But they continue to staff their headquarters at Jefferson Barracks in St. Louis, which also houses a small museum. Other museums can be found in Michigan, Vermont, Minnesota, California, Virginia, Illinois, Georgia, Connecticut, Wyoming, and New Hampshire. At least three of their surviving camps—Birch Creek Camp in Beaverhead National Forest in Montana, Camp Rabideau in Chippewa National Forest in Minnesota, and Bear Brook Camp in New Hampshire—are on the National Register of Historic Places, as are many of their individual buildings. Though the CCC lasted only nine years and three months and some of the enrollees served only six months in it, they have, in a sense, spent their entire lives working for the corps, making sure we remember what they did and what it meant to them. And in so doing, we can discover what it means to us and will continue to mean.

Fig. 2.7. Red Rocks, near Denver. The magnificent views and superior acoustics were already present, but it took the CCC to turn this into a concert theater capable of hosting the Beatles. Photograph by R. D. Leighninger

Chapter 3

▪ THE PUBLIC WORKS ADMINISTRATION ▪
1933–35

The idea that public works might be useful to smooth out business cycles gained popularity during the 1920s, and the Hoover administration gradually tried to put it into practice to alleviate the Depression. First trying to speed up already-planned federal projects, then offering loans to private banks and corporations, and finally including state and local governments in the loan program in the final months of 1932, Hoover struggled to find a workable delivery system for this new weapon. The Emergency Relief and Construction Act, however, was much too little and much too late. He did not get another chance.

The new Roosevelt administration was emboldened by its youthful enthusiasm and the growing desperation that surrounded it to try a much more comprehensive attack. After creating the Civilian Conservation Corps and setting up an agency to deal with relief, the Federal Emergency Relief Administration (FERA), it then turned to agriculture and industry. The Public Works Administration (PWA) arose as part of Roosevelt's strategy for revitalizing industry

Stabilizing prices and wages was seen as useful to both propping up business confidence and eliminating the problem of overproduction. Rather than imposing controls, a cooperative approach was envisioned whereby business and labor, with the help of government mediation, could voluntarily come to an agreement on codes of operation. Production could be planned, destructive competition curtailed, and wage minimums established within a framework of collective bargaining. Industry would have to talk with labor and government but would be left free to regulate itself. This was the premise of Title 1 of the National Industrial Recovery Act (NIRA).[1] To implement it, the National Recovery Administration (NRA) was created and Gen. Hugh Johnson selected to head it. Johnson was a West Point graduate who had served on the War Industries Board, had worked with important industrialists like Bernard Baruch, and was vice president of a company that made farm machinery. He had a quick temper and was not known for diplomacy. In the army he was known as "Iron Pants."

To spur the economy into action while Johnson was trying to coordinate this grand discussion between industry and labor was Title 2 of the NIRA. This created the Federal Emergency Administration of Public Works. It became known almost immediately as the Public Works Administration. It was given $3.3 billion to work with, the largest amount ever allotted to a public works scheme. The man who would soon be empowered to spend it described it this way: You could drive a fleet of trucks from coast to coast, shoveling out a million dollars every mile, and still have enough left over to build a fleet of battleships.[2]

The PWA's first goal was to stimulate the economy by creating a demand for building materials and putting money into the hands of workers to spend. It was not technically a work-relief program such as those being run by the FERA and later by the Works Progress Administration (WPA). Hirees did not have to be currently unemployed. They were paid wages that prevailed for similar work in their part of the country, not an amount based on a calculation of their household needs. But part of the philosophy that drove the work-relief programs also drove PWA. This was the conviction that taking money from the government, known then as being "on the dole," was demeaning regardless of one's need. It was feared that unemployed workers would lose both their self-respect and their skills. Direct relief, providing money or groceries to the unemployed, would have been cheaper, but public works provided an investment in workers as well as in their communities.[3]

Some of the money allotted to the PWA was to go to branches of the federal government—$400 million to the Bureau of Public Roads and $238 million to build ships for the navy. Other agencies had their own lists of projects that they had prepared at the request of the Hoover administration in 1931. The NIRA did not lay out a rationale for giving one federal agency money to distribute to others. Centralization could have been an efficiency consideration or a way of ensuring that appropriations not get snarled in Congress.[4]

Money was also to go to state and local projects. It was to be a combined grant and loan package, with PWA paying 30 percent of the cost of labor and materials and loaning the project sponsor (referred to in the contract as the "owner") the remainder if it had no other resources. The loans would bear a 4 percent interest rate, which was thought low enough to encourage participation from hard-pressed communities but not so low as to eclipse private lenders.

Working directly with communities was without precedent in American politics. However, state public works departments had no experience with making grants and loans to local units, so it was felt that a federal-local connection would get projects started faster. Direct contact also made it easier to determine the local capability to secure and service a loan.[5] Furthermore, it circumvented regional rivalries in state politics and gave local governments more control over what was built in their communities and how it should look.

But the locals did not have a free hand. This was not a block grant. It came with rules governing procurement, labor practices, accounting methods, and other business procedures. This oversight was grounded partly in the fact that the federal government was not just a donor but also a creditor and partly in the desire to ensure efficiency and guard against waste. At least three audits were conducted by federal personnel, and a resident engineer-inspector (REI) was assigned to the building site.

When PWA was created as Title 2 of the NIRA and signed into law on June 16, 1933, it had only a temporary administrator, Col. Donald H. Sawyer, as its head. Given the need for rapid implementation, it is unclear why Roosevelt did not put someone with full authority in charge. Perhaps he was waiting to see what the national reaction would be to this highly experimental agency before deciding what kind of leadership it should have. Perhaps he was buying time to assess the capabilities of two likely candidates for the job, a strategy he would employ again when the Works Progress Administration was created two years later.

General Johnson thought he had the inside track. He believed the logical role of PWA was to serve as leverage for gaining compliance with the NRA. A large project requiring large amounts of cement, for example, could be held out as a reward for cooperation from the cement industry. Others in the Departments of Commerce and Agriculture shared this view. They wanted public works linked to the control of industry and not undertaken immediately and for their own sake. Considering that in 1934 PWA orders were 74 percent of the entire cement industry's business, this might have been a formidable weapon.[6] However, PWA would have been irreparably entangled with the ill-fated politics of the NRA and would most likely have suffered the same fate the NRA met in 1935 when the Supreme Court declared it unconstitutional. Fortunately, PWA was given a separate base of operations and told to begin at once.

Johnson went so far as to draw up a table of organization, create application forms, and even draft telegrams to people he planned to appoint. He had office space in the Commerce building picked out and a staff ready to occupy it. The general was not short on self-confidence.[7]

There was, however, another candidate—Secretary of the Interior Harold LeClair Ickes. Ickes was a crusty Chicago lawyer and a renegade Republican who had followed Theodore Roosevelt into the Progressive Party. He was unimpressed with Herbert Hoover and voted unenthusiastically for Democrat Al Smith in the 1928 presidential election. When Hoover's response to the Depression lived up to Ickes's negative expectations, he had no trouble preparing to vote for another Democrat.[8] But in Franklin Roosevelt he found more than a non-Hoover. He found someone he could support with gusto. He was "head over heals for the nomination" of FDR.[9]

Ickes's skilled service in the campaign earned him consideration for an appointment in the new administration. His first interest was in being commissioner of

Indian Affairs; he had a home in New Mexico and had fought for Indian rights. But he also had a deep commitment to conservation and knowledge of hydro-electric power. When he discovered that Roosevelt was looking for a western Progressive to serve as secretary of the Interior, Ickes put himself forward. Roosevelt had never met him but knew he was an effective and tireless organizer and administrator. They talked, and Roosevelt decided he was the man. "I liked the cut of his jib," said the experienced sailor.[10]

The new secretary soon established his command over the broad and varied Interior empire. He took on other responsibilities as well, becoming known as the "Secretary of Things in General."[11] Still, Roosevelt did not immediately name him public works administrator. He did, however, ask him to chair the Special Board for Public Works, its advisory body.

The special board consisted of the secretaries of War, Agriculture, Treasury, Commerce, Labor, and Interior, the director of the Bureau of the Budget, and the attorney general, an all-star cast. The presence of many of these cabinet officers made sense since they had units already engaged in public works. Treasury built federal buildings, particularly post offices. Agriculture had the Bureau of Public Roads. The War Department built military bases and the materiel deployed from them. But technical expertise was a minor part of their function. They brought political and policy-making experience to this new agency that had to invent itself from the ground up and become, as rapidly as possible, an accepted arm of the New Deal. With vast amounts of money and few precedents for spending, the PWA needed the involvement of the highest level of government to give it legitimacy.[12]

The special board met once a week, and the attendance record of the cabinet members was quite good, showing that they realized the importance of this new agency and their contribution to shaping it. An early and crucial decision was how to divvy up the money. Budget director Lewis Douglas told the board they had no legal obligation to spend any of the money and it would be bad for the economy if they did. Others felt that it should all be spent on federal projects. It did not matter where people were employed or where the materials were used. Labor secretary Frances Perkins argued that it *did* matter. Instead of improving the quality of army bases that most of the population would never inhabit, it would be far better to improve the health, education, and quality of life in the communities where the workers and their families lived. Fortunately, she won the argument and transformed the face of America.[13]

Thus there were to be "Non-Federal Projects" as well as federal ones. The label seems to have been an artifact of Colonel Sawyer's early filing system. Anything that did not fit into one of the existing federal agencies went into this residual pigeon hole. He was not expecting this part of the program to assume the major proportions that it did.[14]

The rules for nonfederal submissions had to be established. In addition to the 30 percent grant, the applicant could apply for a 70 percent loan, and the board had to decide how tough PWA should be in this financing. Many municipalities were already heavily in debt. Securing further loans would take both faith and hope on the part of the lender. Some on the board were willing to extend it. Interestingly, it was an assistant Treasury secretary, Lawrence Robert, who argued that it might be time to deviate from standard banking practice. Banks, he noted, sometimes propped up shaky businesses without adequate security simply because a default would get them nothing; their only hope for a return on their investment lay in the survival of the business. Likewise, the survival of the country was now at stake, and it was no time to be overly worried about repayment.[15]

Nevertheless, the board decided that PWA should try to establish "reasonable security" for its loans. In practice this would come to mean that the loan had a better-than-even chance of being repaid. If the prospects of return were only even, the loan might still be made if "the amount of employment and purchases of materials involved were considered a balancing factor." In theory, this looks pretty risky; in practice it was not. The default rate was low, and profits from the later sales of PWA securities more than made up for the losses.[16]

The special board also made labor policy. The NIRA, in its section 7a, gave federal recognition to the right of collective bargaining. PWA thus gave unions first call on its jobs; but if unions could not fill them within twenty-four hours, the U.S. Employment Service would take over. Local workers were to be preferred to out-of-towners, though a contractor might bring along a certain number of specialists if needed. Veterans were to get preference; but local nonveterans were given an edge over out-of-town vets, and union members were preferred over nonunion vets.[17]

At the suggestion of Secretary Perkins, a Labor Advisory Board was created to consult with organized labor and establish a wage policy. It was headed by Dr. Isador Lubin, who worked out a scheme of minimums for skilled and unskilled labor that varied according to three geographic regions of the country: northern, southern, and central. Skilled laborers earned $1.20 an hour in the North, $1.10 in the central zone, and $1.00 in the South. Unskilled wages were fifty cents, forty-five cents, and forty cents, respectively. A Board of Labor Review representing workers and contractors was established to arbitrate any disputes over wages. To spread the jobs farther, PWA employees were to work no more than thirty hours a week. Wages were to correspond to what was being paid in 1933.[18]

It was agreed that the three essential considerations in reviewing a project were its engineering soundness, the legal authority of the owner to undertake the project, and the ability of the owner to bear the financial burden of the construction. The latter would be particularly important if PWA was loaning money to the owner. Thus PWA began with three divisions: engineering, legal, and financial.

Because public works had been tainted by graft in the past, particularly in the machine politics of the big cities, Ickes and other members of the special board were concerned that the popular acceptance of the program would be imperiled if there were any perceptions of waste or corruption associated with it. Robert argued that local bond elections that might be required for communities to cover their part of the project were unlikely to pass if graft was expected to be part of the deal. More important, Ickes was known as "Honest Harold" from his days as a reformer in Chicago, and he was not about to risk his reputation for probity. As one with long experience in urban machine politics, he knew that a "tradition of lax local inspection was intrenched in American practice. Too often local inspectors winked at substandard materials or wage 'kick-backs.'"[19] Thus an inspections division was created to pursue any complaints about dishonesty in a PWA project. Investigators, usually with legal, accountancy, or law enforcement experience, were sent from Washington to try to nip any trouble in the bud. They would back up the on-site resident engineer-inspector (REI).[20]

The REI played an interesting and difficult role. He was someone with engineering training or contracting experience, sometimes even an architect.[21] He was paid out of the project budget but was responsible to PWA. He made sure that the bidding process was fair and open, proper building procedures were followed, hiring practices were in conformity with federal policy, specified wage levels were maintained, no corners were cut, no substitutions were made, no kickbacks by workers or suppliers to contractors were given, and no PWA materials or workers appeared in the mayor's driveway or at the governor's summer home.

Overall, REIs seemed to have managed good working relationships with owners, contractors, and laborers. They knew firsthand what delays were unavoidable due to weather conditions. They protected workers' interests but also came to the defense of contractors falsely accused by scheming workers. Their services are mostly lost to history. The names of the politicians, architects, and contractors appear on the bronze plaques affixed to each project. The names of the REIs survive only in the PWA microfilms at the National Archives.

Proposals for PWA projects were soon flowing in. Some were quite imaginative. A midwestern mayor wanted his office redecorated; a Kansas preacher wanted new Bibles for his flock. More interesting were the proposal for a moon rocket and the one for "a moving road, something like an escalator, from New York to San Francisco, along which would be built drug stores, theaters, churches, etc."[22] The special board probably got chuckles out of both ideas, little realizing they foreshadowed two great public works programs of later decades.

The need for communities to find ways of covering their 70 percent of the project inspired some creative accounting that spanned the spectrum from cradle to grave. One proposed a maternity hospital that could be paid for in twenty years. However, every woman in town would have to have a baby every year during that period. Another community wanted a cemetery, which would be paid off in seventeen years provided everyone in town died. A far bigger problem was the political pressure that businesses tried to apply in order to get their companies funded as "municipal projects."[23]

Contrary to expectations, however, inappropriate proposals were a minority. The board was expecting 85 percent of the submissions to be "dogs and cats." In fact, more than half of the nonfederal proposals passed the tests of all three divisions in spite of the fact that many communities were ill-equipped to furnish the technical information required on the application.[24]

In the first two years of the agency, Ickes maintained tight control of the state offices. Mimeographed instructions were issued daily. In some cases it amounted to what PWA historian J. Kerwin Williams describes as "administrative barbed wire." This, of course, guaranteed that the PWA would not have the rapid start hoped for by many in the administration. The *New Republic* Washington columnist TRB said the program "moved with glacial slowness, although with a glacier's gleaming purity."[25] And that was just how Ickes wanted it.

On July 8, Roosevelt appointed Harold Ickes PWA administrator. It was a blow to General Johnson. Labor secretary Perkins was present when the president informed Johnson. She reported that he turned "red, then dark red, then purplish." Roosevelt asked Perkins to stay with Johnson after the meeting and "keep him sweet." She drove him around the city for an hour while he calmed down.[26]

Having chaired the special board, Ickes had already exerted considerable influence on the character of the PWA. Now he had the authority to move but at his own deliberate speed. Public works projects, large or small, took some planning. And Ickes was determined that all proposals would get the most careful scrutiny. To make sure that he could count on his staff to be thorough, he prepared a fake proposal into which he had typed a large section from *Alice in Wonderland*. When all three divisions signed off without realizing that they were endorsing the undertakings of the White Rabbit and the Mad Hatter, Ickes rattled the windows with outrage. This ensured that every page was read but did not make for a speedy approval process. One impatient observer complained, "They're trying to run a fire department on the principles of a conservative bond house."[27]

After the legal, financial, and engineering divisions had signed off on the proposal, it went to Ickes, then to the special board, and then to the president. The approval of the board was usually granted with dispatch, probably because they had come to trust Ickes's cold eye. The president, however, was no rubber stamp. He would sometimes turn back projects the board had approved and call up ones they had not. Do not think, said Ickes, that "he just signs on the dotted line. He goes down the line and asks questions."[28]

Getting something going amidst all this careful deliberation was a challenge. Some communities had a head start. When the part of Hoover's Reconstruction

Finance Corporation that made loans to self-liquidating projects was closed down on June 26, 1933, PWA took over all projects that had received RFC approval and gave new life to those rejected because they could not pay for themselves.[29] Starting new projects was harder. Among the easiest projects were those involving road building, because it was a common, well-understood state activity. However, even these were delayed because state and local governments had laid off their engineers as the Depression got deeper.[30]

The board sent out a memo indicating the types of projects that would be preferred. Water, sewer, and waste disposal facilities were the top three. This may have reflected a carry-over of the RFC mindset that focused on projects that would be at least revenue producing if not self-liquidating. More likely, it was an indication of the dire state of public health in the rapidly growing cities where pollution-caused disease was a threat growing even more rapidly.[31]

States and municipalities were under serious legal constraints that prevented them from borrowing to fulfill their part of the contract with PWA. States set about modifying this legislation and coming up with new bond codes. PWA's legal department contributed by guiding communities in the issuance of revenue bonds and the creation of special authorities to undertake projects outside of normal fiscal jurisdictions. By mid-1935 over five hundred bills had been drafted, with the help of PWA, to deal with debt-limit laws. This horrified fiscal conservatives, who saw PWA as encouraging delinquency by enticing communities to borrow more than was good for them. But how much is "too much"?[32]

Williams argues that the existence of the PWA actually saved the credit ratings of state and local governments. The public works they needed could not have been put off for long without danger to the health and safety of their communities. With rising relief expenses and declining revenues, they would have gone under, making them ineligible for any future private borrowing. By allowing them to borrow, build what they needed, and pay off their debts, PWA preserved their credit until recovery arrived. Their dire straits were less a matter of imprudence than a matter of the fundamental inadequacy of a tax base. PWA contributed greatly to the future well-being of communities by getting them out of "needless financial strait-jackets."[33]

The legal entanglements of the new grant and loan program; the fierce desire of Harold Ickes to protect his program, his president, and his country against the threat of graft or waste; and the inexperience of many states and local governments in planning and executing public works projects all contributed to a very slow start for PWA. Out of the original NIRA appropriations of 1933, PWA had funded almost 16,000 federal projects but only 3,735 nonfederal ones. The gleaming glacier only increased the chill of the approaching winter of 1933–34. The economic effects of PWA's large projects were too far in the future. Too many people, particularly people without skills, were still unemployed and growing more desperate. It was time for another experiment.

Chapter 4

• THE CIVIL WORKS ADMINISTRATION •
1933–34

The Civil Works Administration (CWA) must be seen in the context of the Federal Emergency Relief Administration (FERA), from which it emerged, which it briefly dominated, and into which it dissolved when it fell victim to its own success. This dual history will be easier to follow than it might seem, because both organizations were led by one man, Harry L. Hopkins.

He was one man, but he had the energy of several despite frail health. His father was an optimistic but ne'er-do-well Iowa harness maker. His mother was a devout churchgoer who became president of the Iowa Methodist Home Missionary Society. Hopkins learned the "social gospel," a conviction that true religion required social justice, at Grinnell College, where he majored in history and political science. He was familiar with unemployment, poverty, and desperation well before the Depression. He worked at a settlement house in New York City and with the Association for Improving the Conditions of the Poor (AICP).[1]

Hopkins was a social worker often at odds with traditional social workers. While helping run the Emergency Work Bureau in New York City in 1930, he offered jobs without screening or a means test. When some complained about this, he simply told them where they could go. "Although he retained his acerbic personality," says biographer and granddaughter June Hopkins, "Hopkins soon learned . . . to defend government jobs programs with more appealing rhetoric."[2]

When Franklin Roosevelt was governor of New York and trying to deal with the mounting disaster of the Depression, he created a Temporary Emergency Relief Administration (TERA). Hopkins became its executive director. The fact that the agency had not one but two words in its title referring to its expected short life is probably not an accident. Everyone fervently hoped that the Depression was a nightmare from which they would soon awake. They were also concerned that any hint from government officials that it might not be temporary would be bad for morale. President Hoover had set the tone by trying never to utter the word "unemployment," preferring instead to see the problem as "employment stabilization."[3]

This is only one aspect of a continuing theme during the Depression: the framing of economic problems and their solutions in terms of perception and attitude. "Morale," "business confidence," and "consumer confidence" were on the minds and tongues of both pro– and anti–New Deal economists. Liberal John Maynard Keynes and conservative Henry Morgenthau both crafted their policy recommendations based on assumptions about what would persuade businesses that it was again safe to invest. Hoover's Treasury secretary Ogden Mills declared in 1932 that there was "nothing the matter with the United States except that it has the worst case of 'nerves' in history."[4] But the view was most memorably presented by Roosevelt in the assertion, "We have nothing to fear but fear itself." Economics sometimes seemed a branch of social psychology.

Hopkins shared this concern for morale but wanted to improve it with concrete action, not impression management. He quickly overhauled New York's administration of relief, bringing efficiency and accountability to the process. He oversaw TERA's distribution of eighty-three million dollars without corruption or political favoritism. The Federal Emergency Relief Act, which created the FERA, was signed on May 12, 1933.[5] On May 19, Hopkins got the job of heading the new agency.[6]

From colonial times, following the tradition of the Elizabethan Poor Laws, relief for the poor and unemployed generally rested with the local communities. Churches, private charities, and county "poor boards" were expected to take care of widows, orphans, and people with disabilities who were unable to support themselves. The Depression quickly overwhelmed what public and private resources existed for this purpose. Who could have imagined that a quarter of the population would be thrown out of work and a third of the nation would have difficulty putting food on the table? Even those counties and cities willing to raise taxes to meet this responsibility—and there were some—could not keep up with the need. Birmingham and New Orleans raised money for relief through bond issues. Chicago was spending an average of one hundred thousand dollars a day in December 1931.[7]

Local governments turned to the states. Some states denied either the existence of a problem or their responsibility for dealing with it. Others did what they could. The Pennsylvania legislature, after acrimonious debate, voted to send ten million dollars to the local poor boards in September 1931. That seems like an enormous sum, but it did not go far when divided among 1,150,000 unemployed people. The next year they voted another twelve million dollars and imposed a sales tax to raise the money. Illinois closed its relief stations on June 5, 1932, after spending twenty-three million dollars.[8]

Very quickly, the states began looking to Washington. The best President Hoover would do was to create a President's Emergency Committee on Employment to study the matter. When it recommended federal action, Hoover refused and its chairman resigned. Hoover finally allowed the creation, over his objections, of the Reconstruction Finance Corporation (RFC), and within it a modest public works program discussed in chapter 1. It was of little help in the crisis, but it was at least a recognition that the federal government bore some responsibility to solve it.[9]

Thus considerable pressure to do something about massive unemployment had already built up by the time the Roosevelt administration entered office. The FERA was to give $250 million to the states on a one-to-three matching basis. Another $250 million was available as grants at Hopkins's discretion to help those states with the worst problems.

The organization of FERA was makeshift. State relief organizations were newly formed. Relying on existing county administrators was inevitable. To get some control over this combination of inexperienced ad hoc groups and tradition-bound, small-town bureaucrats, Hopkins decided on a regional approach with a limited number of field representatives instead of a new Washington bureaucracy. The field representatives would travel widely, consult with the local administrators, help solve problems, and get things going as soon as possible. But he also hired a few people to establish a system of data collecting and record keeping so that there might be some kind of central accountability for the millions of dollars he was spending.[10]

For the most part, "relief" meant giving money or food coupons to people without incomes or other resources to care for themselves. It was usually referred to as "the dole" and was universally disliked by both those whose taxes made it possible and those who had to accept it. The dole was seen as an insult to the pride of workers who were accustomed to providing for their families through their own labor. Many who qualified for relief refused to apply for it.[11]

Another reason to refuse the dole or denigrate oneself for taking it was the application process. It involved a home visit by a social worker whose job was to determine if the applicant really needed relief and, if so, how much. Even when the social worker was sympathetic and sensitive, it was hard not to feel this household inspection as a violation of privacy.[12]

To avoid the stigma of taking something for nothing, the concept of "work relief" was invented. This involved not just handing out money but having people work for it. Applicants still had to endure the home visit and the means test, and their wages reflected the social worker's evaluation of what they needed. But they were no longer getting "something for nothing." They were working.

Work-relief projects were not without their own stigma, however. They were usually characterized as "make-work." The assumption behind this label is that this was work that did not need to be done. It was not useful in itself. The assumption was reinforced by reports from early projects of workers raking leaves from one side of the courthouse lawn and then raking them back again or ditch diggers filling in the ditches they had earlier dug.[13] For the most part, however, work-relief projects did things that needed doing and would not have been done otherwise: fixing a leaky roof at a school, paving roads and sidewalks, planting trees, draining swamps, building outdoor privies, and turning a vacant lot into a playground. The stigma of make-work remained, however.

The county and state relief administrators were inclined toward direct relief, because it was cheaper and it was what they were used to. Efforts from Washington to encourage work relief met with mixed results. Local administrators set up the projects. They were in a great hurry, had no time to plan, and did not have much experience with work projects. Local contractors did their best to keep projects off their turf, which meant that relief administrators had to avoid the more obviously useful things like building new schools. It is understandable that most of the projects conformed closely to the stereotypes of make-work. In the opinion of Corrington Gill, FERA's newly hired statistician, "they left much to be desired."[14]

When Hopkins took over FERA he shared Roosevelt's hope that the economy just might be turning upward. However, the data he was collecting suggested otherwise. One of Gill's first assignments was to conduct a nationwide census of those on relief. He found 12.5 million people out of work. He also found that they cut across a variety of sectors and levels of the economy. Hopkins reported these findings to the National Conference of Social Work, saying that the problem "is no longer a matter of unemployables and chronic dependents, but your friends and mine."[15] His field representatives observed not only increasing desperation but increasing anger and hints of potential violence.[16] Winter was closing in; it was Roosevelt's first winter in office, and it promised to be a severe one. A more drastic response was called for.

Several of Hopkins's lieutenants had been pondering the problem and had concluded that what was called for was a genuine public jobs program. This meant real jobs at real wages, not make-work. They convinced Hopkins, who convinced Roosevelt. The Civil Works Administration was born November 9, 1933. Its herculean goal was to put four million people to work in thirty days.[17]

Hopkins had four hundred million dollars to do the job. He got it from Harold Ickes and the Public Works Administration. Ickes was proceeding at his own deliberate pace and was not going to be hurried. He did not need that money during the winter of '33, so he gave the program his blessing. The next question was how to enlist the four million workers. It was decided that half would come from FERA work projects already begun and the other half would be recruited through the recently created United States Employment Service (USES).[18]

The two million FERA workers were already on the job or waiting to be transferred from direct relief to work projects. Nine million people swarmed to the USES offices to apply for the other two million slots. There were seventy thousand lined up before dawn in the parks of Chicago where the recruitment stations were located. Idaho, where word traveled more slowly, still managed to fill its quota of six thousand in two weeks.[19] On January 18, 1934, the goal was met: 4,263,644 people were at work.

For those FERA workers who had been on the job from the beginning, the first payday was Friday, November 23, 1933. How does one cut checks for a million people on such short notice? The Treasury Department and the General Accounting Office agreed that it was physically impossible to print and distribute the necessary payroll forms and checks. But the Bureau of Printing and Engraving put on three shifts a day. Hopkins asked the Veterans Administration, which had check-writing machinery in offices across the country, to disburse the payments. Army planes carried the checks across the country. The CWA issued identification cards to workers so that banks could be sure they were cashing checks for the right people, and banks agreed not to charge for the service. It was a logistical triumph that took the cooperation of thousands of people and numerous government agencies, the peacetime equivalent of the evacuation of Dunkirk. The first CWA payroll, 814,511 workers, was met on time.[20]

Another logistical problem was equipping the workers. The easiest projects to get started—and the least likely to threaten the private sector—were brush clearing, road grading, paving, ditch digging, and building repair efforts. They were also natural choices because they involved more unskilled workers. But such projects required hand tools. In November, CWA officials called tool manufacturers to see if they could meet the need. No problem, they were told; there was plenty of inventory in their warehouses. But they were completely unprepared for the speed and efficiency of the CWA mobilization. Supplies were exhausted by December, and factories had to resume production (which was exactly what Roosevelt hoped for). Even twenty-five thousand wheelbarrows a day was not enough. The army helped, opening warehouses untouched since World War I. But many CWA projects were begun without the tools to execute them.[21]

Of course, this did nothing to help the public image of the CWA. Visitors to a work site seeing two men sitting by while a third used the only available shovel were not likely to have a high regard for CWA workers or administrators. Nonetheless, two hundred thousand projects were soon under way with all the tools, muscle, and energy the CWA could muster. Overall, public reception was enthusiastic. *Time* magazine called it the most popular part of the New Deal and noted the "storm of protest" against ending it. Though no friend of the New Deal, *Time* put Harry Hopkins on its cover and wrote a very complimentary story about him.[22]

Compared with traditional work relief, the CWA was unique and unprecedented. There were no means tests nor home visits. Workers were paid in cash, not vouchers or coupons, and were free to spend it as they chose. Wages were "real" in the sense that they were based on prevailing standards and not calculated to meet the minimum subsistence requirements of the worker's family. CWA also paid workman's compensation in the event of on-the-job injuries or deaths. This was unheard of in a work-relief program.

The initial CWA projects were construction related and involved manual labor, much of it unskilled. But Hopkins was well aware that manual laborers were not the only people out of work. They were also "your friends and mine," he told the social workers. Teachers, nurses, clerical workers, musicians, architects, and others had also lost their jobs. Hopkins had employed teachers in early FERA projects that offered literacy classes, vocational education, and other adult-oriented learning opportunities. FERA also supported nursery schools. He went further with the CWA.[23]

Working with the USES, Hopkins established the Civil Works Service (CWS) specifically for white-collar employment. Nurses worked in public health programs. Librarians kept libraries open. Statistical surveys of community needs were conducted. Child nutrition was investigated. Archeological digs were supported. Architects began the Historical American Buildings Survey (HABS), which provided an invaluable record of our architectural heritage and which is still at work. The Public Works of Art Project (PWAP), begun in cooperation with the Treasury Department, put painters, muralists, and sculptors to work decorating public buildings. Theater and concert programs were also begun. Involving artists was a risk, because they were not popularly regarded as "workers" nor seen as an important sector of the economy, but Hopkins knew they had to eat like everyone else.[24]

The holidays of 1933 were actually joyous in the homes of CWA workers. Bonnie Fox Schwartz, whose history of the CWA is both comprehensive and trenchant, summarizes the impact of the program on its participants: "The array of projects, which encompassed the broadest range of skills, liberated an enthusiasm long imprisoned in idleness. CWA wages gave the first real cash—and freedom to spend—that many had in months and even years. Observers saw individuals back on their feet, their families once again secure. But just as significant was the transformation in the consciousness of those on the job. No longer grateful clients, appreciative of the dole and grocery tickets, CWA employees felt they had 'earned' their way."[25]

The *Wall Street Journal* announced at the center of its front page: "Merchandisers' December Sales Big; Aided by Heavy Holiday Buying; Woolworth Tops 1932." Not just the retail economy, it said, but "all sectors of the economy are participating in the upturn." It attributed this to the "general revival in purchasing power." In its story three weeks later, headlined "January Setting Retail Records," it was willing to give some credit to "the government's payroll expenditures on public works programs."[26]

The euphoria did not last. The CWA was expensive. It was costing two hundred million dollars a month. FERA spent only sixty million dollars on both direct and work relief. CWA also offered employee benefits that meant the prospect of further expenses down the line. Both Roosevelt and Hopkins had seen the program as an experiment and time limited. CWA's impact on the economy was tangible, but its enemies were accumulating. The fact that it was hugely successful at what it tried to do was not enough to embolden FDR to consider carrying it on in the face of growing opposition. Nor was Hopkins willing to try to overcome his president's resolve.

Complaints came from all directions. Contractors were frozen out, because CWA, unlike PWA, operated by "force account," essentially doing its own contracting. Farmers and small manufacturers were afraid that the CWA would dry up the pool of cheap labor they depended on. Southerners and southwesterners feared the experience of earning decent wages was going to "spoil" African Americans and Hispanics. Social workers attacked it from both sides. Some did not approve of providing jobs without proper casework to determine the extent of family needs. Others thought the program did not provide adequate work and relief from poverty. Particularly toward the end, when Hopkins cut hours and allowed rotation of jobs, the CWA lost its distinctiveness as a program offering "real jobs at real wages." In some places, "too little money, and too many people in need turned the CWA into just another work-relief project."[27]

Accusations of political favoritism from both parties were a continuing problem. Though both Roosevelt and Hopkins decreed that political patronage should play no part in hiring, it was predictable that this wish would be disregarded. It was also predictable that even where no preference was being given, those who did not get jobs would believe there was. According to Schwartz, the key people in most state CWA organizations were engineers, often followers of Frederick Taylor, the father of "scientific management." Their first allegiance was to efficiency. Politically, they tended to come from the Progressive wing of the Republican Party and were unlikely to have any sympathy with the patronage system of either party. Hopkins also made use of officers of the Army Corps of Engineers to project political neutrality. None of this quieted the howls of state and local politicians seeking work for their constituents.[28]

The speed with which CWA went into action also left it open to corrupt practices. Bribes, kickbacks, price gouging by suppliers, and other criminal manipulations were hard to expose as millions of dollars passed through the makeshift organization. One reason why PWA moved so slowly was that Harold Ickes was determined to prevent these things. Hopkins had other priorities. Thus real and imagined scandals were reported regularly in newspapers around the country. Hopkins did his best to root out corruption and counteract the bad publicity. He could and did fire state and local administrators and even whole organizations. He enlisted Ickes's PWA Investigations Division to pursue reports of attempts by unions to control projects. His field representatives moved from place to place trying to serve as watchdogs as well as troubleshooters. But his major job was putting people to work on useful projects. Running a squeaky-clean organization was impossible under the circumstances. All things considered, however, "it was remarkably well managed."[29]

Roosevelt was nervous about both the cost and the criticism of the program, and he continued to believe in the virtues of a balanced budget. His Treasury secretary, Henry Morgenthau, and budget director Lewis Douglas believed a balanced budget to be the highest virtue and were increasingly anxious about Roosevelt's every deviation from the true path. Douglas also articulated the fear of many that people might become "dependent" on government jobs. On top of all this, all of them, Hopkins included, were still hoping for an upturn in the economy. Brought to life in just two weeks and allowed to live only four and a half months, the CWA's demise would also be quick.[30]

On February 15, 1934, Congress approved $950 million for relief, of which $450 million was directed to closing out CWA.[31] Ickes had refused to divert any further money from the PWA, now gathering steam. This freed Hopkins, who up to this point had been bound by PWA rules because he was using PWA money, to cut wages and hours and rotate workers in and out of jobs, allowing him to stretch the appropriation to the end of March. Layoffs progressed throughout the month. Pleas to continue the program were loud but ineffective. On March 31, the Civil Works Administration experiment ended.[32]

Hopkins and his aide Jake Baker did their best to continue the most promising CWA projects through FERA. Though most projects were selected because they could be completed quickly, many were both of obvious long-range value and only partially finished. Some would become totally useless if they were *not* finished—for example, ditches dug for sewer pipes that would soon cave in if the pipes were not laid. Fortunately, FERA could pick up some of them.

Projects begun by CWA and completed by FERA included an incinerator in Charleston, South Carolina, a tuberculosis hospital in Phoenix, the administrative center at Newark Airport, the Cathedral of Learning in Pittsburgh, the Boise Art Museum, and a community center in Florida that was the largest building of its kind ever constructed of coquina, the shell-and-lime combination used in the historic fortress in St. Augustine. A differential analyzer—a three-ton piece of calculating equipment—reputed to be the largest in the world was built for the University of Pennsylvania. The overhaul of the Detroit streetcar system was also finished by CWA.[33]

On its own, CWA accomplished much of lasting value, and most of it is invisible to the contemporary eye. The thousands of miles of paved roads and the bridges and culverts that accompanied them helped move manufactured goods from factories to stores and fresh meat and produce from farm to market. But how can one know what agency in what decade is responsible for this ability to travel quickly along this route? One mile of road looks much like any other. The water and sewer pipes improved public health greatly, but they are mostly out of sight.

Even when individually recognizable structures are involved, the fingerprints of CWA workers are difficult to find. Reports do not distinguish between repair and new construction and rarely mention individual places and structures, so it is impossible to identify each project without digging up information community by community. There is nothing like the project-by-project files kept by the PWA. The state summary reports are the best guides to particular accomplishments, but these, too, tend to concentrate on aggregate statistics rather than identification of specific communities and projects. Nevertheless, one can get some idea of its impact in the totals recorded (see table 4.1) and find mention of particulars here and there.[34]

In Chicago's Lincoln Park, 2,500 sprinkler pipes were installed. A massive playground improvement was carried out throughout Los Angeles. In New York City parks, repairs were made to 145 comfort stations, 678 drinking fountains, and 22,500 park benches. Eleven thousand trees were planted and 7,000 dead ones removed. Eight golf courses were renovated and every playground was resurfaced and reequipped with jungle gyms, slides, and sandboxes. Phoenix parks were similarly overhauled, and every alley in the city was surfaced with gravel. Liberty Memorial Park in Kansas City was cleared, graded, and enclosed with stone walls.

Table 4.1 Accomplishments of the Civil Works Administration

New roads	44,000 miles
Road repairs	200,000 miles
Drainage and irrigation ditches	9,000 miles
Levees	2,000 miles
New water mains	1,000 miles
Sanitary and storm sewers	2,700 miles
Bridges	7,000
Large culverts	10,000
Sanitary privies	150,000
Pumping stations	400
Playgrounds	2,000
Swimming pools	350
Athletic fields	4,000
Schools, new or repaired	4,000
Airports, new or improved	1,000

Sources: Harry Hopkins, *Spending to Save* (New York: W. W. Norton, 1936), 121, 168; Bonnie Fox Schwartz, *The Civil Works Administration, 1933–1934: The Business of Emergency Employment in the New Deal* (Princeton, N.J.: Princeton University Press, 1984), 183.

City Park in New Orleans was extended and an eighteen-hole golf course constructed.[35]

Most of the work in the four thousand school projects was repairing and refurbishing existing facilities. But the modest CWA efforts were no doubt well appreciated. A typical project in Natchitoches Parish, Louisiana, consisted of reroofing the school building, painting the teachers' cottages, repairing desks and chairs, and landscaping the grounds.

Higher education was assisted as well. For example Louisiana State University got extensive sprucing up with new drill fields for the cadets, sidewalks, sewers, drainage canals, and landscaping. A swamp to the north of campus was drained to combat malaria, and a lake to the east was enlarged from sixty-one to three hundred acres. A botanical garden was constructed. Buildings were termite proofed. The most ambitious project, however, was the moving of Alumni Hall from its site on the abandoned downtown campus. The stone building was completely dismantled and put back together on the new campus several miles south.[36]

In Prescott, Arizona, CWA made three important contributions to cultural and economic life. The Sharlot Hall Museum, described by one local writer as "one of the most beautiful and historically important museums in all of the Southwest," is the centerpiece of a complex of nine historical or newly constructed buildings interpreting the experiences of Arizona pioneers. Its namesake, a pioneer herself who helped run her family's ranching and mining operations and slept with a gun under her pillow, became a civic leader and territorial historian. She organized the CWA effort to build the museum.[37]

The Smoki Museum was built to house a large collection of Native artifacts that local citizens had collected. CWA workers also crafted a diorama depicting life at the cliff dwelling known as Montezuma's Castle. The museum and the Hopi dances organized by its founders helped educate residents and tourists about the culture of their ancestors and neighbors. The dances are no longer held, but educational programs continue.[38]

Prescott is also home to what is billed as the "oldest rodeo in the world." CWA built a grandstand that has served continuously as the focus of the rodeo. The project is atypical for CWA, because heavy equipment and materials were needed. The city probably provided the steel beams and concrete for the enterprise. And a wise investment it was. The rodeo and other events held at the rodeo grounds attract over one hundred thousand tourists and over $2.5 million to the city each year. The grandstand was immortalized in 1971 by the Hollywood film *Junior Bonner,* directed by Sam Peckinpah and starring Steve McQueen, Robert Preston, Ida Lupino, and Ben Johnson.[39]

In its extremely brief life, the Civil Works Administration showed that public works projects conducted on a large scale could be beneficial to both the well-being of individuals and the health of the economy. Even more important, from a

Fig. 4.1. The Smoki Museum houses a collection of Native American arts and artifacts. The CWA built it along with a diorama inside showing Montezuma's Castle and its early inhabitants. Photograph by R. D. Leighninger

Fig. 4.2. Prescott Fairgrounds, home of the oldest rodeo in the country. Steve McQueen played a bronc rider here in the film *Junior Bonner*. Photograph by R. D. Leighninger

perspective seventy years later, CWA demonstrated that public works projects could make enduring contributions to the nation's physical and cultural infrastructure. The CWA was clearly more than temporary work relief; it was long-range public investment.

Hopkins appreciated this, though his priority remained the individual worker. Toward the end of *Spending to Save,* his personal account of the CWA and WPA, he says: "The regeneration of the individual worker no longer needs to be the only concern of a national work program for the unemployed. We have come to a second concept which is that his work is necessary to enrich the national life. In adopting this second principle we have not, however, abandoned our first. Our work must be work for the worker by the worker. He is the first figure. He must be the first and last digit in all government accounting."[40]

Yet in between the first and last digit, Hopkins had time to appreciate what his "second principle" had accomplished. "Long after the workers of the CWA are dead and gone and these hard times are forgotten, their effort will be remembered by permanent useful works in every county of every state. People will ride over bridges they made, travel on their highways, attend schools they built, navigate waterways they improved, do their public business in courthouses and state capitols which workers from CWA rescued from disrepair."[41]

Hopkins banked the fires of CWA and let the steam out of the engine. The engineers went on to other things, and the social workers regained control of FERA, which absorbed as many of the work projects as it could, chugging along on its limited resources. Hopkins was exhausted, and the president sent him to Europe to study European social security programs and to recuperate. But his own fire had not gone out. He was making new plans for a federal work program that was to rise a year later from the ashes of CWA.

Chapter 5

THE WORKS PROGRESS ADMINISTRATION
1935–43

What people remember about public works in the New Deal, if they remember anything at all, is the Works Progress Administration (WPA). It has come to stand in the public mind for *all* Depression-era public works programs. This iconic status was achieved probably because the WPA was larger and closed down later than most of the building agencies. It possessed the same initials, slightly altered, as its rival, the Public Works Administration (PWA). Even at the time, both citizens and politicians were frequently confused about which agency was building what project. Some were probably unaware that there were two separate agencies.[1] So, from the distance of a few decades, it is understandable that PWA and WPA would blur into each other and the rest would be forgotten.

The prominence of the WPA also likely arose from the fact that it had projects in almost every community; it was more deeply enmeshed in politics than other programs; its organization was messier; and, for all of the above reasons, it was the easiest target for New Deal critics. The sheer variety of its efforts made it inevitable that almost everyone could find something it was doing that they thought was unnecessary or worthless. The favorite word for projects one did not like was "boondoggle," which became synonymous with government waste.[2]

Finding real boondoggles was easier in the press than on the ground. One local WPA officer finally decided that the definition of a boondoggle was a project in some other town. "I've been hunting all over the state for one," he explained, "but everywhere I go I'm told it's in the next county. So far, I haven't been able to catch up with a real, live one."[3]

Boondoggles may have been in the eye of the beholder, but there were concerns about WPA patronage and efficiency inside the administration as well as outside. Harry Hopkins, with ferocious energy and dedication, was able to coordinate numerous federal agencies to get the Civil Works Administration (CWA) running in two weeks. He was able to fight back when state and local politicians tried to use CWA jobs for their benefit. Organizing and running WPA was more complicated.

The convoluted circumstances of its creation determined its initial disorganization. The inadequacy of its funding in comparison to the expectations it bore required numerous damaging compromises. The political vulnerability it suffered throughout its existence was a near-fatal handicap. But by attempting to comprehend this supreme messiness we gain a better understanding of the magnitude of its accomplishments.

In late 1934, the fervently wished-for economic recovery was showing no signs of rewarding supplicants. The boost that CWA salaries gave to the economy in December and January was hardly enough to restart production. There were no private jobs waiting for the CWA workers when the program was closed down in March. Those worried that public jobs at real wages were competing with the private sector found no serious competitors in sight. Even after the WPA was running at full steam, this concern was difficult to substantiate. When one state contractors' organization complained that federal programs had taken away all the electricians and they could find no one to work for them, WPA sent them a list of three hundred unemployed electricians. The contractors apologized but did not hire any electricians. Even *Fortune* magazine could find no evidence for WPA competition.[4] Skilled workers needed jobs. Unskilled and semiskilled workers were even more desperate.

So Hopkins went to work on a new program. Initially he was hoping only to extend the Federal Emergency Relief Administration (FERA) work program with money from the Reconstruction Finance Corporation. But Roosevelt had larger ideas.[5]

Roosevelt had become reconciled to the necessity of further measures to combat unemployment. He was also beginning to think of work programs as an instrument of recovery in their own right. The main purpose of the PWA was to stimulate heavy industry through its demand for iron, steel, cement, and other building materials. The effects of CWA proved that wages to common laborers could also stimulate the economy. One FERA document recommended that government money should go "to the lowest economic strata because it is there that occurs automatically the greatest number of respendings."[6] Roosevelt was not completely converted to this position until the recession of 1937, when he saw the results of cutting the public works programs. But the idea was percolating within the administration.[7]

Roosevelt was also thinking about how the political and economic imperative to put people to work related to the problems of those who could not work, usually referred to as "unemployables." He began to put together an economic security package that involved what sociologist Edwin Amenta, in his masterful analysis of American social policy from 1880 to 1950, has called America's "first welfare reform."[8]

Both Roosevelt and Hopkins shared the general public distaste for "the dole." This is why FERA had work projects added to its original mission of direct relief and why CWA was totally focused on jobs. Roosevelt described direct relief for employable workers in words that might surprise modern conservatives. It was, he said, "a narcotic, a subtle destroyer of the human spirit."[9] He proposed to return it entirely to the local level where it would be available only to those who could not work. Anyone who could work should have a job. If the market could not provide them, the government should.

There were those who could not or should not work: people with disabilities like blindness, elders who had already put in a full work life and were entitled to some rest in their final years, and widows with young children who should be supported as they raised their families. For them a system of "social security" was necessary, a national system not determined by local circumstances or prejudices. To this end, he had appointed a Committee on Economic Security, which included some who were working on the work program, like Hopkins and Labor secretary Frances Perkins, and some who were not. They took each other into account but submitted separate reports.[10]

This new work effort, then, was not just another desperate measure to meet an immediate crisis; it was a comprehensive work and relief program that could prepare the country for future challenges. Roosevelt saw the WPA as part of a package, just as he saw both titles of the National Industrial Recovery Act—its National Recovery Administration (NRA) and Public Works Administration—as a package. He told Congress on June 8, 1934, that he was "looking for a sound means which I can recommend to provide at once security against several of the disturbing factors of life—especially those which relate to unemployment and old age."[11]

Both packages came apart quickly under the pressure of American politics. The NRA was declared unconstitutional, and no one attempted to revive it. The PWA, however, carried on until 1942. The WPA lasted until 1943 and was equally productive. But only the Social Security Act, the WPA's partner in the work and security package, survived the New Deal to become a permanent part of American social policy.

The story of the conception, launch, operation, defense, and demise of the Works Progress Administration is complex and convoluted. Perhaps that is why no one has undertaken to tell it in recent times. It sprawled across eight tumultuous years and spanned all levels of government. The best history of WPA is still the one written at the time, *The Administration of Federal Work Relief* by Arthur W. Macmahon, John D. Millett, and Gladys Ogden. It provides solid analysis with stylistic flair. For example many have commented on Roosevelt's style of administration, which dispersed responsibility and authority, creating competitive as well as complementary centers of activity. But few have summed it up as well: "a planetary system wherein many would have a place in the sun."[12]

In late 1934, the planetary system was about to expand. The congressional elections sent new recruits to enlarge the forces sympathetic to the New Deal in both the House and Senate. It gave those who were favorable to government spending as a weapon to fight the Depression a majority of twenty-three in the House and two in the Senate.[13]

Roosevelt was reenergized by the election; Hopkins was turbocharged. He told his core staff members: "Boys—this is our hour. We've got to get everything we want—a works program, social security, wages and hours, everything—now or never. Get your minds to work on developing a complete ticket to provide security for all the folks of this country up and down and across the board."[14] He, too, was thinking about an economic security package, not just a work program.[15]

Both Hopkins and Harold Ickes were natural candidates to run the new program. They had the experience. Both had supporters and detractors in and out of Congress. Each had his own style and priorities. Ickes was known for care and deliberation, tight budgeting, and strict oversight. Hopkins embodied speed and flexibility, capacity for hard work, and disregard for hierarchy. He also "tended to regard money (his own as well as other people's) as something to be spent as quickly as possible."[16] Roosevelt, all too aware of the considerable strengths and vulnerabilities of his deputies, took his time deciding how and by whom to have the new program administered.

Roosevelt's conclusion, characteristically, was to give total control to neither. He named himself as titular head. Under him he created a triumvirate, giving Ickes and Hopkins each a role and placing Frank Walker between them. Walker was a "quiet, gentle, trustworthy, unquenchably friendly man who was invaluable to Roosevelt through the years as a spreader of oil on troubled administrative waters."[17] This, Roosevelt hoped, would prevent open combat between the two public works warriors; but the resulting structure did not work well for either of them or anyone else. It had other consequences too.

As Roosevelt planned it, Walker's Division of Applications and Information (DAI) would receive proposals for public works projects. Hopkins would make sure there were enough workers on relief in the community proposing the project to carry it out. Ickes, heading the Advisory Committee on Allotments (ACA), would get the proposals after Walker had sorted and Hopkins had checked them. The president would have the final decision. Hopkins could also carry out "small useful projects" of his own under a branch called the Works Progress Administration (WPA). When the scheme was finally announced, it took Roosevelt four press conferences to explain it to the public.[18]

The purpose of the Emergency Relief Appropriations Act of 1935 was to relieve unemployment by financing labor-intensive projects that would be useful but not compete with private business.[19] The appropriation was to be spread among existing relief agencies and new ones that the president might create. The relative importance of these agencies and their interrelationships was unclear. Indeed its most important creation, the WPA, was an unnamed seedling in the policy forest.

The clearest part of the proposal was that it would require $4,880,000,000. What the money would be used for was less clear. To some members of Congress, it gave the president an alarming amount of discretion. Sen. Arthur Vandenberg, a Michigan Republican, called it "the most amazing legislative proposal in the history of this or any other democracy. It represents four or five billion dollars worth of lost liberty and the erection of a corresponding Presidential speculation. It was born in a mysterious dark; it has defied intelligent illumination; its only merit is a pious, puzzling hope; its program is a lottery; its only justification is the counsel of desperation."[20] Quoting an unnamed journalist, Vandenberg said the bill could be simplified by "striking out all the text and substituting two brief sections: "SECTION 1—Congress hereby appropriates $4,880,000,000 to the President of the United States to use as he pleases. SECTION 2—Anybody who does not like it is fined $1,000."[21]

The number was not pulled out of a hat, but it might as well have been. It was the product of too many conflicting goals being funneled into a single program without the time to reconcile the ingredients or accurately assess the political possibilities of enacting it. One focus was to be permanent, self-liquidating projects such as Hoover had wanted, ones that would pay for themselves and others over time ($8.5 billion). Another focus was work relief ($4 billion). However, a long-term project with that kind of price tag was inconceivable to Treasury secretary Henry Morgenthau.[22]

Hopkins was thinking in terms of $5 billion a year for five years. Sen. Robert LaFollette was ready for an initial appropriation of $9 billion. But in the end Roosevelt and Morgenthau picked the numbers that came from the focus on relief: $4 billion for jobs and another $880 million to keep the CCC going and to close out FERA. A two-year limit was set. But the permanent, big-ticket items remained on the wish list. The result was to be too little and over too soon to fulfill any of the hopes it carried. With neither Hopkins nor Ickes involved in the final shaping of the bill, the policy behind it was a hash and its implementing organization an obstacle course. It went to Congress "still invertebrate."[23]

There were a number of important consequences of the modest amount of money the president asked for the program. To call five billion dollars "modest" may raise eyebrows, but in the context of the amount of public works needing attention and the numbers of citizens needing employment, a far larger sum might have been more appropriate. Since the administration did not think it could or should expect more, it guaranteed not only that the program could not accomplish all its architects had hoped for it but also that WPA workers would be subjected to both the "security wage" and the means test that had been temporarily suspended by the Civil Works Administration. The money had to be spread as widely as possible and go to those who were recognized as most in need—those "on relief."[24]

This restriction sprang not just from the desire to spread the money as thinly as possible. There was political motivation as well. If public wages were not appreciably below what might be paid in the private sector, it was feared that WPA workers might be reluctant to go back to private employment. This concern was shared by Roosevelt and Ickes as well as New Deal opponents. Evidence to support this fear was lacking, because there was so little in the private sector to compete with public jobs, but the ideological conviction ran deep.[25]

Another consequence of the need to stretch the appropriation as far as it would go was that it necessitated the use of "force accounts" in managing construction. The PWA used private contractors who bid competitively on projects and, if they bid wisely, made a profit. The force account cut out the contractor and the profit entirely. The workers and materials would be assembled by WPA itself, and it would manage the project. This saved the government money but exposed the program to direct criticism should anything go wrong. It also guaranteed an active lobby of contractors working against it.[26]

The name of the organization that Hopkins would lead was itself the subject of some controversy, at least for Ickes. He was convinced that Hopkins had intentionally picked initials, WPA, that would be confused with those of his own organization, PWA. The first two initials, however, came about naturally, because Roosevelt intended that the organization would keep him advised about the *progress* of the *works* programs. However, it was originally to be called the Works Progress Division. This was changed to Works Progress Administration in Executive Order 7034, which followed. No biographer has offered an explanation for the change, so the conspiracy theory remains alive.[27]

In the confusion of the early discussion of the new works program, few noticed the reference to "small useful projects" that was tacked onto the end of Executive Order 7034 after a lengthy description of WPA's various bookkeeping functions.[28] It was to become a tail that wagged the dog. "Although oblique and hardly more than a subordinate clause," said Macmahon, "those words were the most significant ones in the whole series of initial orders." Sherwood described them as a "loophole" that Roosevelt provided for Hopkins, knowing that for Hopkins it was more than enough. It was, in fact, wide enough to push ten billion dollars through.[29] But the push would be exhausting.

Getting the works program enacted was an accomplishment. Actually getting something built with it was an even bigger one. A proposal went first to the Division of Applications and Information (DAI). Then it was referred to WPA to make sure that there were enough workers on relief in the area of the proposed project to carry it out, unless it was a project originated by WPA, in which case it could go on to the next step. The next step was to the Bureau of the Budget to have its administrative costs checked. The proposal proceeded then to the Advisory Committee on Allotments and from there to the president's desk. Those the president approved went back to the Bureau of the Budget, where a formal letter for the president's signature was drafted. Duly signed, the letter went to the Treasury Department where a warrant for appropriation of money to launch the project was prepared. Finally, it went for countersignature to the comptroller general. Woefully complicated in theory, this scheme only got worse in practice.

Two days after Frank Walker's appointment as head of DAI was announced on May 6, the proposals began arriving. He also got fifteen thousand applications for employment in his new agency. The project applications averaged 163 a day at the beginning and rose to 1,067 per day by September. The agency got as many as 1,812 phone calls in a day and an average of 755 pieces of mail. Walker collapsed in early June, and when his agency suffered a similar fate in September, he retired. The DAI, in Macmahon's words, managed to serve as a "breakwater" against the storm surge of applications and, to a limited extent, a "dam and conduit." It also kept Hopkins and Ickes in rough equilibrium within the New Deal planetary system, which is what it was created for in the first place.[30]

The next stop, the WPA review, was in one sense a conflict of interests. The main goal of the new works program was to fund labor-intensive projects with low materials costs. And the WPA was busy developing just such projects. But the projects from other agencies that were heavier on materials and machinery, such as PWA's, were likely to be turned back for just these reasons. Thus WPA was favoring its own projects over others, because that was the purpose of the program as they saw it. Those who saw the program in less focused terms felt that the WPA was an obstruction.[31]

Ickes's domain, the Advisory Committee on Allotments, was presumably the decision-making body. But it included everyone in the government who might engage in public works projects, plus representatives of labor, farming, the American Bankers Association, and the U.S. Conference of Mayors.[32] It was an ensemble suggesting the choruses of "The Twelve Days of Christmas." Among the lords a-leaping were Sears, Roebuck president Gen. Robert E. Wood and New York City mayor Fiorello LaGuardia. Ickes expected that it would either be a great waste of time or that, after a period of initial confusion, he would whip it into shape to suit his own needs. Neither prediction was realized.

The committee actually featured a note of efficiency amidst the scramble of adhocracy, and it was not Ickes's doing. President Roosevelt took seriously the position he had assigned himself. He attended all the meetings, often surprising the committee by being the best informed member present about both project details and agency procedures. Given the number of proposals to be considered, discussion was never extensive. But the committee gave the president both a sounding board and an opportunity to assert his priorities. As with the PWA, he was no rubber stamp. He made the decisions, then worked after the meeting with the budget director so that they could be taken immediately back for the preparation of approval letters.[33]

And there, at least for the WPA proposals, expedition stalled again. The bureau had only one person assigned to prepare all WPA projects. He worked sixteen-hour days, sometimes not leaving his desk for forty-two hours at a stretch. Things relaxed in mid-October, and he only had to work fourteen-hour days.[34]

Once the proposal cleared the Bureau of the Budget, was signed by the president, and had its Treasury accounts set up, it went to the General Accounting Office (GAO) for countersignature by the comptroller general. This proved an even greater nightmare for Hopkins. The comptroller general was no friend of the New Deal. John McCarl was a relic of the Coolidge administration, meaning not only that he thought like Coolidge but that he had actually been *appointed* by Coolidge. He had already been in office fourteen years when WPA was born. He would not do business with subordinates, only the principal; nor would he delegate. He would not use the telephone. When he rejected a proposal, he would not say why.[35]

Roosevelt would have happily sent McCarl into retirement, but the Supreme Court had just rendered a decision that made this impossible. Roosevelt had fired another Coolidge appointee in 1933, but on May 27, 1935, the court said that federal regulators could not be removed for political reasons before their appointments were up.[36] So when Comptroller McCarl decided it was his duty to look into all legal aspects of administering the works program, there was no way to stop him. Newspaper accounts of the bottleneck finally provoked the comptroller to compromise.[37]

Hopkins at least had the advantage of a seasoned organization behind him. As FERA had transformed itself into CWA and back again, it now became WPA. His team of devoted aides was willing to work as hard as he did. The lights in the nine different buildings where WPA had offices were seldom out. Elevators and switchboards were staffed around the clock. Business was conducted as much as possible by telephone and telegram. Written instructions were mimeographed, because printing took far too long. When a *Handbook of Procedures* was finally printed, it was loose-leaf in format to permit quick revision.[38]

Among its other problems, the WPA had to work out its relationship with its rival, the PWA. Communities that had previously submitted their desires for consideration as a nonfederal project by PWA now had a choice. They could go to WPA and perhaps not have to contribute as much to the project as they were required to under PWA rules, which was now 55 percent of total project costs. Some tried to transfer their proposals from PWA to WPA. Hopkins agreed not to let this happen. He was less gentlemanly with newly submitted projects. A division based on cost was proposed: anything over twenty-five thousand dollars would go to PWA and anything under would belong to WPA. Hopkins would simply divide a project costing one hundred thousand dollars into four parts.[39]

It was particularly galling to Ickes that Hopkins could veto his projects on the grounds that they did not involve sufficient relief workers. At the same time, he thought WPA projects were going forward without sufficient scrutiny. He was convinced that major scandals lay ahead. His legitimate grievances were mixed with a certain amount of jealousy. He characterized WPA projects as "trivial and ephemeral" but at the same time saw Hopkins as "bent on building up a reputation for himself as a great builder."[40]

It was becoming clear by this time that enterprises like PWA simply did not belong in the work-relief program as it was set up. The PWA could not meet the budgetary restrictions weighted heavily toward unskilled labor and away from materials. The amount of money in the appropriation allowed little else. Roosevelt personally enforced these requirements at the meetings of the ACA. Ickes had little chance of playing by these rules. "The many streams that were supposed to carry the flow of the works program were gradually absorbed by a single great torrent—the WPA."[41]

In September, Roosevelt made an effort to apportion the money still unspent in the appropriation according to his judgment of what would be best for work relief. He gave most of it, 80 percent, to WPA. This required cutting back considerably on PWA's housing efforts. However, he told Hopkins not to veto any more PWA projects. Then he invited them both on a cruise through the Panama Canal on the USS *Houston,* hoping some shared relaxation for the two combative workaholics would lead to a cease-fire.[42]

With the money allocated, the rickety apparatus created to launch the program was allowed to collapse. The PWA and CCC could seek their own appropriations based on their own rationales for aiding recovery. The WPA was now the agency focused principally on relief.

Because of the emphasis on relief and not the products that might come out of it, there was initially no requirement of local financial contribution for a WPA project similar to that legislated for the PWA. States were now expected to bear the cost of the "unemployables," so the federal government would handle the "employables." But because of WPA's need to spread its money as far as possible and to spend most of it on labor, there was some pressure even at the beginning to obtain money, or at least materials, from the local sponsors. By the middle of 1936, the sponsor's contribution was about 10 percent. In its final years WPA was receiving contributions averaging 30 percent.[43]

To no one's great surprise, WPA had not cured the Depression by the spring of 1936. It had made an impressive start, but there was clearly much more to be done. So the president went back to Congress with the Emergency Relief Appropriation Act of 1936, also known as the First Deficiency Appropriations Act.[44] The latter label reflects the legislative arena in which the original works-program bill, and all subsequent appropriations extending it, had to operate. Because the program required funds that could be made available immediately, it went to the House Committee on Appropriation's subcommittee on "deficiencies."[45] This venue helped reinforce the conceptual flaws of the program and dogged it the rest of its life. The context allowed only for defending what was already in place, not for constructing something else. The program that had come together with conflicting goals and improvised rationales was never able to rise above them to make a strong and clear case for what it was or should be.

The WPA survived for eight years. It never met the full need for employment, nor did anyone ever argue that, based on that gap, it should be given enough money to meet the need fully. Its spokesmen continued to ask for what was thought to be obtainable and would allow continuation of the program then operating. WPA was generally attacked on the basis of its being more expensive than a direct-relief program and defended on the basis that it was superior, in human terms, to the dole. The battle never allowed it to be compared to some other alternative, a program that perhaps could have addressed the total problem of work and relief.[46]

Though Roosevelt's original aspirations were for a total work and security package, he never returned to the challenge of integrating the components he had created. After the election of 1936, he was absorbed with his battle against the Supreme Court. This unfortunate initiative sapped considerable energy from the administration and weakened his political supporters. Hopkins and his crew were apparently so busy keeping the program they had running that they had no time to envision a better one. Later, they were swept up in the effort to get the country ready for a global war. Hopkins's successor, Colonel Harrington, "was by training and experience a manager, not a crusader." WPA made do with what it had.[47]

Throughout its life, WPA had to deal with the relentless pursuit of patronage. Hopkins had seen politicians scrambling during the brief life of CWA to gain political control of, or at least credit for, work-relief jobs and then accusing the program of corruption if the other side beat them to it. He fired individuals, even whole office staffs, accused of wrongdoing. He took noticeable delight in nailing Ohio governor Martin Davey for demanding that FERA workers raise money for his campaign and inaugural ball. With Roosevelt's backing, he took over relief operations for the entire state. The nonpartisan nature of this act was particularly pleasing; Davey was a Democrat.[48] But within the CWA and FERA, Hopkins had been able to replace the suspected malefactors with people he trusted. With the WPA it was harder. To increase its opportunities for patronage, the Senate added an amendment to the Emergency Relief Appropriations Act of 1935 that required its approval of the appointment of any WPA employee who would earn more than five thousand dollars.[49]

Hopkins could try to keep politicians from extorting campaign contributions in exchange for jobs or having them assigned on the basis of party loyalty.[50] He could expose those using government workers for their personal campaigns, as

Governor Davey had done, or for construction projects on their personal property, as Louisiana governor Richard Leche had done.[51] Yet it was nearly impossible to prevent politicians, particularly if they had supported New Deal public
works programs, from reminding workers of how their jobs had come to be. Even
journalists with reputations for fairness, such as Hodding Carter, found nothing
wrong with this. In his case he was hoping that gratitude for WPA work would
incline workers to vote for New Deal candidates against the Huey Long machine.
He found, however, that workers had no trouble taking WPA money and then voting for whom they pleased. The New Deal supporters lost.[52]

Hopkins found himself having to look the other way when Democratic or Progressive politicians used the WPA to "shore up their political fortunes." He later
said: "I thought at first I could be completely non-political. Then they told me I
had to be part non-political and part political. I found that was impossible, at least
for me. I finally realized that there was nothing for it but to be all-political."[53]

The "all-political" Hopkins may have bent with the political winds, but he never
countenanced corruption. For the CWA and FERA work projects, complaints of
wrongdoing had been referred to the FBI or the Investigations Division of the
PWA. In October 1934, FERA set up its own Division of Special Inquiry. This became part of the WPA and was renamed the Division of Investigation. It had field
offices in fifteen cities and a staff averaging sixty. It looked into 17,352 cases and
found less than half of them (8,811) to be legitimate concerns. It took action of its
own in 4,496 cases, dismissing or reprimanding guilty parties. Another 2,215 were
referred to the attorney general. In other cases persons being investigated left the
WPA. Macmahon notes that "grafting was usually uncovered quickly, and the guilty
parties punished, if not by criminal prosecution, at least by dismissal." He also
observed that there was a definite correlation between complaints and states with
administrative problems.[54]

Elizabeth Wickenden, who got the task of reviewing complaints against WPA
during the campaign of 1936, remarks, "I saw every one of them and there were
very, very few, considering the fact that the WPA was a huge program employing
3 to 3.5 million workers." She notes further, "Payroll padding . . . and kickbacks
were the two major things and generally they were very petty in terms of amounts."
Historian Roger Biles agrees. "Considering the potential for scandal and the intense
scrutiny by administration foes," he said, "the record of the WPA was remarkably
good." Macmahon concludes that the abuses of the WPA "were not only inevitable
but also relatively small in number." All charges were directed at state and local
offices, not at Hopkins or the WPA headquarters staff.[55]

The field staff was often successful at fighting off patronage as well. The president of the New York City's borough of Queens, George Harvey, hoped to use
WPA to build his own machine. To get control of the program he accused it of
being top-heavy with supervisors. The borough presidents, he argued, could do

Fig. 5.1. Eighteenth Precinct police station, New York City. WPA projects in big cities were often foci of patronage struggles. Photograph by R. D. Leighninger

the job with less overhead. The city's WPA head, Victor Ridder, produced figures showing that Harvey's supervisory ratio in previous efforts was the same as WPA's. Furthermore, most of the WPA supervisors came from the relief rolls.

Harvey's second ploy was to claim that the quality of WPA's paving work was unacceptable. Ridder replied that since the standards of acceptance in Queens were so high, there was no point in trying to meet them; he would have to transfer the workers to another borough. There was then a great outcry from the citizens of Queens, who were quite happy with the quality of their new streets. Harvey decided his political future would not benefit from further attacks on WPA. Queens received 240 miles of new or rebuilt streets with accompanying trees and shrubs, and the WPA stayed out of Harvey's clutches.[56]

Nonetheless, attacks in the press and in Congress were constant. In 1938 the Senate investigated the contest between its majority leader, Alben Barkley, and A. B. "Happy" Chandler in Kentucky. The committee found both sides guilty of trying to use government programs to bolster their campaigns.[57] The House conducted its own investigation in 1939. Its main concerns were alleged Communist domination of the Workers' Alliance, a relief workers' union, and displeasure at the artworks produced with WPA support. It was, according to Macmahon, a "witch hunt."[58]

To a certain extent, an association with patronage was unavoidable. Since most of the people on relief were in urban areas, most WPA projects were also. And since many cities were controlled by Democratic machines, WPA projects were most helpful to the Democratic Party. This may be as it should be, since the Democratic Party made the programs possible. As long as the work was offered to everyone regardless of party, it is hard to see anything wrong with the Democratic Party reaping some rewards for its programs. Hopkins was accused of enrolling more workers prior to an election, but variations in WPA employment correlate more directly with economic conditions and the availability of congressional appropriations than with elections. In some cases WPA rolls went down in key states before important elections.[59]

One way to avoid patronage was to make more use of the Army Corps of Engineers; career officers were not appointed by Congress and not indebted to either party. Hopkins had found this useful on occasion in local battles over CWA operations. The military administrators could use their presumed neutrality to dampen political fires. Another reason for Hopkins's new appreciation for army engineers was his experience with early WPA projects, which made it clear that sound construction would require greater reliance on engineering expertise. Thus, for purposes of immediate political insulation and the long-term survival of his projects, Hopkins overcame his suspicion of "brass hats" and was persuaded to hire Col. Francis C. Harrington as WPA's chief engineer. At first Hopkins ignored him in policy discussions, but as a boss he was always appreciative of the hard work and sound judgments of assistants. Harrington soon proved he could carry his weight, and in six months there were army engineers assigned to every region of WPA's busy empire. Harrington would succeed Hopkins when the latter left in 1938 to become secretary of commerce.[60]

Corruption was not the only problem of patronage. Simple ability was a more basic concern. Faithful supporters sometimes had nothing more to recommend them than faith. One state WPA director was so overwhelmed by his appointment that he retreated to a hotel room and would speak only to a few trusted advisors who were admitted only after giving a password. He did not emerge for weeks. There were sometimes problems not with who was appointed but with who was not. One state relief administrator, quite competent and deserving of the job, had made a few enemies. The senators had someone else appointed. The passed-over director got her revenge. The new appointee soon found himself unable to perform the job. Desks, typewriters, and other necessary items were locked up and unavailable for months.[61]

One of WPA's mandated limitations was not to build anything on private property.[62] But it also had to beware that its projects not *become* private property. A case in point is what is now the San Francisco Maritime Museum, located by the marina near Ghirardelli Square. Its ocean liner–like shape is familiar to millions

Fig. 5.2. Maritime Museum and senior center, Ghirardelli Square, San Francisco. It was designed as a public bathhouse; the city tried to lease it to a private club. The ensuing protest prevented this, but some striking WPA workers did not return to finish the mosaic on the bayside balcony. Photograph by R. D. Leighninger

of tourists. It was intended as a public bathhouse; but before it was completed, the City of San Francisco decided to lease it as a private club and upscale restaurant. WPA artists decorating it went on strike in protest. A mosaic on the balcony overlooking the bay is still incomplete, because its creators never returned. The uproar was sufficient to return the project to its original purposes. It is now a senior center as well as a museum.

The Emergency Relief Appropriations Act of 1936 gave WPA another $1,425,000,000 to continue work relief, but that was not enough to last to the end of the year. The president would have to request another deficiency appropriation. On February 9, 1937, he got $789 million. But he also told Congress that he was going for a balanced budget within the coming fiscal year. He had been listening to Treasury secretary Henry Morgenthau, who was convinced that the recovery was under way and that businessmen would only join in if they believed the president intended to cut spending. Accordingly, he used a "meat ax" on the work programs, "eliminating or deferring all expenditures not immediately necessary."[63] A recession was soon eating larger and larger holes in the presumed recovery. By the end of the year, the stock market, industrial production, corporate profits, and employment had fallen so far that comparisons with 1929 were being made. The administration was shocked into paralysis.[64]

However, the new crisis provided another stimulus to creativity. The debate over how to get the economy going again resumed. This time a different analysis was winning converts. Production was the initial focus of the recovery efforts. Traditional public works, as pursued by the PWA, were supposed to stimulate production. Production would provide employment, which would encourage further production. Seeing the results of CWA in 1934, however, had prompted doubts about the primacy of production. While conceived as emergency relief for starving workers and of little consequence to the machinery of production, the CWA did, as noted, produce a noticeable impact in all economic sectors. The role of consumers began to draw attention away from the fixation on producers. The problem could be as much underconsumption as stalled production. Instead of waiting for producers, getting more consumers into the economy might be the true road to recovery. One way to do this quickly was to hire them to do public work. The struggle to convince the president of this is covered in more detail in chapter 10.[65]

Roosevelt finally decided that public investment was the best choice. He put money back into the works programs. On April 14, 1938, he asked Congress to provide $300 million for housing and slum clearance, $100 million for highways, $37 million for flood control, and $25 million for federal buildings. The PWA got $965 million, and WPA came away with a $1.5 billion. Both agencies were thus able to complete some of their most important projects.[66]

The types of projects WPA supported changed somewhat from appropriation to appropriation. The original legislation was heavily weighted toward physical

Fig. 5.3. Monte Vista Fire Station, Albuquerque, now a popular restaurant. WPA improved fire protection across the country by building 325 new firehouses and renovating 2,384. Almost twenty thousand miles of new water mains helped too. Photograph by R. D. Leighninger

infrastructure: roads, rural electrification, water conservation, sanitation, and flood control. The 1936 Emergency Relief Appropriations Act added new categories. Public buildings, parks, public utilities, airports, and transit facilities were now named. The 1937 act gave billing to educational, professional, and women's projects in addition to construction activities. By 1938 there was a long list of approved projects including eradication of fungus pests and production of marl fertilizer. Hardly anything could be excluded.[67]

Harry Hopkins left the WPA in December 1938 to become secretary of Commerce. By now among the most trusted of Roosevelt's advisors, he turned his attention to the impending war. Colonel Harrington took over and guided the agency ably through its last years. In the government reorganization of 1939, the WPA was combined with the PWA under a new umbrella called the Federal Works Agency (FWA), headed by John M. Carmody. Carmody had played an important role in negotiating working relationships between CWA and professional and labor organizations. The reorganization also brought a new name to the WPA. Since it was no longer in charge of reporting on the progress of the works program, it became the Work Projects Administration.[68]

The Emergency Relief Appropriations Acts (ERRA) of 1939 and 1941 gave the WPA $1,477,000,000 and $975,650,000, respectively. By 1941 WPA's focus was on national defense. In the original legislation, isolationist senators like William Borah had insisted on including prohibitions against any projects that might have military purposes. But now WPA was spending more than a half billion dollars on defense-related projects.[69]

WPA airports would prove crucial to the war effort and to commercial aviation after the war.[72] At Wold-Chamberlain Field, now Minneapolis–St. Paul International Airport, WPA built three major concrete runways in 1936. Shortly after Pearl Harbor, when a counterstrike was being planned, Wold-Chamberlain was selected as the site of the secret refitting of B-25 Mitchell bombers with long-range fuel tanks. The field was selected because of its distance from both coasts and remoteness from likely spy activity. In February 1942 the planes were flown in. The collapsible neoprene tanks were installed in two weeks by 120 mechanics working shifts around the clock. On April 18, they left the deck of the aircraft carrier USS *Hornet* under the command of Lt. Col. Jimmy Doolittle to conduct the first raid on Tokyo.[73]

Later, C-47s practiced performing midair snatches of Waco gliders from Wold-Chamberlain Field. The gliders were manufactured nearby, so it was helpful to have an airport to test this delicate operation. Gen. Dwight Eisenhower came to the field to see off the C-47 pilots on their flight to England, from where they would carry the gliders filled with infantrymen to support the D-Day landing in Normandy.[72]

Harry Hopkins had believed that public works were not just an emergency response to an economic crisis but a normal part of the nation's commitment to economic security for all citizens. If the private economy could not provide jobs to all who needed them, the government should. Roosevelt shared this belief, at least at times. Therefore there were efforts to make WPA and PWA permanent weapons in the national arsenal against the reappearance of depression. But they were unsuccessful. WPA received its last appropriation in the ERRA of 1941. It was officially liquidated on June 30, 1943.

The president's coalition, vital to the inauguration and defense of New Deal legislation, had neither the numbers nor the fervor necessary for the effort to make the FWA or either of its components, PWA or WPA, permanent. The defection of the southerners, who had come to see the advance of the New Deal as a threat to the survival of the white planter aristocracy, was a blow that was not sufficiently softened by the new support of urban immigrant and African American voters. WPA's entanglement in patronage made enemies for the New Deal both when it allowed itself to be used and when it resisted. Those favorable to social spending became a minority in the House after the elections of 1938 and in the Senate after 1940. Finally, the ever-increasing hum of heavy industry coming back to life to prepare for the war, along with the drum of enlistment in the armed forces, made it hard to worry about future unemployment.[73]

Conceived as temporary and kept alive from appropriation to appropriation, WPA was never able to plan much more than a year ahead. This made it exceedingly difficult to carry out complex projects. Its need to be labor intensive and have a minimal materials budget also mitigated against building anything impressive. And indeed, as with the CCC, part of WPA's glory was that most of its achievements were small and humble. But its collective impact was most impressive, and some of its individual projects rival the best of PWA's as long-range investment.

One of the more unusual and multifaceted efforts undertaken by WPA is San Antonio's Paseo del Rio or River Walk. The San Antonio River snakes through the heart of the city. During the early years of the century it had become a sewer and was, moreover, a constant threat to life and property. A flood in 1921 killed fifty people and did fifty million dollars in property damage. Plans for diverting the river and filling in the old channel were discussed. In 1929 Robert H. H. Hugman, a local architect inspired by the survival of the French Quarter in New Orleans as a convivial space, drew sketches of a clean, landscaped river with walks, stairs, bridges, shops, and food stalls. Floods would be controlled with a bypass channel with gates at both ends. In 1938 a local hotel owner became interested in the plan and mustered some financial support among other businesses, but the city council refused to match their donations.

Maury Maverick, a New Deal supporter, was elected mayor in 1939 and quickly arranged a WPA grant of $325,000 to add to the $75,000 raised by river property owners. The final project cost a total of $442,900, of which property owners paid $82,700. River Walk now offers one and three-quarter miles (twenty-two city

Fig. 5.4. River Walk, San Antonio, a multifaceted network of walkways, shops, restaurants, and a theater. River Walk is a venue for community festivals as well as a flood control project. Photograph by R. D. Leighninger

blocks) of landscaped walkways connecting thirty rock and brick stairways (and one made of cedar) with twenty-one bridges. It includes the Arneson River Theater, which has amphitheater seating for one thousand on one bank and a stage and dressing room on the other. The theater connects with La Villita, a complex of buildings that was the city center before the Alamo battle a century before. La Villita was restored by a WPA offshoot, the National Youth Administration.[74]

In addition to the shops and restaurants that line River Walk, a three-story, enclosed shopping mall and convention center now connects with the river. The commercial contribution to city wealth is huge. River Walk rivals the Alamo as the city's strongest tourist attraction. San Antonio had 21.4 million visitors in 2004, and they spent $4.3 billion while in town.[75]

But consumption has not completely eclipsed the other functions of this space. Downtown workers during the day and families at night and on weekends can enjoy the sun and flowers without an entrance fee. Arneson Theater hosts everything from opera to flamenco concerts. River Walk is an integral part of civic festivals and community rituals. The king of the Festival of San Jacinto, who began his reign in 1891, rides a barge through the city. The river also hosts the annual Battle of the Flowers, a counterpart to the Pasadena Rose Parade. La Villita is a focus of this and other celebrations like Cinco de Mayo and Mexican Independence Day. There are two annual art fairs on the riverbanks. At Christmas luminaria line the river as Mary and Joseph lead the Las Posadas procession in search of shelter for the birth of Jesus.

Another multifaceted project can be found on the campus of Louisiana State University in Baton Rouge: Parker Agricultural Center, a copper-domed arena and office complex that seats 6,756 people. Serving a variety of constituencies and functions, like River Walk, it has made a similar contribution to its community. It was the site of graduations and basketball games for over thirty years and has hosted two gubernatorial inaugurations. Hall of Fame basketball player Bob Pettit showed his talent there. It was the home of the LSU boxing team. The baseball team still practices here in bad weather. It has been a venue for Boy Scout circuses and both Senior and Special Olympics. Garden, floral, and craft shows are regular attractions. Its most frequent use, however, is for livestock shows and sales and for rodeos. Polled Herefords, Texas Longhorns, and dairy cows each have their own events. Quarter horses, Appaloosas, Arabians, Paints, and Tennessee Walkers have separate showings and sales. Swine and poultry are on display regularly. As many as four separate rodeos may be scheduled in a given year.

Youth, college students, and adults are all served. The 4–H Club and Future Farmers of America convene here, and one of the most popular events for young people is the Junior Livestock Show every spring. LSU students have their own rodeo. Students of the College of Agriculture and the School of Veterinary Medicine have direct access to this constant parade of animal life. Stock owners and breeders gather to buy and sell and to consult with the staff of the Agricultural Experiment Station and the Cooperative Extension Service. The facility thus provides not only education for all levels but also gives essential service to the agricultural economy of the entire state, a multibillion dollar enterprise. Reckoning the dollar value of this support is yet another impossible task, but it must be considerable.

Another contribution of these shows to the local economy is more easily calculated. For example the twenty thousand participants, family members, and spectators attending the Junior Livestock Show over a four-day period book an estimated twelve thousand rooms at local motels and have an indirect dollar impact on the community of over fifteen million dollars.[76]

In a far different climate is Timberline Lodge on the slopes of Mount Hood in Oregon. Skiers in winter and vacationers in all seasons enjoy its massive shelter embellished with the carving, weaving, and forging artistry of its WPA and CCC builders. Though it did not experience full use until the 1950s, the project's economic impact over the years has been considerable. Every year 1.9 million people use its facilities, including a quarter million skiers.[77] It served as a set for the movie based on Stephen King's novel *The Shining,* starring Jack Nicholson.

With its mandated emphasis on unskilled labor and need to keep the cost of materials low relative to wages, one must wonder how WPA managed to erect such

Fig. 5.5. San Diego County Administration Building. This huge complex
is unusual for WPA projects, which
put most of their budgets into labor.
Local participation, particularly
donated materials, probably made
this possible. Photograph by R. D.
Leighninger

Fig. 5.6. Concrete picnic tables, Pepper Grove, Balboa Park, San Diego. Photograph by
R. D. Leighninger

monuments. There are two answers. One is that the materials could be contributed by sponsors. The other is that the cost and ratio accounting was averaged for an entire city. Thus many road and sidewalk projects could be averaged with one or two public buildings and still maintain good overall ratios.

Some of the labor-intensive projects are equally impressive. In the hills overlooking San Francisco Bay is the Berkeley Rose Garden, described by one landscape architect as a masterful combination of "Old World elegance and New World adventure."[78] Its spectacular vista guarantees an appeal far beyond the ranks of amateur botanists. It has been the site of countless wedding photographs and is a fine place to sit and enjoy the sun on the bay or watch the fog roll through the Golden Gate. Not far away in Oakland is a similar rose garden, less well-known because it lacks the view, but an inviting place to walk or sit nonetheless. Further up in the Oakland hills is Woodminster Theater. A landscaped waterfall and cascade draw the eye up the hill to the theater and are so entrancing that one might easily forget to turn around and enjoy another grand view of the bay. The small outdoor theater has its own professional company. Tilden Regional Park, running along the hilltops of both Oakland and Berkeley, offers many recreational amenities, including a swimming pool.

Another outdoor complex enhanced by WPA is Balboa Park in San Diego. Its original buildings date from the Panama-California Exposition of 1915. But in 1935, the city decided to host the California Pacific International Exhibition. It left behind many permanent amenities, including a gymnasium, an outdoor theater, clubhouses for the golf course and the bowling green, and an array of concrete picnic tables and benches in Pepper Grove.[79]

Most World's Fair architecture is not intended to survive beyond the closing of the last midway ride and hot dog stand. Balboa Park was an exception. Another is Fair Park in Dallas. Built for the Texas Centennial Exposition of 1936 with WPA and PWA labor, this "world of tomorrow" is still intact, hosting the annual state fair and providing exhibit space for trade shows and festivals year-round, including Cinco de Mayo, Kwanzaa Fest, the North Texas Irish Festival, the Islamic Association of North Texas Prayer Service, the Greater Southwest Guitar Show, the *Dallas Morning News* Science Fair, the Gulf Shore Cat Club, Gospel Expo, the Quilters' Guild of Texas, fourteen antiques shows, four job fairs, and Ducky Bob's Driver Training School. It is home to eight museums exploring fish and flowers, pioneers and planets, dinosaurs and diatoms, freight trains, feminists, and freedom riders. Its dramatic Art Deco sculpture and murals have been carefully restored. The original band shell has been renovated and now hosts concerts featuring groups like the Dallas Wind Symphony and Salman Khan. Its promenades welcome strollers and rollerblades. Almost eight million people attended ticketed events in the park in 2000. Annually, 3.5 million come to the state fair, bringing revenues in 2004 of twenty-three million dollars.

Many waterfront areas, now important features of major cities, were stabilized and made usable for recreation by WPA projects. The Chicago lakefront, both above and below the Loop, was anchored with massive stone embankments. Lake Pontchartrain received similar support and embellishment, preparing the way for extensive New Orleans real-estate development. Bradford Beach in Milwaukee and Orchard and Rockaway Beaches in New York City were other waterfronts made available to urbanites for swimming and picnicking, improving the morale of millions of families during the Depression and for decades after.

Almost six thousand schools were built by WPA across the country. Additions were made to over two thousand more, and over thirty-one thousand were repaired and improved. Most are still serving as schools after six decades of hard use and sometimes indifferent maintenance. Some have gone on to new lives. John Marshall University High School in Minneapolis is now a small business incubator known as the University Technology Center (UTEC). Ninety enterprises have office space here. The former gym is now a central atrium used by tenants and community groups for parties, dinners, and concerts. An Indonesian gamelan ensemble plays there. A tai chi class meets at lunchtime, and a square dance group kicks up dust on weekends. Customers of a violin maker who has a workshop in the building come to the atrium to try out his instruments. This for-profit, privately owned facility offers a variety of technical services to its tenants but sees

Fig. 5.7. Hamlin Park Recreation Center, St. Paul, Minnesota, was designed by city architect Clarence Wigington, the state's first African American architect and possibly the first African American municipal architect in the country. Photograph by R. D. Leighninger

"office space as [its] primary 'product.'"[80] A public space created by a public agency has now become the primary product for private profit making.

Zoos are both recreational and educational. WPA built seventeen and contributed significantly to others. Some, like the Como Park Zoo in St. Paul, consisted of standard concrete cages with iron bars, but others benefited from new thinking about the proper way to house wild animals. Zoos in New Orleans, Cincinnati, San Diego, Dallas, Buffalo, San Francisco, and Detroit got new, open, naturalistic habitats for their animals that were more appealing to both occupants and observers than the older confinements.[81]

WPA efforts promoted health. It renovated 2,170 hospitals, expanded 226 others, and built 156 new facilities. One of its most important new constructions was a $450,000 hospital for the Navajo Nation at Fort Defiance, Arizona. With 140 beds, isolation wards, a laboratory, and a dental office, it was the largest and best-equipped health facility in the Indian Service and served until 2003.[82]

Recreation also promotes health. WPA workers added 1,668 new parks—over seventy-five thousand acres worth—to America's communities and made improvements to 6,524 more. Some cities like Kalamazoo, Michigan, might have only one, but cities like Dallas, New York, Chicago, Philadelphia, San Francisco, and Milwaukee developed whole park systems. Though well used for decades, their WPA origins were largely forgotten. Recently, some cities have rediscovered their history.[83] One WPA park, however, will never be forgotten: Dallas's Dealey Plaza, where John F. Kennedy was assassinated.

Even among proponents of public works within the New Deal there were concerns that, with the WPA's emphasis on unskilled labor and low materials cost, there was no way it could produce things that would last. Yet an amazing number of them have lasted. Some equal the work of the Public Works Administration, which could make full use of skilled labor and machinery and was able to—in fact, was expected to—spend more on materials. The WPA transcended its political and statutory handicaps. It outlasted the derision of its detractors. Its legacy stands solidly and quietly all around us.

Table 5.1 Contributions to civil infrastructure through the Works Progress Administration, 1935–43

Urban streets
    Hard surfaced.......... 30,000 miles
    Other................. 37,000 miles

Sidewalks
    New.................. 24,000 miles
    Improved .... 7,000 miles

Curbs
    New.................. 25,000 miles
    Improved............... 3,000 miles

Road and street lighting
    New .... 838 miles
    Improved.............. 1,641 miles
    New traffic signs erected..... 937,000

Rural roads
    Hard surfaced.......... 57,000 miles
    Other............... 515,000 miles

Bridges, viaducts
    New...................... 78,000
    Improved 46,000

Culverts
    New .... 29,805,000 linear feet
    Improved....... 3,288,000 linear feet

Roadside drainage ditches
    New.................. 79,000 miles
    Improved .... 84,000 miles

Tunnels
    Vehicular 26
    Pedestrian 193
    Railway, sewer, cattle underpasses. 800

Parks, new or improved........... 8,000

Athletic fields, new or improved.... 5,600

Stadiums, grandstands,
    new or improved.............. 3,300

Playgrounds, new or improved ... 12,800

Schools
    New 5,900
    Additions................... 2,170
    Renovations................ 31,300

Libraries
    New 151
    Additions..................... 67
    Renovations.................. 856

Auditoriums, gymnasiums,
recreational buildings
    New 9,300
    Renovated 5,800

Swimming pools.................. 900

Wading pools 1,000

Skating rinks................... 1,200

Ski jumps........................ 80

Golf courses
    New .... 2,800 holes
    Improved .... 5,000 holes

Band shells 170

Hospitals
    New 226
    Additions.................... 156
    Renovations................. 2,168

Office and administrative
    buildings 6,400
    New 1,536
    Additions.................... 323
    Renovations................. 4,524

Dormitories.................... 7,000

Storage buildings 6,000

Armories
    New 400
    Renovated 500

Firehouses 2,700

Jails, prisons 760

Airports
    New 350
    Enlarged..................... 700
    Runways, new or
        improved .... 5,925,000 linear feet
    Taxiways........ 1,129,000 linear feet

Table 5.1 continued

Airport buildings
New 1,200
Improved 2,800

Fish hatcheries
New 163
Additions 135
Improvements 169

Riverbank and shore
improvements . . . . 4,419 miles

Water treatment plants, new
or improved 500

Pumping stations 1,800

Water mains, new or
repaired . . . . 19,700 miles

Wells
New 4,000
Improved 2,000

Storage tanks or reservoirs,
new or improved 3,700

Sewage treatment plants,
new or improved 1,500

Incinerators, new or improved 200

Storm or sanitary sewers
New . . . . 24,000 miles
Improved . . . . 3,000 miles

Sewerage service connections, new or
repaired 639,000

Manholes and catch basins
New 815,000
Improved 423,000

Sanitary privies
New 2,309,000
Renovated 40,000

Source: Federal Works Agency, *Final Report on the WPA Program, 1935–1943* (Washington, D.C.: U.S. Government Printing Office, 1946), 50–52, 131–33.

Chapter 6

· THE PUBLIC WORKS ADMINISTRATION ·
1935–42

The Civil Works Administration (CWA) and Works Progress Administration (WPA) had bought time for the gleaming glacier of the Public Works Administration. They had also, of course, taken some of PWA's funding to get them started. Since the focus of the 1935 works program was on unemployment, PWA now had to compete, at least temporarily, on unfavorable terms with the new agency, the WPA. PWA's share of the new works program was to be nine hundred million dollars, but in fact it got a little over a third of this because of the relief labor restriction. PWA was not designed to execute projects using large numbers of unskilled workers. Power and water projects and large public buildings required skilled labor and machinery. However, the competition increased the pressure on PWA to move more quickly.[1]

In addition to congressional appropriations, PWA had another source of income. As recipients of PWA loans began to repay them, this money, with interest, began to accrue. Securities that PWA had accepted as collateral for these loans were also being sold, first to the Reconstruction Finance Corporation and later on the open market. At first this was sent back to the federal treasury, but in 1935 it was made available to PWA for further loans. This added another $395 million to the program.[2] That this "revolving fund" existed at all is testimony to the financial stability of the loan program. Its success vindicated the relaxation of debt limits. Subsequent research indicates that concerns about municipal default were exaggerated and that communities might have been able to assume safely even more debt than they incurred.[3]

The terms of the new grant and loan program were changed to increase the PWA grant from 30 percent of labor and materials to 45 percent of total project costs. These figures, like their predecessors, sprung from political compromise rather than economic calculation. Some wanted the federal government to cover half of each project; others thought that 40 percent was enough encouragement. Henry Morgenthau split the difference.[4]

At this point PWA also began to prefer projects that could be completed without the need of federal loans. This meant less work for the fiscal division and a speedier approval of proposals. It spread the appropriation further because less was tied up in each project. Local owners still had to come up with the other 55 percent, but they were now usually able to do this by selling their bonds on the private market. Thanks to PWA for giving them a chance to prove that they could continue to service debt, state and local governments were now able to entice private investors back into the market. This was another victory for the financial soundness of the public works program.[5]

Additional money was appropriated for PWA in 1936 and 1937. The First Deficiency Appropriation Act of June 22, 1936, gave it another three hundred million dollars from the revolving fund. It also stipulated that new projects had to be completed by July 1, 1938. The Public Works Administration Extension Act of June 29, 1937, gave the agency another two years of life and another fifty-nine million dollars from the revolving fund. No new proposals were to be accepted and no allotments could be made to projects that had not already been approved by PWA examiners. When the president announced in October 1937 that he was cutting the work programs in an attempt to balance the budget, PWA moved to a regional organization. A staff consolidated in seven geographic regions seemed enough to oversee the liquidation of the program.[6]

The recession that followed, discussed earlier, finally persuaded the president to breathe new life into the works programs. The PWA Appropriation Act of 1938 extended the deadline for new proposals to the end of September of that year and provided $965 million. The agency wasted no time in rolling out allotments. Many projects were already in the pipeline when the presidential cutbacks hit. In the first six months of the new program, over 6,200 nonfederal projects were funded, more than quadruple the number put through in a similar period under the 1933 program. The delay between approval and the letting of contracts was cut even more. In the first six months, almost six thousand projects were under contract, compared with 396 in the earlier program. Some of PWA's most useful work occurred under the new program. While the early period saw a concentration on physical infrastructure like bridges and waterworks, the last few years concentrated more on cultural infrastructure: schools, university buildings, courthouses, museums, and recreational facilities.

Success brought new perils. The integrity of the PWA was threatened from many directions. Congress tried hard to make the federal works programs havens of patronage by requiring in the 1935 act that it be able to approve all personnel making over five thousand dollars. The pressure increased with the new appropriations. At the local level, both party organizations did their best to make sure that jobs went to their own people first. Individual workers and contractors kept an eye out for a fast buck. City council and school board members also had opportunities to enrich themselves or their friends. Ickes usually got the better of them.

Harry Hopkins, who wanted immediate results, accommodated national and local politics while trying to run an effective and honest program. Harold Ickes had a reputation as a stickler for propriety when he entered the New Deal. He was proud of his image as "Honest Harold." Interestingly, he was less bothered than Hopkins by patronage. When he discovered that an Interior Department employee in New Mexico was "antagonistic" to Sen. Bronson Cutting, Ickes's friend and fellow Progressive, he fired him without being asked. The same day, he arranged a National Parks Service summer job for the son of Agriculture secretary Henry Wallace.[7] Hopkins seemed to regard such things as a necessary evil. Ickes saw no evil in it at all. Presumably, he felt young Wallace would earn his keep and that Senator Cutting's enemies were also enemies of the public good. He may well have been right in both cases, but he does not seem to have worried much about it. On another occasion he gave a job in the Housing Division to his ne'er-do-well ward Robert. "In my heart I hate nepotism . . . ," he said, [but, other than bad publicity,] "I really can see little harm in giving a minor clerkship to Robert."[8] Hopkins and Ickes were both self-confident men. With Ickes, this seems to have been accompanied by a certain amount of self-righteousness.

In general, PWA was better at keeping out of local politics than was WPA. But in two instances, where the president's interests or animosities were involved, Ickes was not above making some use of PWA's clout. In neither case was he successful. Robert Moses was New York Park Commissioner and also head of the Triborough Bridge Authority. The Triborough was a five-hundred-million-dollar project inherited from the Reconstruction Finance Corporation. It came freighted with considerable inefficiency and graft. Moses was also a longtime enemy of Roosevelt. Ickes suspended the bridge allotment until all previous funds were accounted for, and he ruled that no PWA grant could go to any authority whose officers held other public offices. The latter move was designed purely to get Moses, and Ickes took part in the vendetta reluctantly. Moses did not back down. Mayor LaGuardia finally prevailed upon Roosevelt to put the interests of the state above his personal grudges.[9] Moses went on to be one of the most successful PWA clients in the country, filling New York City with a wide variety of public assets.

Sen. Huey P. Long of Louisiana was an early New Deal supporter but soon transformed himself into an outspoken critic of Roosevelt and a third-party candidate for president. Though some regarded him as a buffoon, many of the president's advisors respected his intelligence, organizing abilities, and campaign effectiveness. Few thought he had a shot at the presidency, but drawing enough votes away from Roosevelt to elect a Republican was thought to be a real possibility. Though Long had made no attempt to control New Deal programs in his state, he was determined not to let his opponents use them. Ickes did not try to steer PWA project towards Long's opponents nor away from his friends. He did, however, announce in September 1934 that Louisiana had reached its quota of PWA money. Since

PWA had never established a quota system, this seems like an attempt to rattle Huey.[10]

Federal patronage went increasingly to anti-Long forces. At the same time, Long used his control of the state legislature to tighten the squeeze on his opponents in New Orleans. Long engineered legislation forbidding any community to borrow without the approval of a state Bond and Tax Board, which he controlled. He also crafted a law against the expenditure of federal money for "political purposes," which might have allowed him to have local PWA or WPA officials arrested. Ickes twice froze PWA projects in the state and finally stopped accepting new proposals. This was less an offensive strike against Huey than a defense of PWA against the new laws. Where this might have led we will never know. In October 1935 Huey Long was shot to death in the back hallway of the towering capitol building he had just built.[11]

At the project level, the system of resident engineer-inspectors, backed up by the Investigations Division, was quite successful in keeping the many attempts to make political or financial profit from becoming full-blown scandals. Though the agency had limited ability to prosecute, the ability to withhold the next payment until policies were observed usually was enough to correct violations. Both outside observers who chronicled the agency concluded that it remained remarkably free of corruption. Williams says in summary: "Looked at as a whole, the agency operated well. The key personnel were on the whole of high calibre; the PWA maintained a marked degree of freedom from partisan politics, both with respect to appointments and in connection with the making of allotments. While administrative costs were not exceptionally low, the public works agency is generally conceded to have functioned without waste or inefficiency."[12] Isakoff reaches the same conclusion: "The general opinion seems to be that the Public Works Administration has not been a haven for deserving politicians. . . . This writer believes that personal and partisan politics have not been completely absent but they have not been permitted to outweigh consideration of merit and fitness."[13]

The PWA also set a high standard for construction throughout the country. Isakoff asserts that "the standards of design insisted upon by the PWA were probably better than those to which public bodies had become accustomed. The careful supervision of construction enforced by the PWA has probably resulted in closer compliance with specifications than would otherwise have been the case." A questionnaire sent to sponsors of school projects was returned by 773 of them. Seventy-three percent credited PWA with introducing higher standards of planning, 67 with higher design standards, 78 percent with higher construction standards, and 76 percent felt disputes were settled with greater fairness.[14]

Public education was among the greatest beneficiaries of PWA. It brought not only better education but in many cases saved lives. The nation's stock of school buildings was in bad shape. One indication of how great that need was can be found in a report made by PWA's traveling engineer-inspector Fred L. Hargett on July 27, 1937, concerning schools in Louisiana. He was sent around the state to verify the claims of local school officials that existing buildings posed substantial health and safety risks to students and teachers. He covered eleven communities and substantiated health or fire hazards in all but one.

In four communities, he confirmed that the schools there were fire hazards. The school at Winnsboro had already caught fire twice. Its open-flame heater was unshielded from the dry pine lumber around it. There were no fire escapes. The building at Liddeville also had no fire escape and had also already suffered fires.[15] High schools in Franklinton and Lake Providence and a school at Hunter had recently burned to the ground.

The other schools posed health risks because of deteriorating building structure, poor ventilation, or contaminated water. At Monticello and at Liddeville, open-pit toilets were located perilously near the well where students drank. In a separate report on Liddeville, PWA director of engineering Arthur J. Bulger described the toilets as "filthy" and measured the distance to the well as only one hundred feet. He also noted that students who could not fit into the existing four-room building had to hold class in a nearby church, which was impossible to heat in winter.[16]

Schools for African Americans may have been even worse. Another of Hargett's reports described a fifty-five-year-old Negro School in Lake Providence as "leaning" and "about rotted down." It "would take very little wind to blow it over," he added. It had "very unsanitary toilets" and only one light. It was "dangerous," he concluded, "and should not be used as a school."[17]

The situation in Jennings was among the worst. John M. Whitney, M.D., the director of the Parish Health Unit, reported to the school superintendent on the "Training School," which served as both elementary and high school for African Americans. He observed siding "rotted or warped beyond repair," window lights missing, window shades "ragged and torn" and affording "no protection against the sun's rays," warped doors, rusty hinges, and rotted steps. "The water supply consists of a drilled well and hand pump which accommodates approximately 600 children, whereas the source of city water supply is but two blocks away. The toilet facilities . . . consist of two sanitary pit privies which are practically full to overflow." There were roof leaks and "bats and lice in the attic from which a very strong odor emits."[18] In replacing schools like this, PWA was a true lifesaver for many communities.

Federal funds permitted school systems to consolidate their many one- and two-room schools, bringing students together where they could share facilities unavailable in even larger buildings. New Deal hard-surfaced roads made it possible to get to the new consolidated schools. Libraries, science and agricultural laboratories, art and music rooms, industrial arts shops, home economics rooms, and other special facilities that existed only in the dreams of educators before the

Depression now became realities even in small communities. Combined gym-auditoriums offered physical education and performance spaces and also became centers for community activities. The importance of these contributions is impossible to calculate.[19]

Roosevelt's Reorganization Act of 1939 amalgamated the PWA and the WPA, now called the Work Projects Administration, into a single agency titled the Federal Works Agency (FWA). It was placed under the direction of John Carmody, an engineer and former troubleshooter for the CWA. By this time Harry Hopkins had gone on to become secretary of Commerce, and WPA was in the hands of Col. Francis Harrington. Col. E. W. Clark took over for Ickes at PWA.[20]

The PWA was closed in 1942; the FWA carried on until 1949. During this period, national resources had to be poured into the war and the efforts to reconstruct Europe and Asia thereafter. Carmody was succeeded in 1941 by Maj. Gen. Philip B. Fleming, who had worked as Ickes's deputy from 1933 to 1935. Fleming made an energetic and eloquent defense of the need for a permanent federal public works agency but was unable to turn back the growing Republican determination to repeal as much of the New Deal as the American public would allow. Herbert Hoover, brought out of retirement to chair the Commission on the Reorganization of the Executive Branch in 1947, was actually in favor of a permanent Department of Public Works. Opposition from the Army Corps of Engineers scuttled the plan. The FWA became the General Services Administration, the agency that

Fig 6.1 Physical infrastructure: The north span of the bridge from Natchez, Mississippi, to Vidalia, Louisiana, was constructed by PWA. Downstream at New Orleans another PWA bridge, named after Huey P. Long, crosses the Mississippi. The latter was begun under Hoover's Reconstruction Finance Corporation. Photograph by R. D. Leighninger

maintains federal offices. The proud builders of the backbone of national infrastructure became the nation's janitor.[21]

More than any other New Deal agency, however, the Public Works Administration has left dramatic reminders of this age of public building. For example New York City benefited from 107 PWA projects, beginning with vital parts of its transportation system: the Triborough Bridge, the Lincoln and Queens-Midtown Tunnels, the East River Drive, the Henry Hudson Parkway, major sections of the Eighth Avenue (Independent) subway line, and three Staten Island ferries. Those ferries have now been replaced, but one can still see the ferry terminal PWA built on Ellis Island. Additions to dock and pier facilities totaled $5.6 million, and another $1.5 million was spent on barges. Four garbage-disposal projects improved the city's health and cleanliness at a cost of $34.6 million. The garbage incinerator at Fifty-sixth Street and Twelfth Avenue and the attached garage that houses 350 garbage trucks is still vital to keeping the city clean.[22] See table 6.1 for a national summary of PWA physical infrastructure projects.

Thirty-three projects added $25.4 million worth of school buildings to New York City's educational system. Three separate college or university projects spent $12.4 million on higher education. PWA established Brooklyn College with a library, academic building, science building, gym, and heating plant costing $6 million. Three courthouse projects cost $22.3 million. The Bronx County Jail was a PWA project. Central Park, where PWA built the original Central Park Zoo, the Conservatory Gardens, and most of the playgrounds, is only the most famous of the scores of parks, many with swimming pools, built across the city.[23] See table 6.2 for a national summary of PWA's cultural infrastructure projects.

On Staten Island, a large merchant marine hospital complex is now serving as a private hospital, Bayley Seaton. The seven eight-story buildings that form the core of Belleview Hospital and the twelve-story Nurses Home at Kings County Hospital are also PWA projects. There were twenty-four different hospital and clinic projects adding $22.7 million in health facilities to the city.[24] See table 6.3 for a national summary of health-related PWA projects.

On the opposite coast, the San Francisco Bay Area is also studded with PWA landmarks, beginning with the Bay Bridge, which was taken over from the RFC and completed by PWA. Another essential feature of Bay Area transportation is the Caldecott Tunnel, which connects the East Bay and the city with the bedroom communities in the valley beyond the coastal mountains. It is now a commuter's nightmare, but it has made the suburban dream possible for millions and enriched several generations of developers.

The San Francisco Mint, a three-million-dollar office building, and Pier 19 on the Embarcadero were federal PWA projects. A $2.6 million sewage treatment plant constructed in Golden Gate Park ended the practice of dumping raw sewage into San Francisco Bay. To provide water to the city, PWA doubled the size of Hetch

Table 6.1 Physical infrastructure projects completed by the Public Works Administration (federal and nonfederal)

	Federal	Nonfederal	Total cost (S million)*
Streets and highways	9,928	1,500	920.8
Engineering structures			
Bridges and viaducts	9	379	221.9
Wharves, piers, docks	62	53	38.5
Subways and tunnels	0	14	207.0
Other	110	27	18.9
Aviation projects			
Airports	354	30	25.4
Improvements to landing fields	193	0	21.1
Other aids	101	0	3.2
Railroads	0	32	201.0
Sewer projects			
Disposal plants	21	873	326.1
Sanitary sewers	72	463	90.0
Storm sewers	5	116	20.8
Combined sanitary and storm	0	75	32.6
Sewer and water systems	29	196	24.4
Garbage and rubbish disposal plants	20	41	11.0
Water projects			
Reservoirs	21	182	27.2
Filtration plants	1	118	18.8
Water mains	38	252	31.5
Complete waterworks	103	1,867	237.8
Electrical power projects			
Electrical distribution systems	39	53	20.5
Power construction projects	53	230	91.7
Gas plants	1	25	1.9
Water navigation aids			
Channels and levees	164	6	105.9
Dams and canals	29	2	93.1
Locks	35	0	31.0
Lighthouses	212	0	3.9
Other	256	37	42.9
Flood control, water power, and reclamation			
Channels	18	3	3.8
Dams and canals	149	32	92.4
Storage reservoirs	18	8	9.7

Table 6.1 continued:	Federal	Nonfederal	Total cost ($ million)*
Water power development	10	16	184.5
Soil erosion	93	3	15.2
Flood control	0	25	64.0
Miscellaneous	51	44	85.4
Game and fish protection	193	0	2.2
Nonmilitary vessels	100	0	5.4
Improvements to federal land	285	0	22.9
Surveying and mapping	610	0	18.1

*Total est. cost as of February 28, 1939. Includes PWA grants and loans as well as local funds.

Source: Public Works Administration, *America Builds: The Record of the PWA* (Washington, D.C.: Government Printing Office, 1939), tables 10, 11, 13, 19, and 20, 279–82, 288–91.

Table 6.2 Cultural infrastructure projects completed by the Public Works Administration (federal and nonfederal)

	Federal	Nonfederal	Total cost ($ million)*
Educational building projects**			
Primary/secondary	206	6,450	940.9
College/university	36	662	204.0
Other educational buildings	21	65	24.9
Public libraries	0	105	12.0
Courthouses and city halls	30	629	127.8
Auditoriums and armories	1	102	30.2
Post offices	406	0	43.6
Penal institutions	75	178	52.0
Social and recreational buildings	28	131	18.2
Residential buildings	551	6	75.5
Office and administrative buildings	211	130	74.9
Warehouses, laboratories, shops	678	83	48.7
Parks	0	61	6.8
Swimming pools	0	65	0.1
Fire and police stations**	0	128	12.5
Markets**	0	21	8.3
Abattoirs**	0	4	0.1
Farm buildings**	0	7	2.9
Miscellaneous	756	218	78.7

*Total est. cost as of February 28, 1939. Includes PWA grants and loans as well as local funds.
**These categories come from table 14 and are not broken out in table 19. Therefore they may be included under "Miscellaneous" in that table.

Source: Public Works Administration, *America Builds: The Record of the PWA* (Washington, D.C.: Government Printing Office, 1939), tables 14, 19, and 20, 283, 288–91.

Table 6.3 Health projects completed by the Public Works Administration (federal and nonfederal)

	Federal	Nonfederal	Total cost (\$ million)*
General hospitals	* *	261	88.4
Tuberculosis hospitals	* *	134	67.9
Hospitals for epileptics	* *	12	5.2
Insane asylums	* *	205	121.9
Schools for the feeble-minded	* *	29	16.8
Homes for the aged	* *	40	12.4
Other hospital projects	* *	81	18.2
Hospitals and institutions	151	* *	43.6
Pest and disease control	146	0	5.7

*Total est. cost as of February 28, 1939. Includes PWA grants and loans as well as local funds.
**The table on federal projects does not break down by type of facility.

Source: Public Works Administration, *America Builds: The Record of the PWA* (Washington, D.C.: Government Printing Office, 1939), tables 12 and 20, 280, 290.

Fig. 6.2. Cultural infrastructure: Zimmerman Library, University of New Mexico, Albuquerque, was designed by the regionally renowned architect John Gaw Meem. Photograph by R. D. Leighninger

Fig. 6.3. Cultural infrastructure: Monterey County Courthouse, Salinas, California. Architect Robert Stanton hints at modernism with an unusual amount of glass in his Greco-deco design. Photograph by R. D. Leighninger.

Hetchy Reservoir at a cost of $2.3 million. The Cow Palace, a familiar landmark just south of the city, was originally constructed for livestock exhibition, though it has served as host to political animals as well. Both national parties have had their preelection conventions here.[25]

In Oakland, the imposing Alameda County Courthouse dominates Lake Merritt. It was used by PWA as an example of the wide-ranging economic impact that its projects could have. Materials used in its construction came from eighteen states, including lumber from Oregon, steel from Ohio, glass from Oklahoma, marble from Tennessee, valves from Michigan and Massachusetts, pumps from Illinois, copper pipe from Connecticut, iron pipe from Alabama and Utah, electrical equipment from New York, boilers from Pennsylvania, radiators from New Jersey, and plumbing from Rhode Island.[26]

As in New York and other major cities, millions of dollars were spent on school construction in the bay area, including George Washington High School, Marina Junior High and the Sunshine School for crippled children in the city, and multiple buildings at Berkeley High across the bay. One San Francisco school project alone cost $5.6 million. Libraries were built in Berkeley and Alameda. There was also a $2.4 million hospital project.[27]

The PWA was busy in Houston. Its ten-story city hall with many fine art deco details cost $1.7 million. The Jefferson Davis Hospital was also a skyscraper with

Fig. 6.4. Called a "livestock pavilion" when PWA constructed it, the Cow Palace in San Francisco became better known for its hosting of Republican and Democratic political conventions. Photograph by R. D. Leighninger

Fig. 6.5. Alameda County Courthouse, Oakland, California, was used in PWA's report *America Builds* to illustrate the national impact such a project could have on stimulating the many industries that provide building materials. Components came from eighteen different states. Photograph by R. D. Leighninger

a central section reaching eleven stories and two ten-story wings. It cost $2.4 million and remained in service until 1989. The Sam Houston Coliseum and Music Hall, a $1.3 million project, entertained circuses and symphonies until it was replaced with an even larger music hall in 1998. The Houston Federation of Garden Clubs got its own Garden Center in Hermann Park. With a $3.9 million school project, twenty-five elementary schools and sixteen high schools were built, including Mirabeau Lamar and Stephen F. Austin High Schools. PWA dredged the Houston Ship Channel an additional two feet, which cost $2.8 million. There were five million dollars worth of street and highway improvements and over two million dollars for a new waterworks and storm sewers. The PWA also provided a commemoration of the state's birth by erecting a tower crowned by a lone star at the site of the battle of San Jacinto.[28]

Arizona, the last of the original forty-eight states to enter the union, was not the least participant in the PWA program. Over seventeen million dollars was spent there on 122 PWA projects. Much of it went for irrigation and roads, but it also had many school and university projects. The University of Arizona in Tucson received eight buildings, all but one of them still in use but whose plaques give no

Fig. 6.6. Joseph Finger's design for Houston City Hall was called "ultramodernistic" by the mayor, who would have preferred something in Spanish Renaissance. Photograph by Greg Gilman

credit to PWA. Arizona State University in Phoenix and the University of Northern Arizona in Flagstaff each got a new building and several additions. Six buildings each were constructed for a new junior college and a city high school in Phoenix. A large city park in Phoenix was graced with a clubhouse, boathouse, golf club office, and band shell. Arizona has nationally known landmark buildings as well. The tribal headquarters of the Navajo nation at Window Rock was constructed with PWA aid. The Painted Desert Inn was a PWA project, though its role is not mentioned in the historical material in the building; all the credit is given to the CCC boys who provided the labor.[29]

Fig. 6.7. (left) The original Arizona State Museum sits on the campus of the University of Arizona in Tucson. The plaque gives credit to its architect, Roy Place, but none to PWA. Photograph by H. Anderson Photography

Fig. 6.8. The Council House in Window Rock, Arizona, is the seat of government for the Navajo Nation. PWA built schools across the reservation so that children would not have to be sent away to boarding schools. A large hospital was built in nearby Fort Defiance by the WPA. Photograph by R. D. Leighninger

The University of Washington in Seattle was one of the first institutions of higher education to take advantage of the opportunities offered by the PWA. It first added a $460,000 wing to its library, then built women's dormitories, an infirmary, and a power plant addition for almost one million dollars. Another million got them a huge chemistry building, Bagley Hall. Finally, it added a $206,000 swimming pool to its physical education building. An important contribution was made to the soon-to-blossom military-industrial complex by the wind tunnel constructed by the College of Engineering's department of aeronautics to test new types of aircraft. The navy, the Army Air Corps, and the Boeing Corporation all used it.[30]

There are other projects in Seattle, but one of the most interesting in terms of systematic rebirth is the $98,000 armory. Armories were common New Deal projects, in part because National Guard and Army Reserve forces were receiving attention as the prospect of war increased and in part because they usually provided a community with meeting and recreational facilities. Most still serve the latter purposes. The armory in Seattle, however, has had a more interesting life. In 1962 it was converted to support the Century 21 World's Fair; it stands at the base of the famous Space Needle that became the fair's, and the city's, icon. It is now the Center House for the Seattle Center complex, a tourist destination of museums and entertainment venues connected to the downtown by monorail. It is a streamline moderne design that houses a children's museum; a food court; two theaters, one of which serves the Seattle Shakespeare Society; offices for cultural organizations, including the Northwest Folklife Festival; and an experimental high school specializing in the arts.

In New Orleans, PWA reconstructed and modernized the historic French Market, making it a world-famous tourist magnet while still a place to get fruits, vegetables, and prepared foods. Not far from the French Quarter rises the twenty-story hospital known as "Big Charity," a monument to public health and an engineering curiosity as well. Erecting such a giant on the mud and sand of this city below sea level was a considerable risk. It stopped sinking at eighteen inches below grade, but not before the anxious owners arranged an inspection by high-paid, Ivy League consultants. Outside the city, the rumor circulated that one could now enter the building at the second floor.[31] Because of damage sustained during Hurricane Katrina, hospital administrators want to tear it down; but local doctors say it is still serviceable.

Elsewhere in the state of Louisiana, eleven parish courthouses were being built. In no other period in the state's history, before or since, have so many courthouses been constructed. All are still serving as the primary seats of justice in their parishes. Entire campuses for seven regional universities were also springing up. Classroom buildings, laboratories, libraries gymnasiums, art and drama facilities, heating plants, and dormitories of concrete, brick, and stone replaced temporary and dilapidated quarters occupied by these fledgling institutions. Grambling, an important

Fig. 6.9. The former Seattle Armory now houses museums, a food court, and other cultural amenities for the Seattle Center complex at the base of the city's iconic Space Needle. Photograph by R. D. Leighninger

Fig. 6.10. The French Market in New Orleans's famous French Quarter had existed since 1784, but PWA turned it into an internationally known tourist destination. Photograph by Greg Gilman

Fig. 6.11. This streamlined bas-relief characterization of justice on the Rapides Parish Courthouse in Alexandria, Louisiana, reminds citizens that "justice delayed is justice denied." With PWA's help, Louisiana built more parish (county) courthouses than during any other period in its history, before or since. Photograph by Greg Gilman

Fig. 6.12. Law barracks, the Citadel, Charleston, South Carolina. The chapel of this famous military school, a classroom building, and a series of officers' houses also were built by PWA. Photograph by R. D. Leighninger

historically black college, received its first six permanent buildings at this time. Southern University in Baton Rouge, another historically black university, got a stadium, a gym-auditorium, and several handsome dormitory buildings. Nor was the state's flagship institution, Louisiana State University, neglected. Two classroom buildings, three dormitories, a faculty club, and an experimental sugar mill were added to its campus.[32]

In other cities, famous structures were made possible by PWA, though none are identified in the public mind with the New Deal. How many people are aware that Charleston's well-known military school, the Citadel, has a chapel, a barracks building, officers' quarters, and several other amenities courtesy of PWA? At least two famous Chicago historians are unaware that the Outer Drive Bridge in the center of city's waterfront is a PWA project.[33] How many know that the Orange Bowl in Miami, the gold bullion depository at Fort Knox, the Tennessee Supreme Court building in Nashville, the Jewel Box floral conservatory in St. Louis's Forest Park, the University of Minnesota's Coffman Memorial Union, the University of Texas tower, the stadium and track at William and Mary College in Williamsburg, Will Rogers Coliseum in Fort Worth, city hall in Kansas City, the Municipal Auditorium in Oklahoma City, the Oregon State Capitol in Salem, the Suffolk County Courthouse in Boston, and the Key West Overseas Highway were all PWA projects?

Less glamorous but vital to health and prosperity were the many water, sewage, and electrical projects made possible by PWA across the country. Rapidly expanding cities had outgrown their capacity to treat sewage; some never had such capacity. Raw human and industrial waste was flowing daily into our lakes and rivers. Even small towns had trouble getting uncontaminated drinking water. Massive sewage systems in cities like New Orleans, Cincinnati, and Chicago and modest ones in thousands of small communities prevented a national public health crisis.

Electrical power made widely available spurred the economy and raised the quality of life in all the households it reached. Hoover Dam, the grandest of these projects, was one of many. Ickes called it Boulder Dam on the grounds that this was common usage until his predecessor at Interior decided to name it after Hoover. It had been authorized by Congress (but not funded) as Boulder Dam in 1928. When someone complained that he continued to use Boulder, Ickes fumed: "Hoover had very little to do with the dam and in fact was supposed to be opposed to it. To call it Hoover Dam is to give him credit for something for which he is not entitled to credit, and ignore those who dreamed of this proposition and brought it to successful conclusion after years of effort. The dam was never officially named Hoover."[34]

The project was so huge that no single contractor could undertake it. A consortium of six, including Henry J. Kaiser and Stephen Bechtel, both of whom used their experience to build vast industrial empires after the Depression, was required for the task. At the time it was the biggest dam in the world. It provided electricity for far-off Los Angeles and irrigation for the Imperial Valley. It was soon followed by other large power projects: Fort Peck Dam in Montana, a photograph of which by Margaret Bourke White was on the cover of the first edition of *Life* magazine; Parker Dam in Arizona; the Big Thompson Project in Colorado; Alcova Dam in Wyoming; Bonneville Dam on the Columbia River between Oregon and Washington; Grand Coulee, also on the Columbia, made famous by Woody Guthrie; and many others. The Bonneville project involved the construction of a "fish ladder" so that salmon could continue to spawn in the river.[35]

Not all PWA dams were huge, and not all are in the West. The Muskingum Watershed Conservancy project in southeastern Ohio constructed fourteen dams for flood and erosion control and created reservoirs to save the flood waters for dry spells. Eleven lakes were created with two hundred miles of shoreline, which added recreation to conservation. The project cost forty-four million dollars and involved the cooperation of the CCC, WPA, National Youth Administration, the Forest Service, the Soil Conservation Service, and the Biological Survey.[36]

The Bonneville salmon were not the only animals to be served by PWA. Many zoo projects provided more naturalistic habitats for a variety of species. Elephants

Fig. 6.13. Hoover Dam, an incredible project that took the combined efforts of six contracting firms, two of which—Bechtel and Kaiser—became giant, multinational corporations. Ickes called it Boulder Dam because he believed Hoover had had nothing to do with it. Photograph by Arthur Rothstein, Farm Security Administration

Fig. 6.14. Parker Dam on the Colorado River between Arizona and California diverts water into a 238-mile aqueduct flowing to Los Angeles. Photograph by H. Anderson Photography

and chimpanzees in Washington's National Zoo, antelopes in St. Louis, and bears and snakes in Cincinnati all got new quarters. Landscape architect Phoebe Cutler says, "The grounds and structures [were] carefully detailed with cascading plants, figurative reliefs, and picturesque bowers for the animals."[37]

PWA built many airport buildings, most of which have been superseded because of the vast increase in air travel since the 1930s. One terminal building that still stands at the heart of its airport is Washington National. It is now known as Reagan National Airport. The president who spent most of his political career trying to discredit "big government" programs now has his name attached to one of the jewels of a classic big-government program. At the time of the renaming, no one seemed to know about the origins of the building, and there was no public comment on the irony of the honor.

An important adjunct to the PWA's many contributions to domestic infrastructure was its ongoing support of the national defense build-up (table 6.4). The military significance of some of the WPA airports has been noted. The PWA had an even greater role. This included a huge expansion of the Army Air Corps' Barksdale Field in Louisiana, which later played a major role in Operation Desert Storm and in the 1999 NATO operations in Kosovo. It also sheltered President

Fig. 6.15. National Airport, now named after Ronald Reagan, is a product of the type of "big government" program that he spent most of his political career opposing. Photograph by R. D. Leighninger

Fig. 6.16. Port Allen (Louisiana) Middle School, originally a high school, across the Mississippi River from Baton Rouge, is a small art deco gem by Bodman and Murrell. Photograph by R. D. Leighninger

Bush after the September 11 disaster. An allotment of $1.5 million to the Coast Guard built several kinds of airplanes for patrol and rescue operations. Another $2.8 million produced five 165-foot Coast Guard cutters. Most impressive was what PWA did for the navy. It might surprise most people to learn that the aircraft carrier *Yorktown*, sunk in the Battle of Midway, was a New Deal public works project. In addition to the *Yorktown*, PWA funded the carriers *Ranger* and *Enterprise*, seven heavy cruisers, four light cruisers, five submarines, and thirty-two destroyers.[38]

PWA claimed to have built projects in all but three counties in the United States.[39] This is a slight exaggeration, but probably not much of one. There are more than three parishes in Louisiana alone that have no PWA projects within their boundaries. However, it might be possible to assert that PWA money was spent in every county in the country. Wages from workers in urban areas may have been sent back to family members in isolated parts of the country. We need not take this boast literally to agree that the reach of this agency was enormous and that it changed the face of the country from city to rural crossroads, border to border, and coast to coast.

Table 6.4 Defense preparation projects completed by the Public Works Administration

	Federal	Total cost ($ Million)*
Naval vessels	60	240.0
Coast Guard vessels	99	26.5
Aircraft	48	19.2
Ordnance	50	7.1
Machine tools for navy yards	81	4.1
U.S. Military Academy, West Point	20	3.5
U.S. Naval Academy, Annapolis	36	5.3

*Total estimated cost as of February 28, 1939.

Source: Public Works Administration, *America Builds: The Record of the PWA* (Washington, D.C.: Government Printing Office, 1939), 136, table 20, 290–91.

Chapter 7

▪ THE TENNESSEE VALLEY AUTHORITY ▪
1933–

Like many New Deal agencies, the Tennessee Valley Authority (TVA) had multiple purposes, though no other had so many. It was an experiment in regional planning, a conservation effort, an assertion of the public right to provide electrical power, a flood control project, an extension of river navigation, an attempt to stimulate the economy by improving agricultural practices and attracting industry, a novel form of bureaucratic organization, and a promotion of grassroots democracy. Along the way, it ventured into town planning, revival of traditional crafts, and archeological excavation. A focus on the built environment precludes discussion of all these features in equal detail. However, one of the fascinations of the TVA is that it was conceived as a package, one so stunning that it stood out even in the context of the many creative improvisations of the early New Deal. According to one of its chroniclers, it was "in many ways the most unique government agency ever set up in the United States."[1] It attracted international attention and waved, however briefly, lofty ideological banners. It was, to one of its most vigorous agents, "democracy on the march."[2] Thus one must stand back and look at the package before considering any of its component parts.

As a bold experiment in regional planning, the dream of the Tennessee Valley Authority was born in one war and died in another. It still exists as a system of dams and reservoirs and as a producer of electricity, but as a vision of the American future it had evaporated within five years of its conception. In some areas, particularly conservation, it even became the negation of its original aspirations. For a while, however, it captured the imaginations of many. "It begins with the watershed . . . the silver rivers yellowing and widening with weight of clay, which bind this valley into unity deeper than man can fence his states; a linkage and veinage of moving waters ill-kempt for navigation, capable of apoplectic flood, but muscled with a munificence of power that man has scarcely touched." This was written by James Agee for a feature in *Fortune* magazine. The article is a masterpiece of poetry, anthropology, and economic analysis, one of the best appraisals of the TVA at the time or since. He did not get a byline.[3]

Comprehensive planning for the Tennessee Valley did not originate with the New Deal. The complex interplay of river, farm, and factory began much earlier. During World War I, the National Defense Act of 1916 mandated a domestic source of the nitrates needed for explosives. The production process required large amounts of electricity. Muscle Shoals, Alabama, was chosen as the site for a phosphate plant, because it had already been identified as a good site for hydroelectric power generation. Eventually, Wilson Dam was built here. But national defense was not the only intent of the act. The role of the dam to provide flood control and to aid navigation was also featured. Moreover, it was apparent that a single dam could not accomplish the necessary flood control. Even the hydroelectric project could not run year-round unless upriver dams were added to regularize the flow of water to Wilson. The seeds of a watershed plan were already sprouting.[4]

The 1916 act also recognized that the plants could be used to produce nitrates for fertilizer as well as explosives. Thus a contribution to regional economic development was foreseen. The nitrate plants were experimental. Two different technologies, the Haber and cyanamid processes, were developed in two separate plants so that their relative advantages and problems could be compared. Research therefore was central to the whole operation. The project also involved housing for plant workers. The myriad ramifications that would spin out of the TVA were foreshadowed from the beginning of the Muscle Shoals enterprise.

In 1921 Henry Ford offered to buy the property, complete the dam complex, and lease it to the government. He would produce fertilizer and electrical power. He would also tie the complex to new industries. His workers would live in small towns near his factories and raise their own food using Ford tractors. He even had a scheme to defeat the boll weevil and improve cotton production. The idea of mixed-use development foreseen in the 1916 act was greatly elaborated in Ford's vision.[5]

Ford's proposal also got attention in Congress, but there it ran up against the opposition of Sen. George W. Norris of Nebraska. Norris had been concerned with the interrelation of erosion, flood control, and navigation in the Mississippi valley and was also an advocate of public control of hydroelectric power from the beginning of his service in the Senate in 1913.[6] Norris had studied Muscle Shoals carefully and was convinced that Ford's offer was far too low. He also thought the nitrate plants were more appropriate for research than commercial production. Most important, Norris was an advocate of public ownership of the capacity to generate electrical power. He saw "an irreconcilable conflict between those who believe the natural wealth of the Unites States best can be developed by private capital and enterprise, and those who believe that in certain activities related to the natural resources, only the great strength of the Federal Government itself can perform the most necessary task in the spirit of unselfishness, for the greatest good to the greatest number."[7] Failing to get congressional cooperation, Ford withdrew his offer in 1924. Norris was equally unsuccessful in getting his own vision of the development of Muscle Shoals enacted in law. Even when his bills got through Congress, they met vetoes by Presidents Coolidge and Hoover, who were strong opponents of public power.

Though his focus was on hydroelectric power, Senator Norris also had a broad view of what could be done with the valley. In addition to the fertilizer, the flood control, and the navigation benefits that could be obtained by government action, he was proclaiming the potential for new manufacturing opportunities, indeed a "complete and modern economic development" that electricity would bring. "As early as 1922 Norris proposed a multipurpose corporation with powers remarkably close to those enjoyed by the later TVA."[8]

In Franklin Roosevelt, Norris at last found a supporter. As governor of New York, Roosevelt had worked for a public use of the St. Lawrence River to generate electrical power. His perspective on rivers, however, did not stop with power. In their current state, rivers were agents of destruction as well as progress. They were carrying off the topsoil farmers needed to survive. As much as 70 percent of the farmable land in some areas of the Tennessee Valley had been ravaged by erosion. Much of the forest land was also being harvested to extinction. By one estimate, only four million out of twenty-seven million acres in Tennessee were undamaged.[9] Agee's *Fortune* magazine assessment summed up the plight of the valley dramatically: "These past four generations, we have wrung the very blood from the land and shipped its health to market and seaward by the sewers and left it exhausted and misplanted for the rain to do the rest. Left to its own devices and the rain's, that whole land could be desert before another century had passed."[10] It is interesting to find in a conservative business journal such a strong case for government intervention.

Roosevelt was well aware of the human dimension of the devastation explicit in Agee's indictment. This was a man-made calamity, not an act of God. Farmers had to learn new ways of gaining a living from the land without destroying it or else be moved to land more suitable for cultivation. He saw, as he had seen in creating the Civilian Conservation Corps, that reclaiming the land also involved reclaiming its people within some kind of sustainable balance.

People, land, and water interacted in many ways. The erosion of the farmland and the removal of the forests were not only threatening the survival of the farmers but also putting at risk the lives of the city dwellers downstream. The strong spring rains could no longer be held back by fields and forests and went crashing on to flood the valley. Annual flood damage was estimated by the Army Corps of Engineers to be $1,780,000 along the Tennessee, and that says nothing about what that river contributed to floods further down on the Ohio and Mississippi.[11] In order for dams and reservoirs to have a chance at preventing this destruction, erosion control and reforestation would first have to reduce the runoff. This meant starting with the entire watershed, working down from the mountains, restoring the forests, stopping the erosion of soil and the families who worked it, and containing the rivers with engineering feats that would not only prevent the wild waters from sweeping away the towns but also put them to work to bring electricity to homes and businesses in the valleys.

The National Defense Act of 1916, the Henry Ford proposal to buy Muscle Shoals, and the vision of Sen. George Norris had all included multiple functions and purposes interacting in complicated ways. But none of their plans included the entire Tennessee River watershed from Virginia to the Ohio, extending over six hundred miles and involving seven states.[12] That vision was Roosevelt's. He proposed a project that "if envisioned in its entirety, transcends mere power development; it enters the wide field of flood control, soil erosion, afforestation, elimination from agricultural use of marginal lands, and distribution and diversification of industry. In short this power development of war days leads logically to national planning for a complete river watershed involving many States and the future lives and welfare of millions. It touches and gives life to all forms of human concerns."[13] Roosevelt's advisor Rexford Tugwell regarded the TVA as having "more significance for the future than any other single attempt of the Administration to make life better for all of us." It was not an emergency measure but "a deliberate turning toward the future, a commitment toward an ideal."[14]

The authorization for fulfilling this commitment was embodied in sections 22 and 23 of the TVA legislation.[15] The former allowed the president, subject to congressional approval, to "make surveys of and general plans for . . . [the] physical, economic, and social development" of the region. The latter called for the development of legislation based on these surveys and plans that would promote the "economic and social well-being of the people living in the said river basin."[16] The vagueness of these sections made possible the many imaginative experiments in the early TVA, and they were made part of the law with very little debate. Though this may seem strange, it is of a piece with the latitude granted the president in the legislation enacting the Civilian Conservation Corps. The widely felt need to get things going and the willingness to experiment suppressed the fears and prejudices that otherwise would have been given full voice.[17]

The legislation called for a unique organizational structure. The TVA was to be an independent government corporation, not part of any cabinet department but responsible directly to the president and Congress. It would be governed by a three-person board appointed by the president. Even before the legislation was approved in April 1933, Roosevelt had chosen its chairman. Arthur Ernest Morgan, often called "A. E.," was a civil engineer and president of Antioch College. The fact that he was a college president despite having dropped out of college after only one semester says something about the force of his intellect and personality. One of his several qualifications for the TVA job was the fact that he had created an innovative system of dams and reservoirs for flood control and land reclamation along the Miami River in Ohio. He shared Roosevelt's grasp of the interdependence of riparian engineering and conservation. He also shared Roosevelt's appreciation of social factors: his construction camps were planned to provide the amenities of a community to the workers and their families instead of being the usual random assemblage of shanties, bars, and brothels.[18]

Morgan stepped easily into Roosevelt's broad but vague scheme of regional planning. He was comfortable with thinking on a grand scale and had plenty of ideas of his own. His promotion of these ideas was forceful and confident. He was convinced that they were of the highest moral and intellectual quality and would be assented to by all reasonable people once they had heard him expound them. As an engineer and construction boss he was also used to giving orders and having them carried out without debate. He disdained political patronage and influence peddling. If there was any opposition to what he wanted to do, it had to be a result of ignorance or political conspiracy. He was the sort of person destined to build an efficient, comfortable, and beautiful railroad and die in a train wreck.[19]

A. E. Morgan was on the job for three months before the other board members were appointed. He had already made key appointments and begun work on many projects by the time he was joined by David Lilienthal and Harcourt Morgan. This was both fortunate and unfortunate. It laid the groundwork for immediate friction within the board. It is also likely, however, that some of the TVA's more creative accomplishments would not have happened had he not been able to get them going before locking horns with the other two board members.

David Lilienthal was a Harvard Law School graduate who had studied with Felix Frankfurter. He was politically well connected and was very articulate both on the podium and on paper. TVA excelled in public relations, and one of the reasons for this was Lilienthal. He was a specialist in utility regulation and an advocate of public power, which made him a natural choice for the TVA board. In fact A. E. Morgan had recommended him for the position.[20]

Harcourt Morgan was a college president, like A. E. His specialty was agriculture, and he had built the University of Tennessee into a respected center of agricultural research. He had strong relationships with the farming communities across his state, and his network included the bankers and journalists in those communities. He could draw on the support of the valley's agriculture schools and had worked closely with the agriculture department's Cooperative Extension Service and with the farmers' lobby, the American Farm Bureau Federation. His agricultural interests did not extend to forestry or an appreciation of the overall watershed. To him, woods were just places outside farms. Also he tended to focus on the larger farmers. Grassroots to him "meant the power structure, not ten farmers."[21]

Harcourt Morgan was older than Lilienthal and less assertive, but both soon found themselves chafing under the dominion of A. E. Morgan. They did not share all of A. E.'s passions, which they were inclined to regard as utopian if not crackpot. Nor did he ask for their approval. Thus they soon engineered a division of labor giving them considerable autonomy in their own areas of expertise—Lilienthal with the power projects and Harcourt Morgan in agriculture. They also outvoted him on anything that required board approval. A. E. was not pleased with this development and tried to use his personal relationship with Roosevelt to mitigate or undo it. He had charge of the overall management of TVA, however, and plenty of his own projects to oversee, so he allowed his resentment to simmer.

As work got under way and people came to view the progress, some of the president's hope for the future blossomed in the observers. Journalist Lorena Hickok, who had been dispatched by Harry Hopkins to check on CWA and WPA activities around the country, reported to him on the TVA in June 1934: "A Promised Land, bathed in golden sunlight, is rising out of the grey shadows of want and squalor and wretchedness down here in the Tennessee Valley these days."[22] *Fortune,* while much more cautious, was willing to give the TVA the benefit of the doubt and even allow the comparison of Roosevelt's vision with that of the founding fathers. "[For if you] . . . think that their road is steep into dubious frontier and their whole endeavor a gamble, remember that roads which lead to high places commonly have that character; and that, for an instance, the establishment of this government was in its time a gamble. And: if some gambles have turned out worse than that, others may turn out better."[23]

These fine abstractions had concrete foundations. In fact tons of literal concrete were soon being poured. Norris Dam on the Clinch River, a tributary to the Tennessee, was the first TVA effort to tame the river. Roland Wank, TVA's chief architect, had been hired because of his recently completed Union Terminal in Cincinnati. The imposing streamline deco structure featured a grand promenade that invited people in on one level and a network of tracks and bridges that brought their trains in below. The rotunda where tickets were sold and trains announced was decorated with murals of pioneers and workers. A coffee shop lined with tile from the famous Rookwood Pottery was one of the amenities enjoyed by travelers. Its drama, efficiency, and commodiousness was a suitable credential for one who would execute the vision of TVA.[24]

The Bureau of Reclamation had already drawn plans for Norris Dam. It had designed Wilson Dam at Muscle Shoals in a neoclassical style and proposed a similar look for Norris. Wilson was also built of concrete and steel, but the concrete was formed to look like stone. The dam was given the look of a Roman aqueduct and decorated with an array of pilasters and entablatures. Wank asked for a few days to review the plans and returned with a much more severe and functional proposal. He was, in the words of Julian Huxley, interested in "the disposition of

Fig. 7.1. The cant of the Norris Dam spillway is both functional and expressive. It portrays the strength of the dam and the power of the water behind it. Photograph by Farm Security Administration, uncredited

the structure to its surroundings and of its component parts to each other." He wanted "good, honest, efficient structures, and never mind the mayonnaise."[25]

Wank's plans added a visitors' center above the dam and a reception center within the powerhouse. He reasoned that the project belonged to the taxpayers, and they ought to be welcomed and shown what they had invested in. TVA dams always bore a prominent inscription, "Built for the People of the United States," instead of the more common plaque that would have listed the officials overseeing the project and perhaps the architect. Wank's plan also paid attention to how the dam fit into the surrounding landscape. There was no attempt to disguise the structure and preserve an illusion of unspoiled nature as the government rustic architects of the CCC had done. This was clearly a man-made thing brought to control and regulate natural forces. But it did not have to be plunked down athwart the river with no other regard for where it was. Respect for the location was possible, and some harmony where human construction joined natural structure could be achieved. In addition Wank paid attention to how visitors would approach and view the dam. One critic saw comparisons to the siting of the Acropolis. Other activities were also provided for. When stone was quarried and crushed for aggregate in the concrete, the quarry created a boat harbor. With the help of the CCC, three recreation areas were built. They included cabins, beaches, stables, and dining facilities.[26]

The simplicity of Wank's design magnified the sheer size of the dams themselves and created a new kind of monumentality that thrilled observers. *New Yorker* architecture critic Lewis Mumford noted that "the mere cant of a dam . . . makes one think of the Pyramids of Egypt." Both were examples to him of the "architecture of power." The cant, or angled edge, was not a feature common to dams. The neoclassicism of Wilson Dam is predominately vertical with an angled spillway only at the very bottom. The cant is impressive only when water is flowing over it. In Wank's design that effect is always present, water or no water, symbolizing the power of the water it is holding back. The depth of the concrete splaying out on the downriver side also emphasizes the strength the dam must have to hold back the water.[27]

Critics were impressed with the total integration of architecture and engineering. The structures worked well and looked good at the same time. Architectural critic Talbot Hamlin saw TVA's engineers and architects as "true partners." Another critic, introducing a thirty-page spread of TVA photographs, found "a consistent logic and sensibility running through all these structures, small as well as great. Everywhere the arrangements are adjusted to the human being, not only as a worker in and user of buildings and accessories, but also as one who sees and feels and enjoys. The observant designer . . . will find many ideas that are worth incorporating in his own work. That way progress lies!"[28]

This is not just engineering. In a neoclassical treatment, the concrete would have been faced with stone or shaped to imitate stone. Instead, Wank used the concrete-pouring process itself to make the surfaces interesting and give human scale to the immense masses. He had the rough-sawn boards of the forms within which the concrete was poured nailed together in alternating horizontal and vertical panels. When the forms were removed, the grain of the wood remained visible and the subtle checkered pattern stood out so that, in Hamlin's words, "the walls have life."[29] Moreover, this effect was achieved at a fraction of the cost of traditional ornamentation.

Wank's new scheme did not suit everyone, so Morgan called in the nation's premier industrial architect and builder of vast automobile plants in Detroit, Albert Kahn, to consult. Kahn gave it a strong endorsement. Wank could then proceed to design subsequent TVA dams with the same aesthetic and site planning, and never mind the mayonnaise.[30]

The TVA's first dam was named for Sen. George Norris. Norris was not just a dam, a power generator, and a series of parks; it was also a place for people to live. As Morgan had done for his construction projects on the Miami, he also provided Norris Dam with a community of houses, a school, shops, and other amenities. Careful planning preserved most of the trees on the site. Norris's houses combined the vernacular Appalachian "dog-trot" style using cedar shake roofs and board-and-batten siding with, of course, the latest electrical appliances. Streets curved following the gentle contours of the landscape. By classic town-planning standards it was low density, with only 2.7 families per acre.[31] Near the Norris school was an athletic field, a town common, and a few public buildings. In addition to residences, Norris accommodated a few poultry and dairy farms and the nation's first all-electric creamery. Though originally conceived for construction workers, Norris was soon inhabited by the executives, technicians, and managers. It eventually became a suburb of Knoxville. This connection was facilitated by the Norris Freeway, a twenty-five-mile stretch of limited-access highway designed by Wank. It brought construction materials to the site and later encouraged visitors and commuters. It was "sound and attractive highway engineering," and its attractiveness was preserved by a ban on billboards within the 250-foot right-of-way.[32]

Unfortunately, there was a destructive side to this glorious new construction. Once the dams were complete, the valleys behind them would fill with water. People lived in these valleys and had for hundreds of years. Their ancestors were buried there. Residents had to be persuaded to move. They were offered new land and assistance in getting to it. Whole houses and churches were taken apart and rebuilt. Entire cemeteries were moved when descendants would allow it. Some

Fig. 7.2. Norris Dam and powerhouse. The simple technique of alternating the direction of the boards on the forms into which concrete was poured enlivened the surfaces of otherwise stark geometric walls. Photograph by Farm Security Administration, uncredited

resisted. One man maintained that his hearth fire had been going since his ancestors entered the valley 150 years ago and he was not leaving without it. Though skeptical of this presumed eternal flame, TVA moved it. Another valley dweller, an elderly woman known as Aunt Rachel, refused to sell her land. She said she would just sit on her porch and let the water rise around her. The TVA agent described all the wonderful things that the dam and power plant would bring to the valley and implored her to cooperate in this monumental effort. "Cooperate?" she cried. "I'm goin' to die for the government. What more do you want?"[33]

In general, the valley residents accepted the money TVA offered for their land. The appraisers were local. *Fortune* magazine's reporter judged the offers as "entirely fair." Less than 5 percent of the land acquired was contested, and court settlements awarded only 16.8 percent over the prices offered. Nonetheless, the relocation broke up long-established communities, disrupted family ties, and buried generations of memories under tons of water. Norris Dam alone displaced thirty-five hundred people. Many of the valley's poorest residents paid a high price for the new opportunities TVA brought. Agee captures the unspoken, and perhaps unspeakable, pain of this dislocation in a brief graveside vignette. "And there was also the woman who stood very silent, not crying, in the rain, in rain-sagged calico, and watched the walnut coffin raised and fitted into its new board box; and who lifted her wet skirt to take her tears only when the box was crayoned with 'TVA.'"[34]

Of the twenty-eight dams built by TVA, ten had been completed and seven more begun by 1942. Some were main river dams that included lock facilities for navigation. Others were storage dams with huge reservoirs behind them to control floods and regularize the flow of water to the electrical plants (see table 7.1). They are the material achievements that caught the eye of the world. There were other, more modest but still important, contributions to the physical infrastructure of the Tennessee Valley. Many old roads and bridges went under the waters of the impounded lakes and reservoirs. New roads and bridges had to be built to reconnect the population. The same care in design devoted to the dams also went into the bridges. Four of them were sufficiently impressive that they were included in a Museum of Modern Art publication.[35]

Building dams, bridges, and model towns was just the beginning of Morgan's plans for transforming the valley. Even as he was doing his best to bring high technology to the hills and hollows, he was also aware that there was much worth preserving in the rural way of life. He encouraged the teaching and production of traditional crafts: furniture making, metalwork, weaving, basket making, and others. He saw to it that some of the homes in the town of Norris included shop space. He encouraged local craftspeople to use Wank's visitors' center at the dam to display and sell their work, and he opened craft shops in Chattanooga and in the Rockefeller Center in New York. This was not just an attempt to maintain continuity in the valley culture—what Walter Creese calls a symbolic "splicing of value systems"— but a recognition of the possibilities for supplemental income in a transitional economy. Morgan helped the Southern Highland Handicraft Guild market its products across the country. By 1938 the guild was issuing stock and representing twenty-five hundred craftspeople.[36]

Morgan had other ideas for using construction as a vehicle for social development. Workers at Norris Dam were put on a five-and-a-half-hour, six-day work week and encouraged to use the rest of the day in academic study or training in electrical work, automobile repair, pipe fitting, dairy technology and other vocational skills. One of Morgan's goals was to help workers move up to foreman rank. Workers and their families could also learn or develop traditional craft skills or attend lectures, concerts, or plays. There was a "home demonstration center" with classes in cooking, child care, and budgeting.[37]

Some of Morgan's other inspirations were less well received. He wanted to develop his own currency to stimulate and supplement a barter system in rural areas where cash was scarce. He wanted to reduce the number of counties in Tennessee from ninety-five to eleven in order to streamline negotiations with local governments. He thought that farmers who failed to participate in the soil erosion

Table 7.1 TVA dams (New Deal)

	Construction	State	Main River	Storage Cost
Norris	1933–36	Tennessee	x	$31,500,000
Wheeler	1933–36	Alabama	x	$48,200,000
Pickwick Landing	1934–38	Tennessee	x	$47,000,000
Guntersville	1935–39	Alabama	x	$39,000,000
Hiawassee	1937–40	North Carolina	x	$23,200,000
Chickamauga	1938–40	Tennessee	x	$41,000,000
Watts Bar	1939–42	Tennessee	x	$35,600,000
Kentucky	1939–44	Kentucky	x	$119,200,000
Cherokee	1940–41	Tennessee	x	$36,300,000
Fort Loudoun	1940–43	Tennessee	x	$43,000,000
Hales Bar*	1940–52	Tennessee	x	$35,600,000
Ocoee # 3	1941–43	Tennessee	x	$8,700,000
Chatuge	1941–42	North Carolina	x	$10,000,000
Nottely	1941–42	Georgia	x	$8,600,000
Appalachia	1941–43	Tennessee	x	$23,700,000
Douglas	1942–43	Tennessee	x	$46,200,000
Fontana	1942–45	North Carolina	x	$75,800,000

*Remodeling; originally built 1905–13.

Source: John H. Kyle, *The Building of TVA: An Illustrated History* (Baton Rouge: Louisiana State University Press, 1958).

Fig. **7.3.** Chickamauga Dam and powerhouse. The traveling gantry supporting the crane at the top of the dam is typical of Roland Wank's functional aesthetics. Photograph by Farm Security Administration, uncredited

control program should have their property confiscated. One can see the appeal of these ideas to Morgan's engineering mind. He no doubt expected others to see the logic, too, and agree immediately. Unfortunately, he could not see the political drawbacks. These schemes furthered the impression that Morgan was at best a dreaming utopian and at worst a dangerous kook. His fellow board members sometimes shared this impression and let others know.[38]

This, of course, lent credibility to Morgan's perception that there were conspiracies against him. Because he was convinced of his own rectitude, there must be immorality behind the opposition. Eventually, his pot of resentment boiled over. He tried unsuccessfully to block Lilienthal's reappointment to the board in 1936. When this failed and his threat of resignation produced no solicitations from the president, he also began to make public comments about his colleagues, which included accusations of dishonesty. In 1938 Roosevelt finally had to step in. Morgan refused to substantiate his charges in a personal interview with the president, calling instead for a congressional investigation. Roosevelt had no choice but to fire him.[39]

Meanwhile, Lilienthal was engaged in a legal and public relations war to establish the right of TVA to generate electricity and offer it to citizens of the valley. Private power companies were not about to accept this intrusion without a fight. They had strong ideological objections to any government operation of utilities, and they did not want what they regarded as unfair competition. They maintained that TVA was unconstitutional, and they were determined to go as high as necessary to prove it.

The power companies entered the engagement with a few disadvantages. They had heretofore shown no interest in extending the benefits of electricity into rural areas, because they did not believe there was any market for it. Their early argument against TVA was that there was already sufficient generating capacity in existence. TVA would be producing wattage no one would use.[40]

The private power companies had an even bigger problem in their public image. They were under investigation by Congress and the Federal Trade Commission for fraud and corruption, including the creation of a billion dollars worth of "watered" stock. The companies had discovered a variety of ways to artificially inflate their investment so that they could charge higher rates and still be within the 6 to 8 percent return that state regulators were supposed to hold them to. Agee described this as an accounting "jungle from which none but the natives have ever returned alive."[41]

More than three hundred communities in the valley had applied to TVA for electrical power, but the injunctions filed by the Commonwealth and Southern Companies, the private utilities' representative, prevented most from getting it. These were appealed by TVA, but the trial did not begin until late 1937. A circuit court upheld the constitutionality of TVA in 1938. An appeal to the Supreme Court was unsuccessful. The court also ruled that private utilities had no standing to block PWA projects. At this point the private utilities decided to sell their facilities to TVA, local municipalities, or rural cooperatives. The lights could finally be turned on in the valley.[42]

Some constitutional issues remained, and the full federal mandate was not clarified until 1940 and 1941 when the Supreme Court decided two final cases.[43] The eight-year struggle had cost valuable time and much money. Richard Lowitt concludes: "The damage done the defendants throughout this extensive litigation far outweighed the damage that would have occurred to the plaintiffs had the work continued. More serious was TVA's inability to help provide the blessings of cheap electricity to many deprived people during these Depression years." The episode did, however, establish that there was a broad rural market that both public and private utilities would proceed to serve. The supposedly surplus wattage was being eagerly absorbed in communities that had escaped the injunctions. Electric lights, washing machines, stoves, refrigerators, pumps, milking machines, and other appliances were soon in use throughout the valley.[44]

Unfortunately, not all citizens of the valley were well served by TVA. African Americans made up 11 percent of the watershed. Early promises to hire representative numbers, pay equal wages, and provide equal housing impressed *Fortune*

Fig. 7.4. Julien Case and his wife, farmers in Lauderdale County, Alabama, enjoying their electric stove. Private power companies told TVA there was no market for electricity in rural areas. When they discovered otherwise, they took TVA to court, blocking service to most areas of the valley until 1938. Photograph by Arthur Rothstein, Farm Security Administration

magazine. However, these employment opportunities were largely menial and temporary. Applicants with skills were turned down. Blacks could not live in Norris. Jim Crow policies were unquestioned.[45]

Some of this may be due to the counterco-optation documented by Philip Selznick in *TVA and the Grass Roots*. By advancing an ideology of grassroots democracy to facilitate its survival in a hostile environment, the TVA ultimately ceded considerable control to those it sought to co-opt. It adopted the racial attitudes of local farmers and Cooperative Extension officials just as it compromised on conservation issues with local strip miners.[46] A. E. Morgan, however, did not need to be co-opted on race. He believed that "the universal immorality of the Negro is a bigger blight on the country than people realize."[47]

As with the CCC, CWA, and WPA, it is remarkable that the TVA with its three-headed board worked at all. Like them, however, it did. The unlikely administration survived five years until the train wreck. And, of course, the departure of A. E. Morgan was not the end of the TVA. It survived and grew in size and influence. But survival brought compromise. TVA continued to generate electricity but increasingly with coal-fired steam generators that encouraged strip mining and polluted the air. It continued to build dams, though ones that undermined the farm economy and threatened rare wildlife. It contributed mightily to the war effort by providing the electricity for the secret Oak Ridge atomic bomb research complex and for plants producing aluminum for airplanes and other war machinery. It brought new recreation facilities to the Tennessee Valley. It continued to bring commercial benefits to valley industries and save billions of dollars through flood control. It was however, no longer the bold experiment in regional planning that its creators and well-wishers had hoped would change the face of America.

Nonetheless, the accomplishments of the TVA during the New Deal were sufficient to earn it worldwide admiration and provide it with insulation from criticism that lasted for decades even as its negative impacts were accumulating. Per capita income in the valley had been less than half the national average in 1929. By the early fifties it was up to 79 percent. Muscle Shoals revolutionized fertilizer production in this country and abroad; most is now made with the aid of TVA technology. Crop yields have increased appreciably. Reforestation was so successful that a major paper company moved in to exploit it. With the help of the Civilian Conservation Corps, TVA taught farmers to terrace their land to retard soil erosion. They also planted a variety of fast-growing ground cover, including honeysuckle, which some observed "will grow not merely all over your land but in your ears at the slightest encouragement."[48]

Freight traffic on the Tennessee was four million mile-tons in 1980, more than one hundred times what it was in 1933. Oil, grain, coal, steel, chemical, and even frozen chickens are able to travel the river from Paducah to Knoxville because of TVA locks and dams.[49] Flood damage has been virtually eliminated in the valley. Even by 1937, with only three dams and reservoirs in place, a flood that left a million people homeless in the Ohio and Mississippi valleys had little effect on the Tennessee. In 1971, when five to ten inches of rain fell in the valley within forty-eight hours, flood waters at Chattanooga were held to seven feet above crest. Without the dams and reservoirs it would have been 22.5 feet above. The city incurred thirty-five million dollars in damage, but the impact estimated without the flood control system was five hundred million dollars.[50]

The New Deal in general did much to improve the nation's public health, but one of the more dramatic side effects of TVA was the elimination of malaria. Drainage ditches, channels, and pumping stations opened stagnant areas, and the regular raising and lowering of water levels in the system made it impossible for the anopheline mosquito to propagate.[51]

In 1941, when many of TVA's efforts were completed and open for inspection, the Museum of Modern Art mounted an exhibition of TVA architecture. The critic from *Time* concluded that "TVA's designers had coordinated its myriad parts into a unified symphony of structure." Economist Stuart Chase provided words for the entrance to the exhibit celebrating the "new architecture, bold as the engineering from which it springs. Look at it and be proud that you are an American."

Lewis Mumford, who had seen many of the structures firsthand, decided it was "as close to perfection as our age has come." He went on, "Thanks to these dams, the colossal forces of the Tennessee River are held back or released almost as easily as one turns the water off and on at one's private faucet, and instead of wasted water, there is an abundance of electricity. Aren't we entitled to a little collective strutting and crowing?"[52]

Some of this exuberance must be understood in the context of the approaching world war. Between them, the totalitarian governments of Germany and Russia had swallowed up much of Europe and seemed bent on taking the rest. There was reason to doubt whether democracy could compete with this new form of government. Some believed at the time, and even later, that the New Deal was the only viable middle way between communism and fascism. The success of TVA was seen as evidence that a democracy could engage in large-scale planning without dictatorship. One did not need a Mussolini to make the trains run on time.[53]

The radiant modernity of TVA architecture and the relative efficiency with which it had integrated so many diverse and complex parts were testimony to what David Lilienthal called "the virility and vigor of democracy." Richard Lowitt concludes that, "by almost any standard, TVA in late 1941 was an outstanding American success story—not in the traditional sense based on individual effort but as a planned enterprise indicating what a free people, dedicated and concerned, could accomplish."[54]

Chapter 8

HOUSING

Public Works Administration Housing Division, 1933–37
United States Housing Authority, 1937–42
Federal Housing Administration, 1934–

Some believe that we owe government's discovery that it had an interest in housing to germs. Disease is no respecter of class or wealth and can travel well beyond the location and conditions that spawned it. Once the connection between slums, germs, and sickness had been made by Pasteur in the 1880s, the need to do something about slums became apparent. Others believe that fear of civil unrest was an even earlier cause of government action in housing. Revolution, not germs, inspired governments in Europe in 1848 to improve the housing of the poor.[1]

In any case, European countries were heavily invested in what they called "social housing," shelter for their low-income citizens, by the end of the World War I. The Netherlands began its housing program in 1902, and its government was building some of its most famous projects in Amsterdam and Rotterdam by 1913. Germany and Austria soon followed. Social housing provided more than simple shelter. Kindergartens, libraries, recreation facilities, clinics, and rooms for community meetings and clubs were part of the building complexes. These projects also provided an opportunity to experiment with new materials and construction techniques. This work, and the architects who performed it, became quite famous.[2] Some American Progressives were aware of these developments but were unable to implement them domestically because of the conviction they shared with their conservative countrymen that subsidy of housing was inappropriate and public investment had to produce a monetary return.[3]

The conclusion that the private housing market could not provide decent shelter for low-income people was reached only gradually in the United States. The immigrants and migrant farmworkers who crowded into cities in the latter part of the nineteenth century lived in unsanitary apartment buildings called tenements. Philanthropists and city governments tried to build "model tenements" that would provide safe and healthy living conditions and still return a profit on investment. Some Progressives rejected the idea of model housing entirely and advocated simply weeding out the bad tenements. Jacob Riis, a New York newspaper reporter and photographer, pushed the model tenement movement by showing the horrors of urban housing in his book *How the Other Half Lives.* However, the movement did little beyond raise consciousness. Even philanthropists hoping for only a 5 percent profit were disappointed. Since private developers could get five times that amount of profit in upper-income housing, there was no reason to operate in the lower end of the market. Low-income housing was not a viable private investment. Its payoff was only in public terms: better health, less crime, happier families.[4]

The model tenement movement was not the only private venture in improving housing for low-income workers. The "company town" was a popular idea among creative industrialists in England and the United States for several centuries. Factory owners believed that well-housed workers would be more content and more productive. In other cases the company town was designed to shield workers from the corrupting forces of the city: overindulgence in alcohol or radical politics. Company towns could also be a source of profit. Joseph Pullman's company town outside of Chicago, which he named after himself, charged for the use of the library and the churches he built as well as for the houses, some of which were no better than slum tenements. When hard times hit his business, he lowered wages but not rents.[5]

The biggest government impact on housing had nothing to do with building. In 1913 mortgage interest rates and taxes were made deductible from the new federal income tax. This would become a huge subsidy for homeowners. Other government aid set precedents that would affect the housing market. The Farm Loan Act of 1916, which lowered the cost of borrowing for farmers, provided a model for later legislation that would bring low-cost capital into the residential credit market.[6]

During World War I, there was a brief flurry of government-built housing for munitions workers. Interestingly, the government chose to follow British precedent and build permanent structures rather than cheap, temporary barracks. The program lasted less than a year and died with the armistice.[7]

From the 1890s to the 1920s, economic conditions were good for middle- as well as upper-income housing. Wages were stable, land outside cities was cheap, streetcars allowed home buyers to take advantage of this, and lumber and other building materials were readily available at low cost. After World War I, however, housing prices began to increase while wages did not. An affordability problem developed. While the problem went unrecognized at the federal level, several states tried to help the middle class buy houses. California established a revolving loan fund. New York offered tax exemption for new construction. Massachusetts even built houses (twelve, in fact) for sale to workers on long-term, low-interest mortgages.[8]

These state efforts recognized problems not covered in the standard view of housing economics, still widely held, that the market served all income levels. It is based on the assumption that shelter opportunities will trickle down. As long as construction continues at the upper end, homeowners will trade up and those further down will inherit their older dwellings. Everyone can be housed. This model is vulnerable to several disruptions. If there is less building, the market tightens and there is less movement. If landlords do not lower rents as their buildings age, low-income renters cannot move up. The market will not force them to lower rents if they are dealing with a captive audience. If public transportation does not provide access to cheaper opportunities at the edges of cities, only those who can afford automobiles can take advantage of them. This decreases competition for inner-city landlords while increasing demand, allowing them to keep rents high. It also reduces their incentive to keep their buildings in good repair. Racial and ethnic discrimination confine some renters and would-be home buyers to small segments of the market where they can be charged higher prices for even worse housing.[9]

As the affordability crisis of the 1920s progressed, reformers concerned about slum conditions were not the only voices calling for government intervention in housing. As secretary of commerce, Herbert Hoover established a Division of Building and Housing in 1921 to take leadership in the stimulation of residential building. He also introduced national standards for building under federal contracts. Real-estate interests began lobbying for tax breaks to get more capital into building. New York governor Al Smith offered such tax breaks for low-income housing construction in 1926. As president, Hoover oversaw the passage of the Home Loan Bank Act in 1932, the first permanent federal housing legislation, to stimulate mortgage lending. Even Hoover's secretary of commerce, a strong believer in laissez-faire economics, was forced to admit the "shortcomings in our individualistic theory of housing, and the failure which grows out of expecting each person in our highly complex industrial civilization to provide his own housing as best he may." By then, however, the Depression was reaching its depth. Patience for traditional market solutions had run out. A new administration took over.[10]

Government action was swift. As we have seen, Title 2 of the National Industrial Recovery Act established the Public Works Administration (PWA) in 1933. Section 202.d of the act provided for the "construction, reconstruction, alteration or repair under public regulation or control of low-rent housing and slum clearance projects."[11] Mary Simkhovich, a New York settlement worker and head of the National Public Housing Conference, along with Father John O'Grady, secretary of the National Conference of Catholic Charities, was able to persuade New York senator Robert Wagner to include this section in the legislation. Of the $3.3 billion allocated to the PWA, $125 million was to go to housing. The problem was knotty, the economic interests involved were complex, and the new crop of urban and liberal legislators and their constituents were eager for solutions. Initially, there was no opposition to federal involvement from the real-estate forces, who had been worn out by the crisis and their own failure to handle it. That could not be expected to last long, however.[12]

Indeed the disarray of the real-estate sector was brief; opposing forces would soon regroup. However, there were more important internal problems in the New Deal housing initiative that would hamper its defense and guarantee its continued vulnerability. Housing was not something the new president was particularly interested in. The passion that Roosevelt had poured into programs like the Civilian Conservation Corps or the Tennessee Valley Authority, which embodied his devotion to conservation and stewardship of the land, was not evoked by urban housing. He was happier with resettlement schemes that would send urbanites back to the land. As for slums, he told a group of visitors to the Lower East Side of New York City, "You don't need money or laws; just burn it down." The New Deal was never only about Roosevelt, but his support was important to most programs, and lack of it was a serious handicap.[13]

A second problem was that the housing effort was born in Title 2 of the NIRA, which placed it in the care of Harold Ickes. This was a mixed blessing. It guaranteed that the program would be armor-plated against charges of corruption but also that it would not produce an immediate dynamo of clearing and building. Given the many obstacles in the way of this clearing and building, it is probable that not even Harry Hopkins could have produced immediate results. But with Ickes in charge, an agonizingly slow start was inevitable.

Ickes established a PWA Housing Division to be headed by Robert D. Kohn, past president of the American Institute of Architects and former head of defense housing construction during World War I. Kohn was one of the few people in the country with any experience in running a government housing program. The division had two instruments for addressing the housing situation. It could solicit applications through the nonfederal grant and loan program from communities to construct their own housing. However, there were very few local agencies in existence empowered to construct housing. Housing was not a standard part of the portfolio of local government. The division could also offer loans to private corporations.[14]

Since PWA had inherited Hoover's last-minute public works program, the Emergency Relief and Construction Act run by the Reconstruction Finance Corporation, it began its work there. The RFC was empowered to offer loans to private, state-regulated corporations engaged in building housing for the lower end of the market. Expected to be low-profit enterprises, they were known as "limited dividend" corporations. Because the Hoover legislation was so restrictive, the RFC had managed to fund only one housing project in its thirteen months of life. Like the rest of the RFC program, the housing projects had to be "self-liquidating"— they had to pay for themselves. Since rents would be charged, that might not seem difficult. But the time limit for payoff, the amortization, was thirty years. That could not be done with low rents. Knickerbocker Village on the Lower East Side of New York City was the only project to gain RFC approval. This "village" was twelve stories high. Apartments were small and rents were too high for the people who had lived in the neighborhood and who had been displaced while the project went up.[15]

The restrictiveness of the RFC was not the only problem. Private builders were simply not interested in low-rent housing. Warren Vinton, chief of research for the Resettlement Administration, complained that "the industry has almost exclusively confined itself to the building of homes for families in the upper income bracket . . . to the almost complete neglect of the vastly larger market for modest priced houses."[16] The situation had not changed since the days of "tenement reform."

The division looked at other proposals that the RFC had not approved. One, Carl Mackley Houses, had been submitted by a Philadelphia hosiery workers' union that was looking not for profit but for decent housing for its members. More important, the union had assets of its own to commit. This was unusual. The division loosened the RFC restrictions somewhat. Even so, it was hard to qualify. The PWA was willing to loan applicants 85 percent of the cost of the project at 4 percent interest. However, they still had to come up with equity of 15 percent. Finding that equity was a challenge in the depths of a depression. Those who had it were not eager to put it into low-income housing. New applicants had to be found.[17]

To encourage proposals and, more importantly, to educate communities about what public housing might look like, the division put together a road show. Its representatives went from city to city "to preach the gospel of housing." They promoted the idea that housing should not be just a bunch of buildings but a "complete community." "Homes should be so located as to have adequate sun and air and plenty of protected play space for children. They should be within easy and protected walking distance of schools and shops. Buildings should be low and well built and supplied with at least the minimum of mechanical equipment." Such homes were "long term investments."[18]

Eventually, the division had 533 applications to evaluate, but they were little improvement over the RFC proposals. Some were scams to unload undesirable property; some were efforts to revive speculation in suburban subdivisions; some were fanciful dreams. A group of musicians wanted to build themselves a clubhouse on the roof of a skyscraper. Only seven proposals seemed viable (table 8.1). One was the hosiery union's Carl Mackley Houses.[19]

This was not enough for Ickes, who was under pressure to get the PWA moving. He decided that the division should undertake its own construction rather than wait to find viable private investors. Though many of the public housing estates in Europe had been built under the sponsorship of labor unions or building societies,

Table 8.1 Limited-dividend housing projects sponsored by the
Public Works Administration

Name	City	Units	Site	Cost
Altavista Housing	Altavista, Va.	50	vacant	$100,000
Boulevard Gardens	Queens, New York City	967	vacant	$4,086,600
Boylan	Raleigh, N.C.	54	vacant	$233,600
Carl Mackley Houses	Philadelphia	284	vacant	$1,123,713
Euclid Housing	Euclid, Ohio	72	vacant	$500,000
Hillside Homes	Bronx, New York City	1,416	vacant	$5,717,871
Neighborhood Gardens	St. Louis, Mo.	252	slum	$740,000

Sources: Michael W. Straus and Talbott Wegg, *Housing Comes of Age* (New York: Oxford University Press, 1938), 225–29; Gail Radford, *Modern Housing for America* (Chicago: University of Chicago Press, 1996), 93.

Ickes was impatient with the inexperienced local groups and wanted a more coordinated attack on slums and poor housing conditions.[20]

The PWA suspended the limited dividend program in February 1934 and began acquiring land and recruiting local architects and contractors to build housing under its own supervision. Simultaneously, it began aiding communities to establish their own housing authorities. PWA would work with them as with the nonfederal projects, offering a 30 percent grant and a 70 percent loan. The grant was later raised to 45 percent, as with the nonfederal projects. More important, the amortization rate was extended to sixty years, which gave the projects a fighting chance of paying off with lower rents.[21]

As with other New Deal agencies, the Housing Division began with lofty goals. One was to clear slums. Another was to build high-quality homes, setting standards for a national solution to the housing problem. A third was to provide shelter for the poor as well as the middle class. A fourth was to help communities organize themselves to finance and build their own housing. And of course, like the rest of the PWA, it was supposed to reduce unemployment and stimulate the economy. Unlike other New Deal programs, which came apart only gradually, this one had to confront its internal contradictions and political cross fire from the beginning.

Slum clearance, though politically popular, was expensive, because slums occupied desirable urban land that, despite its current sorry state, was still expensive to acquire. There were also costs involved in tearing down what was there. Land on the margins of the city was much less expensive. Reformers like Catherine Bauer argued that demonstrations should start there, because more resources could be put into the buildings themselves.[22] Yet even with cheap land, there was no magic formula that would allow the construction of decent housing for families with very low income without some subsidy. It was obvious that this could not be done in the market, because the profits were too low and the risks were too high. Nor could philanthropists willing to accept a very low profit do it. Could it be done on a non-profit basis?

Robert Kohn, the Housing Division head, was an architect and more interested in making the PWA a laboratory for experiments in improving housing quality than in slum clearance or housing at the lowest end of the market. Ickes, not willing to choose between conflicting goals, or perhaps calculating that he was unlikely to get very far unless he continued to promise to achieve all goals, soon replaced Kohn. He chose Col. Horatio B. Hackett, a West Pointer who had been an administrator for the large Chicago architectural firm of Holabird and Root.[23]

Hackett increased the staff of the division and moved ahead with Ickes's program. It was not easy. Though real-estate interests had been quiet when the PWA Housing Division was created, they soon began mounting an opposition. Though it was apparent that there was no need to fear competition at the lower end of the market, because private developers were not operating there, there was always the possibility that government success with low-income housing might lead to ventures into middle-income housing. This was not an imaginary threat. There were advocacy groups thinking along these lines and crafting legislation to increase middle-class housing affordability. As for those who owned slum property and derived good profits from it, the division was clear about its attitude toward them. "Every attempt is being made to restrict competition with private enterprise to that restricted field where operators exploit the misery of the underprivileged. Here the competition is deliberate and amply justified." Open war had been declared on slumlords, and they would certainly fight back.[24]

Antipathy was not confined to special interests. Newspapers and general public opinion were more alarmed about housing than about other New Deal programs. Standard ideological opposition to any government involvement in private markets was coupled with anxieties about possible effects on market values of private homes. Injunctions against construction were sought in several cities. In Boston one such suit elicited a countersuit representing a much larger group of property owners demanding that the project proceed, because they felt the upgrading would benefit, not threaten, their interests. In general restraining orders were not granted.[25]

Greater problems were soon encountered, however. Though eminent domain, the government's right to acquire land for public purposes, had been recognized since 1795, a Kentucky district court judge ruled in January 1935 that public housing was not a "public use." This took away the division's bargaining power in acquiring urban land and forced it to turn to the strategy advocated by the reformers: cheaper land further out. Of the fifty-five projects eventually completed by the division, only twenty-seven involved slum clearance. Only one of the limited-dividend projects was on slum land.[26]

There were vocal proponents as well as opponents of the PWA's housing efforts. Some were particularly vocal about the slowness with which Ickes proceeded. They wanted public housing, and they wanted it now. New York City mayor Fiorello La Guardia attacked PWA lawyers for procrastination. He called them "semi-colon boys." Ickes answered him at the dedication of the city's Williamsburg Houses project, a sixteen-hundred-apartment complex, in 1936. "In general I agree with the mayor," he said, "but I would like to express my appreciation of the work of these meticulous lawyers on this particular project for, on several occasions, a 'semi-colon boy' saved us from a large black period marking the end of the whole undertaking."[27]

The division had internal problems as well. Though Ickes believed that housing was "one of the most worthwhile things we are doing," he was unable to defend it against Roosevelt's periodic raids to move its budget to other agencies. When the Civil Works Administration was created in the fall of 1933, it was funded largely with PWA money. Ickes gave this his full blessing, because he could not spend the money at this time anyway. The following year was a different story, however. No sooner had he announced allotments to twenty-seven housing projects on December 8, 1934, than the president impounded $110 million of the Housing Division's $135 million. The money was needed by the Federal Emergency Relief Administration to counteract the devastation caused by severe blizzards and floods. The following July, when the new works program was being launched, the division was able to move again. But in the final budget shuffle in September 1935, the Works Progress Administration got preferential treatment, because it could employ more workers on relief. Housing lost $100 million of its $249 million budget. With such funding shifts, long-range planning was impossible, despite the fact that long-range planning was "the essence of its program."[28]

As long as relief was uppermost in the president's mind, housing was bound to suffer in the competition for funding. Even though, as *Fortune* magazine observed, residential building was 40 percent of the construction industry and the "greatest single factor in unemployment," it was not a sector that could be affected immediately. Housing required planning and, with Harold Ickes in charge, careful planning. It was, according to Michael Straus and Talbot Wegg, "a poor tool to serve the interests of immediate employment." Not until late in 1936 could the Housing Division's work proceed on its merits as housing rather than as an instrument of relief.[29]

The Housing Division, concerned that most American architects had no experience in designing low-income housing, propagated sample plans to ensure that basic considerations like light, ventilation, and safety would be included in all submitted proposals. They even offered specifications for playgrounds and landscaping. The March 1935 issue of *Architectural Record,* the profession's leading journal, was devoted almost entirely to these sample plans. The issue began with an article by Colonel Hackett on "How the PWA Housing Division Functions."[30]

Information was collected, land acquired, and ground broken. Fifty-five projects in thirty-nine cities were built (table 8.2). They were carefully planned and soundly constructed. Apartments were no more than two rooms deep; all had cross or through ventilation. Every bath had a tub, toilet, sink, and medicine cabinet. All bedrooms had closets. At a time when 85 percent of U.S. homes had neither electric stoves nor refrigerators, many PWA homes had both. Bulk purchasing of 16,697 refrigerators cut costs in half. Most projects were able to negotiate lower gas and electric rates with local utilities, though some cities refused to do this even though private developments enjoyed such discounts. In consultation with the U.S. Children's Bureau, PWA constructed playgrounds and included indoor play space for bad weather. Community rooms with kitchens were added for organizations and clubs. If local governments agreed to operate clinics, PWA built them.[31]

Table 8.2 Housing projects built by the Public Works Administration

City	Name	Units	Race	Site	Cost
Atlanta, Ga.	Techwood Homes	718	white	slum	$2,933,500
	University Homes	675	black	slum	$2,592,000
Atlantic City, N.J.	Stanley Holmes Village	277	black	slum	$1,550,000
Birmingham, Ala.	Smithfield Court	544	black	slum	$2,500,000
Boston, Mass.	Old Harbor Village	1,016	white	vacant	$6,636,000
Buffalo, N.Y.	Kenfield	658	white	vacant	$4,755,000
Caguas, P.R.	Caserio La Granja	75		vacant	$275,000
Cambridge, Mass.	New Towne Court	294	white	slum	$2,500,000
Camden, N.J.	Westfield Acres	515	white	vacant	$3,116,160
Charleston, S.C.	Meeting Street Manor	106	black	vacant	$675,000
	Cooper River Court	106	white	vacant	$675,000
Chicago, Ill.	Jane Addams Houses I	723	white	slum	$5,210,902
	Jane Addams Houses II	304	white	vacant	$1,830,858
	Julia Lathrop Homes	925	white	vacant	$5,862,000
	Trumbull Park Homes	462	white	vacant	$3,038,000
Cincinnati, Ohio	Laurel Homes	1,039	both	slum	$7,086,000
Cleveland, Ohio	Cedar-Central Apts.	650	white	slum	$3,384,000
	Outhwaite Homes	579	black	slum	$3,564,000
	Lakeview Terrace	620	white	slum	$3,800,000
Columbia, S.C.	University Terrace	48	white	slum	$278,164
	University Terrace	74	black	slum	$427,836
Dallas, Tex.	Cedar Springs Place	181	white	vacant	$1,020,000
Detroit, Mich.	Brewster	701	black	slum	$5,200,000
	Parkside	775	white	vacant	$4,500,000
Enid, Okla.	Cherokee Terrace	80	white	slum	$557,100

Table 8.2 continued

City	Name	Units	Race	Site	Cost
Evansville, Ind.	Lincoln Gardens	191	black	slum	$1,000,000
Indianapolis, Ind.	Lockfield Garden	748	black	slum	$3,207,000
Jacksonville, Fla.	Durkeeville	215	black	vacant	$948,000
Lackawanna, N.Y.	Baker Homes	271	white	vacant	$1,610,000
Lexington, Ky.	Blue Grass Park	286	both	vacant	$1,704,000
Louisville, Ky.	LaSalle Place	210	white	vacant	$1,350,000
	College Court	125	black	vacant	$758,000
Memphis, Tenn.	Dixie Homes	633	black	slum	$3,400,000
	Lauderdale Courts	449	white	slum	$3,128,000
Miami, Fla.	Liberty Square	243	black	vacant	$969,880
Milwaukee, Wisc.	Parklawn	518	white	vacant	$2,600,000
Minneapolis, Minn.	Sumner Field Homes	451	both	slum	$3,632,000
Montgomery, Ala.	Riverside Heights	100	white	vacant	$411,000
	Wm. Patterson Courts	156	black	slum	$506,000
Nashville, Tenn.	Cheatham Place	314	white	slum	$2,000,000
	Andrew Jackson Courts	398	black	slum	$1,890,000
New York, N.Y.	Williamsburg Houses	1,622	white	slum	$13,459,000
	Harlem River Houses	574	black	vacant	$4,219,000
Oklahoma City, Okla.	Will Rogers Courts	364	white	vacant	$2,000,000
Omaha, Neb.	Logan Fontenelle Homes	284	both	slum	$1,955,000
Philadelphia, Penn.	Hill Creek	258	white	vacant	$2,110,000
San Juan, P.R.	Caserio Mirapalmeras	131		vacant	$500,000
Schenectady, N.Y.	Schonowee Village	219	white	slum	$1,435,000
Stamford, Conn.	Fairfield Court	146	white	vacant	$884,000
Toledo, Ohio	Brand Whitlock Homes	264	black	slum	$2,000,000
Virgin Islands	Bassin Triangle	30		vacant	$220,027
	Marley Homes	38		vacant	(incl. in
	H. H. Berg Homes	58			slum above)*
Washington, D.C.	Langston Homes	274	black	vacant	$1,842,000
Wayne, Penn.	Highland Homes	50	black	slum	$344,000

Sources: Michael W. Straus and Talbott Wegg, *Housing Comes of Age* (New York: Oxford University Press, 1938), 225–29; Gail Radford, *Modern Housing for America* (Chicago: University of Chicago Press, 1996), 100–101; Jack Irby Hayes, *South Carolina and the New Deal* (Columbia: University of South Carolina Press, 2001), 73–74; John Stroman Lofton Jr., "An Economic and Social History of Columbia, S.C. during the New Deal" (Ph.D. diss., University of Texas, Austin, 1977), 136–39; C. W. Short and R. Stanley-Brown, *Public Buildings: A Survey of Architecture Constructed by Federal and Other Public Bodies between the Years 1933 and 1939 with the Assistance of the Public Works Administration* (Washington, D.C.: Government Printing Office, 1939), 666.

Everything that Harold Ickes and the PWA did was solidly constructed. The general philosophy was that it was "economical in the long run to build well." Architectural historian Richard Pommer concluded that the "early work of the PWA . . . remained for many decades the finest urban housing in America."[32] The judgment of Miles Colean, the Federal Housing Administration's research director, rendered in 1944, was that PWA housing was more expensive than it needed to be because of Ickes's "mania for durability."[33] That mania, however, produced structures that are, for the most part, still in use today almost three-quarters of a century later. Considering the fact that hard-pressed housing authorities have, during much of this time, provided only minimal maintenance, this survival is truly remarkable.

The housing was needed and welcomed in the communities where it was built. It delivered one of the benefits promised by the PWA Housing Division: high-quality shelter sensitive to the needs of its occupants. It failed to deliver another. Despite the sixty-year amortization, those with low incomes could not afford the rents. While this might have been obvious from the beginning, those involved probably held the hope that their careful planning and husbanding of resources would bring their products within reach of the poor. The hope also brought them needed political support. As Radford has noted, the question of how much housing should be subsidized is separate from who should build it.[34] One might also consider the continued hard use and survival of much of this construction. Had it been amortized at seventy-five years instead of sixty, the rents would have been still cheaper and would have reached still lower, perhaps even into the ranks of the very poor. Such an amortization would have been politically impossible in Ickes's time. He was pushing the current conventional wisdom to get sixty years. But the plain fact is that most of the buildings *have* lasted well over sixty years even without good maintenance, and some of them could survive to see their centennial. A study of Atlanta's Techwood Homes on its sixtieth anniversary concluded that it was good for another six decades. Carl Mackley Houses, after a recent rehabilitation, is still attracting tenants.[35] Building well *was* economical.

There were those who questioned the whole strategy of amortization or "self-liquidation." Social workers, based on their firsthand experience and on studies like the one conducted in 1934 by the Civil Works Administration, concluded that many people could not afford to pay any rent at all. The CWA survey found 60 percent of families had incomes of less than $750 a year. They were paying from 28 to 63 percent of their income for shelter, even though a Labor Department "Minimum Decency Budget" advised that the $750 was adequate only for food and clothing. As further evidence, the study noted that 50 percent of these families were in arrears with their rent. "The simple fact is," concluded Simon Brienes in *Social Work Today,* a radical journal, "that really low rents cannot be based on factors like construction costs and interest. No amount of actuarial juggling and

Fig. 8.1. PWA housing in Cedar Springs Place, Dallas, Texas, is still in use, as are most PWA projects. Harold Ickes's "mania for durability" was criticized at the time but has proven a good investment. Photograph by R. D. Leighninger

sleight-of-hand can guarantee a rental level within the reach of the majority of families of the U.S." Radical social workers were not the only ones to reach this conclusion. The Rev. Edward Moore, a member of the New York City Housing Authority, said the same thing in the *Saturday Evening Post. Fortune* agreed that "new housing cannot be created to rent at rates within reach of low-income classes except through heavy subsidy." However, it opposed the subsidy. Giving the poor new housing was just an "emotional" impulse. Housing reform should focus on making the oldest dwellings in use "decent."[36]

For those who *could* afford the rent—many of whom were what we call today "the working poor"—PWA housing was a godsend. It was clean, safe, solid, and in many cases had modern appliances that were the envy of many middle-class families. One group for whom this shelter was particularly welcome was African Americans. Housing opportunities even for the middle class were scarce and often miserable. Over a third of the PWA housing projects were built for African Americans. Twenty-one were for blacks only, and another six were integrated. In general the New Deal offered unprecedented opportunities to African Americans but rarely came close to meeting what was actually needed. Many schools and parks for African American communities were built by the WPA and PWA, but they were usually proposed later, were less expensive, and were the first to be cut if projects went over budget. The PWA Housing Division came much closer to being a genuine equal-opportunity program.[37]

Employment opportunities for African Americans were also better on PWA housing projects. Ickes, as secretary of the Interior, had integrated the public facilities of

Fig. 8.2. Logan Fontenelle Homes, a PWA housing project in Omaha, Nebraska. Ickes did not challenge segregation in the South, but a third of PWA housing was built for African Americans. Some projects, like this one, were integrated. Photograph by John Vachon, Farm Security Administration

the Interior Department and hired blacks in executive and professional positions as well as clerical ones. He also appointed Robert Weaver, who would later serve as secretary of Housing and Urban Development in the Johnson administration, as his advisor on Negro Affairs. Ickes and Weaver devised a policy requiring contractors to pay skilled black workers a proportion of the project payroll equal to at least half of their percentage in the local workforce.[38] Such a quota might be illegal today, but it was an oasis of fairness in an arid landscape of Jim Crow America.

The PWA Housing Division was not the only New Deal contribution to housing. The division was barely under way when another federal initiative emerged through Congress. The National Housing Act of 1934 created the Federal Housing Administration to insure mortgages on private, middle-income housing development. This made it far easier for private developers to collect capital and proceed with projects that would have been impossible under the RFC or PWA limited-dividend programs.[39] This brought the private sector back into large-scale housing construction and spurred the postwar housing boom. It was among the more important of New Deal achievements. However, it also paved the way for a two-tier approach to housing that would result in an almost immediate marginalization and impoverishment of the bottom tier.

Several bills aimed at making public housing a permanent government program were introduced into Congress in 1935. Senator Wagner proposed abolishing the PWA Housing Division and allocating eight hundred million dollars to local housing authorities. Pittsburgh congressman Henry Ellenbogen, who knew about public housing from his youth in Vienna, introduced another bill calling for a United States Housing Authority that would work with local authorities but would also offer grants and loans to cooperatives, building societies, and other nonprofit organizations like the labor union that built Carl Mackley Houses. It would be able to build on its own if no local sponsors were forthcoming. Neither bill made it out of committee, so Wagner and Ellenbogen joined forces in 1936 to try again. There was little support from Roosevelt.[40]

Labor unions were prominent advocates of public housing because, though their members were hardly the poorest segment of the population, they too felt unserved by the housing market. The chair of the American Federation of Labor's Housing Committee pointed out that even workers with better than average incomes could not achieve the "famous" American standard of living: a "modern kitchen and bathrooms, central heat, a sunny garden and a quiet neighborhood for the children to grow up in."[41]

Considerable debate ensued. Opponents of the 1936 bill included the U.S. Chamber of Commerce, the real-estate interests, banks, and the lumber industry. The last group was nervous, because they saw the federal building programs experimenting with new materials like concrete and steel to cut costs. Finally, the United State Housing Act, also known as the Wagner-Steagall Act, emerged in 1937. Housing reformers gave their support, because they thought it was better than nothing. Some regretted this later when they saw the results. All power to build was lodged with local housing authorities. There would be no further building initiated by the PWA or any federal body. The local nonprofits were also cut out. The bill required that any new building would have to be matched by an equal number of slum units destroyed. This restricted housing to slum clearance, as local business interests desired, and simultaneously ensured that the low-income housing stock could not increase, keeping rents high. Most important, the act capped the amount that could be spent per unit at a level that guaranteed that public housing would become only the last resort of the poor and no competition with the private market. Even its outward appearance would communicate that this was "poor people's housing." Some believe that this was not just an unavoidable consequence of low budgets but a deliberate stigmatization.[42]

The United States Housing Authority (USHA) was allocated eight hundred million dollars to create loans for low-cost housing. Local housing authorities had to put up 10 percent of the cost of a project; the rest would be covered by a low-interest, sixty-year loan. To keep rents down, the USHA would pay the difference between the rents charged, which were based on 20 percent of the tenant's income, and the cost of operating the project.[43]

The USHA was placed in the Interior Department under Ickes. But Ickes was unable to have his own choice to head the new agency confirmed. Instead, Roosevelt picked Nathan Straus, heir to the Macy fortune and sponsor of the Hillside Homes limited-dividend project built through the RFC. He was an ally of housing reformers like Catherine Bauer. Ickes gave in and had nothing further to do with the enterprise, which now reported directly to the president. This may have been as much prescience as pique.[44]

In order to gain political support, Straus made every effort not only to keep construction costs at the level imposed by the act but to go below it. In the USHA-funded complex built in Red Hook, New York, closets had no doors, kitchens became part of living rooms, partitions were thin, and elevators stopped on every other floor. The exterior was described as "Leningrad Formalism." Radford concludes that this "constrained approach to building under Straus's administration ultimately proved politically disastrous. Those who hated public housing remained hostile, while the minimal building produced by the USHA attracted no new allies and discouraged some of the old ones." The fact that Straus was arrogant, a poor administrator, and totally unable to deal with Congress did not help matters.[45]

Straus appointed some of the reformers to important positions in the USHA. They were able to mitigate some of the more harmful aspects of the bill in its implementation. Catherine Bauer was put in charge of managing slum demolitions and was able to increase the replacement ratio from one-to-one to something closer to three-to-one. There was, however, no mitigating the effects of cheap construction. The sequence of "continuous urban decay" was begun. In 1939 Congress refused to extend the public housing program and would put no more money into it for another decade. Straus resigned in 1942, vainly hoping that his departure would improve the agency's relations with Congress. The USHA continued but with a new focus on defense housing.[46]

Whatever its deficiencies as shelter and as architecture, much badly needed public housing was built by the USHA in this brief period. It was far better than living in the tenements or on the streets. Moreover, the sheer quantity of it must be confronted to put matters of quality in perspective. In 370 separate projects in 174 cities, the USHA put up housing for 120,000 families at the cost of $540 million. Wheeling, West Virginia, put up 302 units at a cost of over $1.2 million. Youngstown, Ohio, built 618 units for $3 million. San Antonio, in five projects, acquired 2,554 units for a bargain rate of $10 million. Memphis paid $9 million for its 1,878 units. Bridgeport, Connecticut, added 1,643 family units with $8.8 million. Louisville used $14 million for 2,669 units. Construction costs were higher in the East, as can be seen in Bridgeport's costs and the $16 million paid for 2,859 units in Philadelphia. Costs were similar in New Orleans, where $26.8 million bought 4,881 units—probably an indication of the rake-off facility of Huey Long's successor, Richard Leche.[47] Efficiency and accountability varied as well as quality. There was no Harold Ickes to ride herd on these efforts. Nonetheless, the USHA managed to shelter tens of thousands of people for half a century or longer.

Though they were not built with the same care as the PWA projects, most of these projects are still in service, and many people still want to live in them. The announcement that the Matthew Henson project in Phoenix would be replaced in October 2003 brought cries of protest from its residents.[48]

The Lanham Act of 1940 formally shifted the government's attention to defense housing. The Federal Works Agency, which had become the umbrella under which the PWA and WPA had operated since 1939, received $150 million from the Lanham Act to build housing in defense industry centers. Between 1940 and 1944, 650,000 units were built; however, most of them were temporary dormitories and trailers.[49]

In general, banking, real estate, and construction interests were never enthusiastic about the USHA. They were much better served by the FHA. Many middle-income home buyers were also well served. By guaranteeing mortgages, the FHA greatly reduced the risk of large-scale housing development. It also subsidized the modernization of the industry by providing research services to builders. The FHA told builders where the greatest demand was and helped them coordinate

Fig. 8.3. A. D. Price Court in Buffalo, New York, was built by the U.S. Housing Authority. Though constructed on a bare-bones budget, USHA housing was badly needed, and much of it is still in use. Photograph by Farm Security Administration, uncredited

their projects with school construction and the provision of utilities and transportation. Economies of scale brought costs down to the point where a new house in 1940 was selling for less than ones in the 1920s. With further federal subsidies in the form of road building, the postwar suburbs blossomed.[50]

The suburban tracts were wildly popular. Among their eager clients were returning veterans, who were aided in becoming homeowners by another important federal subsidy. The Veterans Administration joined the FHA in insuring mortgages. There was a certain monotony to this "crabgrass frontier" that was the product not only of the efficiency of prefabricated, mass-produced techniques used by developer William Levitt but also by the government's enforcement of aesthetic uniformity. It was feared that if houses deviated at all from the mainstream, nineteenth-century notion of a house, their resale value would be jeopardized. Modernist features like flat roofs were specifically ruled out. The layout of suburbs also prepared the way for later family problems: long commutes taking breadwinners out of the family, isolation of homemakers, separation of elders, reinforcement of gender stereotypes, traffic congestion, and increased dependence on automobiles to get to shopping, schools, and medical care.[51] Few noticed this at the time. The main goal was homeownership, and the federal programs and subsidies were making it possible.

The impact of FHA financing and planning was enormous. Its importance continues. Few people would identify it as a New Deal program. It has enabled millions of families who might not otherwise have been able to afford homeownership to achieve this central part of "the American dream." Its success, however, had a cost. By separating the interests of middle-income citizens from those with lower incomes and thus greatly narrowing the political support for the latter's interests, another New Deal policy initiative that began with the interests of all became a two-tiered policy that quickly abandoned the lower tier. The FHA's negative effect on the lower end of the housing market was not just passive. It practiced aggressive racial discrimination. Its manuals made clear that minority presences in neighborhoods were regarded as a danger to property values, and mortgages were unlikely to receive FHA approval if racial restrictions were not written into deeds. The result was that by the late 1950s less than 2 percent of housing built after the war with the help of FHA insurance was sold to minorities, and only 1 percent was built in minority subdivisions.[52]

The FHA also refused to insure mortgages in inner-city areas, a practice known as redlining. Thus families living in these areas, whatever their race or credit rating, could not buy homes with FHA-insured mortgages nor get loans to repair their homes, furthering the growth of slums and the abandonment of the inner cities. Decades later, redlining became illegal.[53]

Thus New Deal housing programs that initially envisioned a better quality shelter for all citizens came unstuck, dividing along racial and class lines. It was both a fabulous success and a dismal failure. Could it have been different? Might the Housing Division have found a way to continue building high-quality communities that appealed to a range of low- and middle-income tenants? Should it have tried to make the argument that adequate housing for the very poor could not be provided without subsidy? Could it have avoided the political vortex that sucked public housing into a downward spiral of cheap buildings looking disreputable and becoming even more so because they could not stand up to hard use and low maintenance?

Gail Radford faults Ickes for trying to keep the program too centralized, making every decision and signing every document, and paying too little attention to the local housing authorities the division had worked so hard to create. But she concludes that the division "was a small fragile operation trying to find ways to introduce new and threatening activities with few resources, little experience, widespread and powerful enemies, and no mobilized mass support."[54] The social housing tradition established in Western Europe was simply not comprehensible to American society at this time.

Chapter 9

RESETTLEMENT

Subsistence Homesteads Division, PWA, 1933–35
Division of Rural Rehabilitation and Stranded Populations, FERA, 1934–35
Resettlement Administration, 1935–37
Farm Security Administration, 1937–46

The Civilian Conservation Corps (CCC) was the New Deal's first response to the dual uprooting of people and topsoil. Young men who were bumming along the highways and rail lines were put to work reforesting the stripped hills and replanting the gullies and grasslands. But what of their parents and younger siblings who had also been uprooted? Families did not fit the CCC format. And those who were not on the road but still attached to their farms were only doing further damage to the depleted soil as they inched closer to starvation. Some people had to be persuaded to move while at the same time new places found for those already moving. Massive resettlement was a problem the nation had never faced before.

The late nineteenth and early twentieth centuries had seen a large population shift from the farms to the cities as industrialization promised new wealth to some and new jobs to many. Life in the new cities, however, was a mixed blessing. New residents faced bad housing and little basic physical infrastructure—clean water, sewers, paved roads. Industrial pollution threatened health and even clean laundry. Crowding intensified sickness and crime. Many felt homesick for life on the farm. Even those who had never lived in the country could imagine its sunshine and clean air. A back-to-the-land movement emerged, and many felt its seductive appeal, which was not only economic but also political and spiritual.

Many of the founding fathers had been farmers. Thomas Jefferson was particularly articulate about the virtues of agrarian society. Farming became fused with self-sufficiency and democracy as the underpinning of the new nation. Being able to grow one's own food, beholden to no one, gave one the feeling of political independence. This doctrine assumed mythic proportions and was still very strong in the 1930s.[1]

Even before the cities became problematic, rural living had acquired a gloss of spiritual improvement over the basics of reliable subsistence. Beginning in the 1830s pilgrims journeyed to the frontier to establish their own religious or philosophical utopias. Brook Farm, Sabbath Day Lake, Zoar, Oneida, New Harmony, and Amana were among many colonies founded as visionaries pursued the good life from New England, across the Midwest, and into the Great Plains. Most fell apart after their spiritual leaders died, but new ones were still springing up a hundred years later.[2]

Thus living close to the land had great spiritual as well as practical appeal. When depression hit industry, there were many individual and collective attempts by struggling city dwellers to go back to farming. However, they ran smack into the agricultural depression that had started a decade earlier. The country did not need any more farmers.[3]

In fact, many of the farmers still making a living on fertile land were themselves an endangered species. Few people realized this in the 1930s, and fewer talked about it. One who did was Milburn L. Wilson. A farm boy from Iowa who managed to get a degree in agriculture from Iowa State University, Wilson was eager to practice what he had learned. He turned down an offer to teach at the university. Instead, he became a tenant farmer in Nebraska. This was a classic way for a young man to get a start toward owning his own land. For many, however, particularly in the South, it was a one-way ticket to serfdom. Wilson avoided the pitfalls and moved on to homesteading in Montana. One of the first things he did there was buy a steam tractor, the biggest he could find. "I was rather aggressively machine-minded," he said.[4]

This appreciation for machinery was probably what gave Wilson insight into the future of American farming. He could see the transition under way from the family farm, which was primarily about feeding itself, to the commercial farm, which produced for the market and fed itself from the profits, to agribusiness, where feeding farm families was entirely incidental. To survive this transition, families would need more land, more efficient machinery to work it, and more capital to keep it all going. Families would become corporations, work for corporations, or cease being farmers.[5]

This realization may have made Wilson more intent on solving the resettlement problem, because he knew it had long-term as well as short-term ramifications. In any case the short-term problem was pressing enough. There were four groups that needed resettling. First, there were farmers already forced off their land by soil exhaustion, drought, and dust storms. They were the "Okies" of John Steinbeck's novel *The Grapes of Wrath*, whose faces would later be shown to the nation by photographers like Dorothea Lange and Arthur Rothstein. Next there were farmers on land that could no longer support them, still rooted but, like the land, drying up. They were written about by James Agee and photographed by Walker Evans in *Let Us Now Praise Famous Men.*[6] Then there were unemployed workers in the cities, some of whom had come from farms and knew farming and therefore might want to move back to a semi-agricultural life. Finally, there were workers in rural areas whose work—coal mining, for example—had disappeared, leaving no alternative employment. They were labeled "stranded workers."

It occurred to Wilson and others that there might be some kind of compromise between a life that was totally urban and one that was totally rural, a new hybrid. This might not only provide survival but also have advantages that such polarized existences did not. Again, Wilson's own experience pushed him to seek this compromise. He had grown up on a farm and had experienced all the advantages of the rural life. But he was not blind to its disadvantages. His mother had been a teacher, musician, and painter before committing herself totally to her husband's occupation: farming. When she was seventy, Wilson bought her an easel and some paints. He was delighted and a bit saddened by the joy that she got from this. "Between the time that she was twenty and the time that she was seventy, that side of her never really had a chance to live at all." Was the glorious independence of the life on an isolated farm worth such a price?[7]

Wilson had seen Mormon farming villages in Utah where the farmhouses were grouped together, not set apart on little islands surrounded by their own fields. This lessened the workload of the individual farms, because they could share some tasks or specialize in certain skills; it also allowed conveniences like running water and electricity and provided a community life. They had the fresh air and sunlight denied the city dwellers, but they also had some of the social and cultural amenities of the city that farmers rarely enjoyed.[8]

Wilson was not the only one looking for some alternative to farmer isolation on the American landscape. Visitors to Europe found the clustered settlement of rural hamlets appealing. Elwood Mead, a civil engineer and water policy expert who had worked in rural Australia, came home to plan model rural communities in California. He persuaded the state government to fund two of them. They attracted considerable attention but did not survive the early years of the Depression. Mead's ideas, however, would soon reappear.[9]

Was there also a compromise between aggravating the agricultural depression by sending people back to farming and allowing people to starve on unproductive land, in cities, or on the road looking for work? Could places be found where families could be kept nourished by growing most of their own food while deriving a small income from part-time, nonfarm work? If they had skills like woodworking or weaving, they could make things to sell. They might find part-time work in industries in nearby cities or ones that were setting up operations outside cities. Those who still had jobs had probably already suffered a cutback in hours. Those who had been picked up by the new work-relief agencies like the WPA were also working only part-time, because the programs wanted to spread the work as widely as possible.

The food they grew would not upset depressed agricultural markets, because they would still have to buy staples like flour and sugar. The things they would grow, fruits and vegetables, were not things they were now buying. It would not just keep them alive but improve the balance of their diets. And, with a little luck, it would not be their only form of sustenance.[10]

This would work best if the industrial jobs were not too far away. The idea that industries might not always remain in the cities was a new but plausible one. Some were already considering decentralization to cut the costs of transportation. Food processing and clothing manufacture could be done closer to raw materials. Taxes and rents would be lower in rural areas. Henry Ford had been broadcasting his plans for moving into the Tennessee Valley to take advantage of the new electricity and improved navigation, and the directors of the Tennessee Valley Authority were doing their best to encourage such relocation. The TVA-constructed town of Norris included in-home workshops and kitchen gardens to encourage this hybrid opportunity. Though Ford was denied the leadership role in Tennessee, he pursued his own decentralization program in Michigan, setting up satellite factories for the manufacture of automobile parts and providing homes with gardens for his workers. In fact gardening was compulsory. Ford was convinced that "the man too lazy to work in a garden in his leisure time does not deserve a job."[11]

These urban/rural hybrids became known as "subsistence homesteads." Their first legislative embodiment was in section 208 of Title 2 of the National Industrial Recovery Act. Since Title 2 was the origin of the Public Works Administration,[12] PWA soon had a Subsistence Homesteads Division, with M. L. Wilson at its head. Wilson had gone from homesteading to teaching agriculture at the University of Montana, directing a Rockefeller-funded experiment in farm ownership for tenant farmers and studying economics with John R. Commons at the University of Wisconsin. By the time of the New Deal, he was a widely respected agronomist and had been appointed head of wheat programs for the Agricultural Adjustment Administration.

Subsistence homesteads would help to re-anchor the floating population of displaced farmers and factory workers. They would allow submarginal land—farms on exhausted soil or soil that should never have been planted in the first place—to be returned to forest or grass. They would also offer a chance of ownership to those who had lost their homes or tenant farmers who had never owned one. Like many New Deal programs, it was a multipronged attack on variety of problems. And like most New Deal programs, it was a godsend to some and anathema to others. In retrospect it has been written off as a silly idea. Sidney Baldwin, the principal historian of the Farm Security Administration, called it "little more than an esoteric experiment."[13] In its historical and economic context, however, it made sense to a lot of thoughtful people.

It did, however, depend on the assumption that the relocating industries would not take unfair advantage of their part-time workers. A few critics at the time, including Rexford G. Tugwell, who as head of the Resettlement Administration would reluctantly inherit the program two years later, were skeptical. There were already places in the South where part-time factory work was combined with part-time farming. The wages there were the lowest in the country. Russell Lord, an Agriculture Department employee, attended an early meeting to discuss subsistence homesteads. He sensed that the industrialists present thought they would be able to pay the semirural workers "not so much in money as in sunlight and fresh air."[14]

The word "subsistence" was probably used to make clear that the homesteaders' output was for their own use and would not compete with established farmers. It had an air of grim survival to it, however. Lord noted that it "did not march along with the pipes and trumpets of . . . New Deal optimism. It sounded rather like the muffled drums of an enforced retreat."[15]

The Subsistence Homesteads Division was endowed with twenty-five million dollars and empowered to offer loans for homestead purchases. Otherwise, like other early New Deal legislation, little was specified and much was left to the president. This gave the new agency considerable elbow room, which it took, thus laying the groundwork for congressional resentment that was to simmer for several years. Later resettlement programs were quite different from subsistence homesteads in important ways, but they all had a few features in common: "a preference for self-help approaches to relief, an effort to reconstitute basic economic relations, a touch of agrarian romanticism, and a strong emphasis on collective, or community, values."[16]

Like PWA's nonfederal projects, initiative for a subsistence homestead loan had to come from a sponsoring community. Like its parent organization, the Subsistence Homestead Division received its share of bizarre proposals. One applicant wanted to perform eugenics experiments. Another sent blueprints for dairy barns housing two thousand cows apiece, equipped with electric milkers, manure buckets, and fly zappers. The electricity would be generated by twenty-four bulls on treadmills. Still another suggested that farmers wear Greek robes.[17]

The division soon had $4.5 billion worth of requests for loans. About four hundred proposals looked promising and were sorted into three groups. First were the archetypal subsistence homestead colonies for part-time farmers located on the periphery of industrial centers. Then there would be rural colonies for those being resettled from submarginal land. Finally, there were villages for the stranded workers. These were the ones that would be particularly dependent on the attraction of decentralizing industries. Thirty-four communities were planned; twenty-seven were hybrid colonies for the industrial periphery, three were for resettled farmers in rural areas, and four for stranded workers (table 9.1).[18]

Table 9.1 Subsistence homesteads

State	Name	Location	Type	Units	Cost
Ala.	Bankhead Farms	Jasper	hybrid	100	$1,046,421
Ala.	Cahaba Homesteads	Birmingham	hybrid	287	$2,760,610
Ala.	Greenwood Homesteads	Birmingham	hybrid	83	$827,835
Ala.	Mount Olive Homesteads	Birmingham	hybrid	75	$618,162
Ala.	Palmerdale Homesteads	Birmingham	hybrid	102	$938,865
Ariz.	Phoenix Homesteads	Phoenix	hybrid	25	$104,859
Calif.	El Monte Homesteads	El Monte	hybrid	100	$292,477
Calif.	San Fernando Homesteads	Reseda	hybrid	40	$102,065
Ga.	Piedmont Homesteads	Jasper Co.	farm	50	$649,651
Iowa	Granger Homesteads	Granger	hybrid	50	$216,190
Ill.	Lake County Homesteads	Chicago	hybrid	53	$554,746
Ind.	Decatur Homesteads	Decatur	hybrid	48	$157,280
Minn.	Austin Homesteads	Austin	hybrid	44	$213,228
Minn.	Duluth Homesteads	Duluth	hybrid	84	$983,984
Miss.	Hattiesburg Homesteads	Hattiesburg	hybrid	24	$75,649
Miss.	Magnolia Homesteads	Meridian	hybrid	25	$73,556
Miss.	McComb Homesteads	McComb	hybrid	20	$91,453
Miss.	Richton Homesteads	Richton	farm	26	$216,469
Miss.	Tupelo Homesteads	Tupelo	hybrid	35	$139,247
N.J.	Jersey Homesteads	Hightstown*	hybrid	200	$3,402,382
N.C.	Penderlea Homesteads	Pender Co.	farm	195	$2,277,286
Ohio	Dayton Homesteads	Dayton	hybrid	35	$50,000**
Pa.	Westmoreland Homesteads	Greensburg	stranded	255	$2,516,470
Tenn.	Cumberland Homesteads	Crossland	stranded	251	$3,267,345
Tex.	Beauxart Gardens	Beaumont	hybrid	50	$143,028
Tex.	Dalworthington Gardens	Arlington	hybrid	79	$325,712
Tex.	Houston Gardens	Houston	hybrid	100	$283,568
Tex.	Three Rivers Gardens	Three Rivers	hybrid	50	$162,943
Tex.	Wichita Gardens	Wichita Falls	hybrid	62	$178,528
Va.	Aberdeen Gardens	Newport News	hybrid	159	$1,353,896
Va.	Shenandoah Homesteads (7)	five counties	farm	160	$1,060,125
Wash.	Longview Homesteads	Longview	hybrid	60	$194,098
W.Va.	Arthurdale	Reedsville	stranded	165	$2,744,724
W.Va.	Tygart Valley Homesteads	Elkins	stranded	195	$2,080,214

*Renamed Roosevelt
**Loan

Sources: Paul K. Conkin, *Tomorrow a New World: The New Deal Community Program* (Ithaca, N.Y.: Cornell University Press, 1959), 332–34; Russell Lord and Paul H. Johnstone, eds., *A Place on Earth: A Critical Appraisal of Subsistence Homesteads* (Washington, D.C.: Bureau of Agricultural Economics, USDA, 1942).

Wilson was a believer in grassroots democracy. His idea was that the home-steads should be turned over to local corporations. He delegated much of the responsibility for the planning and implementation to regional and local offices and encouraged them to work with local people, particularly the land-grant universities. His hopes for a decentralized program were dashed on two large rocks. The first was Comptroller General John McCarl, a consistent nemesis of New Deal experiments, who stripped the local corporations of any financial authority and tied them up in complicated accounting procedures.[19] The second was Harold Ickes, who held the PWA reins tightly. However, it was not only management philosophy that made Wilson's independence a problem. Ickes also had a public relations fiasco to deal with.

One of the first projects, a community for stranded West Virginia coal miners, had attracted the patronage of the president's wife and his chief aide, Louis Howe. It was named Arthurdale, and it soon attracted a lot of publicity, all of it bad. Mrs. Roosevelt and Howe made frequent visits to the site and began to make decisions about it without bothering to involve Wilson or Ickes. Howe impulsively ordered fifty prefabricated houses from a company in Boston. Upon delivery, it was discovered that they did not fit the foundations already poured. They had been designed as Cape Cod summer houses and were too small for a normal family. Worse, their walls were too thin to withstand the cold mountain winters.[20]

This was only the beginning. Because of the thin walls, the houses required oversized furnaces. Each house had its own septic tank with a special grease trap to guard against bacterial infection. It was soon revealed that the traps cost $37.50 each. This was symbolic of several problems. First, Mrs. Roosevelt was convinced that the Arthurdale colonists deserved high-quality accommodations. She had chosen the handcrafted furniture for the homes and had put some of her own money into the enterprise. Wilson was also supportive of good-quality building, because he saw subsistence homesteads not as a Depression stopgap but as a new way of life. Ickes, to the contrary, favored simple shelter; the colonists could add their own plumbing later.[21]

Second, Howe was moving too fast to get this high-quality design. Third, the cost overruns that resulted were making the project and the whole program a national joke. An article in the *Saturday Evening Post* was particularly damaging. The *Washington Post* published a feature soon after headlined "Blunders at Arthurdale." Ickes said in disgust: "We have been spending money down there like drunken sailors."[22]

Congress was creating even greater problems. To replace work in the coal mines, Arthurdale was to have a factory manufacturing furniture for the post office. Politicians with furniture factories in their districts objected to competition from the federal government. To some, it was not just the competition they feared; it was the possibility of "the absolute subversion of free government" that was sure to

Fig. 9.1. The PWA's subsistence homestead community of Reedsville, also known as Arthurdale. The enthusiastic involvement of Louis Howe and Eleanor Roosevelt led to bad decisions and even worse publicity. Photograph by Elmer Johnson, Farm Security Administration

follow. This kind of overheated rhetoric was to haunt the program throughout its existence and complicate the lives of all the agencies of which it was a part.[23]

After the extinction of the postal furniture factory, efforts were made to attract other industries. Some came, but none survived. The stranded workers remained economically stranded. They were, however, well housed. They had a good school, recreational facilities, and lots of visitors from the outside world. "Got so a man couldn't set down to his sow belly and turnip greens without some stranger peeking in at his window or walking in to ask fool questions," said one resident.[24]

While reporters and congressmen focused on Arthurdale, other projects were getting started and running smoothly. Phoenix Homesteads purchased several tracts of good land, hired a respected local architect to design adobe houses, interviewed and selected homesteaders, and began a cooperative dairy and poultry farm. Soon a paved road connected them to a district school and jobs in the city. In a far different climate, Duluth Homesteads also functioned according to plan. Tenants grew food for the table and found nonfarm work elsewhere. Some grew enough to sell in town. There was no reported complaint from established farmers. A cooperative spirit developed that included a community fund to pay the

Fig. 9.2. Phoenix Homesteads, another PWA community, proceeded smoothly and got no publicity. Pictured here is its second phase, designed by Vernon DeMars for the Resettlement Administration. Photograph by Russell Lee, Farm Security Administration

Fig. 9.3. El Monte Homesteads, a subsistence community near Los Angeles, remained popular with its residents even after defense industry jobs became available elsewhere. Photograph by Dorothea Lang, Farm Security Administration

mortgages of those who were sick and could not work. Tenants stayed long enough to own their homesteads and were satisfied enough with the arrangements that they tried to obtain additional homesteads for their community in 1948. The Wagner-Ellender-Taft bill that would have allowed this was passed in 1949 but cut the following year by Republican-led opposition to public housing.[25]

Outside of Los Angeles, El Monte Homesteads, consisting of predominately white-collar families, got off to a good start. The small, six-tenths- to nine-tenths-acre tracts of fertile soil proved quite adequate to produce fruits and vegetables enough to share with friends and relatives as well as keep the family larder full. Community spirit was high enough to resist a heavy-handed manager. Though there was no interest in a consumers' cooperative, homesteaders readily cooperated in buying and sharing tractors. As the Los Angeles sprawl moved out to surround them, their homes became models copied by private developers. Some residents were happy enough with their homesteads that they turned down good jobs in the new defense industries in order to stay.[26]

In Granger, Iowa, a parish priest organized a community of subsistence homesteads for a group of central and southern European coal miners' families living in crowded shacks in mining camps. Their children had no recreation except the pool hall. Two or three of them drowned each summer swimming in the Des Moines River. The Granger elders believed the miners could not possibly appreciate decent housing; they would use bathtubs for coal storage. However, the city government supported the proposal, and the new houses became showplaces with flowers, shrubs, and well-tended yards. The mines remained open, providing at least occasional work, and the homesteads functioned as planned, cushioning the ups and downs of the economy. As in Duluth, the tenants became homeowners in due time. In the entire history of the project there were no defaults on loans.[27]

Despite the fact that African Americans were among the worst hit by the Depression, only one resettlement project was planned for them. Ickes might have wished otherwise. He demonstrated his concern in his housing program, but the homestead projects were not initiated by PWA; they depended on local proposals. So the division became part of the New Deal's neglect of sharecroppers in general and black sharecroppers in particular. The exception was Aberdeen Gardens near Hampton, Virginia. It was sponsored by Hampton Institute and was designed for unemployed shipyard workers living in the slums of Newport News. The homes were planned by a senior architect in the division, Hilyard R. Robinson, who was also African American. He designed brick, colonial revival, two-story houses, most accompanied by chicken coops. Former secretary of energy Hazel Reid O'Leary grew up in one of them. A cohesive community developed in Aberdeen, extending through three generations. In 1994 children of the original tenants organized its placement on the National Register of Historic Places.[28]

Fig. 9.4. A young couple moving into Aberdeen Gardens near Newport News, Virginia. It was the only PWA subsistence homestead built for African Americans. Original residents and their descendants had it placed on the National Register of Historic Places in 1994. Photograph by John Vachon, Farm Security Administration

In 1934 the positive impacts of these and other projects were still in the future, and the projects running without mishap were getting no publicity. Ickes was concerned that the political consequences of public embarrassment caused by Arthurdale would sink the program and damage the whole PWA, which he had worked so hard to keep free of scandal. He wanted to get full control and knew that Wilson would not do it himself. On May 12, 1934, he centralized the program. This did not improve operations greatly. In some places, like Phoenix Homesteads, it caused snags, delays, and mistakes, because regional officials did not understand local conditions. Landscaping was proposed for Phoenix consisting of plants entirely unsuited to arid conditions. One shrub selected was actually illegal in Arizona because of its tendency to harbor a virus hostile to citrus trees. For Ickes these were minor risks compared to the circus at Arthurdale. He hope the program was now locked down until he could unload it.[29]

As the Subsistence Homesteads program was proceeding, a similar effort was under way in the Federal Emergency Relief Administration (FERA). It was called the Division of Rural Rehabilitation and Stranded Populations and had come about because Harry Hopkins had concluded that farmers on relief could be supported less expensively if they could be kept farming. He bundled the rural projects of the Civil Works Administration and the direct relief going to rural areas into an effort that combined loans for purchasing livestock, equipment, or better

Fig. 9.5. Austin Homesteads, near Austin, Minnesota, housed workers from the Hormel meatpacking plant. Photograph by John Carter, Farm Security Administration

Fig. 9.6. Austin Homesteads today. Photography by R. D. Leighninger

land together with something like a subsistence homesteads program. The FERA established twenty-eight communities (table 9.2). They differed somewhat from the PWA's subsistence homesteads in that they were more often rural and based in cooperative farms. Their businesses and industries were usually home-grown rather than dependent on industrial decentralization. All participants were relief clients and usually constructed their own homes and community buildings. The communities had very little economic success, because farming was more central to their survival and the farms were usually too small for efficient operation.[30]

In early 1935, the new work relief program was being planned. In the general confusion, other reorganizations became possible. One of them was the creation of the Resettlement Administration (RA). It would relieve Ickes of the Subsistence Homesteads Division, which he welcomed. The new agency would pick up the FERA's Rural Rehabilitation and Stranded Populations program as well. It would also address the plight of the migrant Okies. Underneath it all would be the effort to plan the use of agricultural land more rationally.[31]

Twenty-five of the FERA communities and all thirty-four of the PWA subsistence homesteads became part of the new agency. It was kept separate from both the Departments of Interior and Agriculture, because neither was fully committed to resettlement and both were wary of the political trouble that such activity

Fig. 9.7. Bosque Farms, a FERA community south of Albuquerque. Photograph by Arthur Rothstein, Farm Security Administration

Table 9.2 Federal Emergency Relief Administration communities

State	Name	Location	Type	Units	Cost
Ala.	Skyline Farms	Jackson Co.	farm	181	$1,230,333
Ariz.	Phoenix Part-Time Farms	Phoenix	hybrid	91	$564,013
Ark.	Dyess Colony	Mississippi Co.	farm	275	$2,306,250*
Ark.	St. Francis River Farms	Poinsett Co.	farm	86	$546,767
Ark.	Chicot Farms	Chicot and Drew Cos.	farm	85	$587,339
Fla.	Cherry Lake Farms	Madison	hybrid	132	$1,913,811*
Ga.	Pine Mountain Valley	Harris Co.	hybrid	205	$2,207,572*
Ga.	Irwinville	Irwin Co.	farm	105	$899,815
Ga.	Wolf Creek	Grady Co.	farm	24	$233,251
Minn.	Albert Lea Homesteads	Albert Lea	hybrid	14	$38,161
Neb.	Fairbury Farmsteads	Jefferson Co.	farm	11	$67,896
Neb.	Fall City Farmsteads	Richardson Co.	farm	10	$102,755
Neb.	Grand Island Farmsteads	Hall Co.	farm	10	$68,127
Neb.	Kearny Homesteads	Buffalo Co.	farm	10	$98,239
Neb.	Loup City Farmsteads	Sherman Co.	farm	11	$101,282
Neb.	Scottsbluff	Scotts Bluff Co.	farm	23	$321,520
Neb.	South Sioux City Farmsteads	Dakota Co.	farm	22	$115,396
Neb.	Two Rivers Farmsteads	Douglas and Saunders Cos.	farm	40	$547,746
N.Mex.	Bosque Farms	Valencia Co.	farm	42	$677,725
N.C.	Roanoke Farms	Halifax Co.	farm	294	$2,191,568
N.C.	Scuppernong Farms	Tyrell and Washington Cos.	farm	127	$779,327
N.Dak.	Burlington House	Burlington	stranded	35	$213,172
S.C.	Ashwood Plantation	Lee Co.	farm	161	$1,874,269
S.Dak.	Sioux Falls Farms	Minnehaha Co.	farm	14	$218,661
Tex.	Ropesville Farms	Hockley Co.	farm	76	$667,489
Tex.	Woodlake Community	Wood Co.	farm	101	$648,256
Tex.	Wichita Valley Farms	Wichita Co.	farm	91	$931,087
W.Va.	Red House	Red House	stranded	150	$1,506,398

*Original FERA investment, not total.

Source: Paul K. Conkin, *Tomorrow a New World: The New Deal Community Program* (Ithaca, N.Y.: Cornell University Press, 1959), 334–35.

Fig. 9.8. Bosque Farms today, with a home restored by its current owners, Joan and Joe Arvizu. Photograph by Joan Arvizu

was heading into. The one person who was fully committed and who was willing to play with political dynamite was Rexford G. Tugwell. He had a vision of what a rational land policy ought to be and of the proper social organization that should carry it out. The Resettlement Administration would be the laboratory for testing his ideas.

Tugwell was a well-published agricultural economist at Columbia University who had been part of the president's Brains Trust prior to his nomination. He had come after the election to work in the Department of Agriculture. He was a little older than the "eager-faced, immature technicians and academicians with lean bodies and no bellies, running around hatless, acting rather breathlessly mysterious and important, calling each other and the President by their first names, and more often than not, reaching his ear more readily than any of the old political hacks" who were flocking to Washington.[32] But he shared their zeal for change. He had rejected the classical economists' faith in the market. He observed the increasing centralization of industries and shared Thorsten Veblen's admiration for industrial engineers who planned efficiently and Veblen's disdain for businessmen who, in their self-interest and greed, tended to gum things up. He thought that governments could learn from industry to achieve national goals through central planning. Tugwell was also angered by the injustices experienced by poor tenant farmers and sharecroppers, which the New Deal's Agricultural Adjustment Administration was only exacerbating. Therefore he was more interested in the retirement of submarginal land and other aspects of land reform than he was in subsistence homesteads. However, taking on "everybody else's headaches," including Arthurdale, was a price he was willing to pay.[33]

A tenant farmer works land owned by someone else and either pays the owner rent in cash or as a share of what he harvests. He uses his own equipment and animals and provides for his own subsistence. A sharecropper, however, has nothing other than what the landowner provides. If the proceeds from the harvest do not cover what the owner has furnished, he is in debt for that amount. He is also dependent on the owner for a fair accounting. Under favorable circumstances—consistently good yields—a tenant farmer can come out ahead and save enough to buy land. In the South in the 1920s, this hardly ever happened. Both tenants and croppers were permanent serfs. It was "the economy of the Middle Ages without the cathedrals."[34]

The Agricultural Adjustment Act had provided aid to landowners and intended that this also help to sustain the owner's tenants.[35] Traditionally, tenants and sharecroppers were "economic shock-absorbers for landowners and planters." As the century advanced, they became increasingly important to American agriculture. In 1910, 37 percent of farmers were working for someone else; in 1930 it was 45 percent. In Mississippi it was 70 percent. When the severe shock of the Great Depression hit, the tenant farmers and sharecroppers were the ones who absorbed it. Landowners were paid for crop reduction and simply evicted sharecroppers from the land to be left fallow. They also used the federal payments to buy farm machinery, further decreasing the need for tenants. Between 1930 and 1940, the number of tractors in Louisiana doubled. In 1933 a million farm families were on relief; by 1935 they had grown to 2.5 million. "The AAA's reduction of cotton acreage," writes William Leuchtenberg, "drove the tenant and the cropper from the land, and landlords, with the connivance of local AAA committees which they dominated, cheated tenants of their fair share of benefits."[36]

The landowner's view of the system was a bit different, of course. Edward O'Neal, head of the American Farm Bureau Federation, the voice of the larger commercial farmers, painted it this way: "When you talk to one of these niggers, you say, 'Robert are you happy out here?' 'Why, Mr. Ed, this is your land, your home. I don't pay you any rent for the house. I've got plenty of water, plenty of wood, a nice garden, some pigs, a couple of Jersey cows. I got a nice little pasture. When I make something, you get it, and when I don't make anything, you don't get anything. It's heaven here.'"[37]

In February 1935, there was a rebellion within the AAA in the form of an attempt to provide legal protection for tenants. The rebels were promptly fired. The purge made clear to Tugwell that he would have to pursue land reform outside the Agriculture department.[38]

As head of the Resettlement Administration, Tugwell waded into the troubled waters with vigor. The RA's staff went from twelve in May 1935 to over sixteen thousand in December. It had plenty to do: loans and grants to farmers and farm cooperatives, the retirement of exhausted land and resettlement of those on it, the care of migrant workers, and the community programs it had inherited from PWA and FERA. It also began its own program of community building (table 9.3), described as "trying to put houses and land and people together in such a way that the props under our economic and social structure will be permanently strengthened." One journalist said the RA's job was "to rearrange the earth and the people thereof and devote surplus time and money, if any, to the rehabilitation of the Solar System."[39]

There was already a surplus of farmers; with the planned retirement of submarginal land, there would be more. Sending them into urban slums with no jobs was not a cheerful prospect. Tugwell did not regard the subsistence homestead idea as a viable solution either, though the RA would continue to support it. He preferred the FERA farm communities. He soon launched another thirty-four of his own. In these he followed closely the model developed by Elwood Mead. He

Table 9.3 Resettlement Administration communities

State	Name	Location	Type	Units	Cost
Ala.	Gee's Bend Farms	Wilcox Co.	farm	100	$418,505
Ala.	Prairie Farms	Macon Co.	farm	34	$201,684
Ariz.	Casa Grande Valley Farms	Pinal Co.	co-op	60	$817,548
Ark.	Lake Dick	Jefferson and Arkansas Cos.	co-op	97	$663,851
Ark.	Biscoe Farms	Prairie Co.	farm	77	$373,224
Ark.	Clover Bend Farms	Lawrence Co.	farm	91	$483,535
Ark.	Desha Farms	Desha and Drew Cos.	farm	88	$511,873
Ark.	Lakeview Farms	Phillips and Lee Cos.	farm	141	$899,652
Ark.	Lenoke Farms	Lenoke Co.	farm	57	$254,485
Ark.	Plum Bayou	Jefferson Co.	farm	200	$1,634,922
Ark.	Townes Farms	Crittenden Co.	farm	37	$163,734
Ark.	Trumann Farms	Poinsett Co.	farm	57	$278,937
Fla.	Escambia Farms	Okaloosa Co.	farm	81	$585,819
Ga.	Flint River Farms	Macon Co.	farm	146	$727,611
Ky.	Sublimity Farms	Laurel Co.	forest	66	$419,825
Ky.	Christian-Trigg Farms	Christian Co.	farm	106	$971,425
La.	Transylvania Farms	E. Carroll Par.	farm	163	$847,640
La.	Terrebonne Plantation	Terrebonne Par.	co-op	73	$514,504
La.	Mounds Farms	Madison and E. Carroll Pars.	farm	149	$803,616
Md.	Greenbelt	Washington D.C.	garden city	885	$13,701,817

hoped they could be developed into cooperative farms that would prove to be a more rational, humane alternative to the cutthroat competition of the market.[40]

Sensitive to congressional passion for the fee-simple tradition of land owner-ship, the RA planned only one community, Casa Grande Farms in Pinal County, Arizona, as a true cooperative where land was held in common by the homestead-ers. On the others, the land would be sold to the occupants after a five-year trial lease. This would allow the farmers time to adjust to their new circumstances and learn new and more efficient ways of farming under the tutelage of an RA farm manager. They would have new or rehabilitated homes and outbuildings. They would be eligible for loans to buy livestock and equipment. The land would be chosen carefully, its productivity and market potential assessed by experts. Each family would have a home and farm budget drawn up under the supervision of the farm manager. They would also, it was hoped, learn to cooperate in the pro-duction and marketing of their harvests.

Thus Tugwell hoped to bring to the rural landscape a new fruitfulness and har-mony through careful planning and wise administration. His vision did not stop

Table 9.3 continued

State	Name	Location	Type	Units	Cost
N.C.	Pembroke Farms	Robeson Co.	farm	75	$613,268
Mont.	Kinsey Flats	Custer Co.	farm	80	$874,741
Mich.	Ironwood Homesteads	Ironwood	hybrid	132	$1,373,138
Mich.	Saginaw Valley Farms	Saginaw Co.	farm	33	$365,958
Miss.	Hinds Farms	Hinds Co.	farm	81	$294,485
Miss.	Milestone Farms	Holmes Co.	farm	110	$744,721
Miss.	Lucedale Farms	George and Green Cos.	farm	93	$449,946
Mo.	La Forge Farms	New Madrid Co.	farm	101	$769,535
Mo.	Osage Farms	Pettis Co.	farm	86	$967,056
Ohio	Greenhills	Cincinnati	garden city	676	$11,860,628
S.C.	Orangeburg Farms	Orangeburg and Calhoun Cos.	farm	80	$535,519
S.C.	Tiverton Farms	Sumpter Co	farm	29	$117,988
Tex.	McLennan Farms	McLennan Co.	farm	20	$244,050
Tex.	Sabine Farms	Harrison Co.	farm	80	$436,674
Tex.	Sam Houston Farms	Harris Co.	farm	86	$607,778
Wis.	Drummond Project	Bayfield Co.	forest	32	$246,377
Wis.	Greendale	Milwaukee	garden city	572	$10,638,466

Source: Paul K. Conkin, *Tomorrow a New World: The New Deal Community Program* (Ithaca, N.Y.: Cornell University Press, 1959), 311, 314, 315, 336–37.

there. He might not be prepared to rehabilitate the solar system, but he was willing to replan cities. They, too, would have to change to reabsorb the wandering, jobless exiles from both farm and city in a more humane environment. His inspiration was the garden city movement, which had originated in England and found enthusiastic supporters in the United States. It provided a model of a carefully planned, large-scale integration of housing, commerce, and industry in a nature-preserving, aesthetically pleasing package. The result would be three satellite communities known as greenbelt cities.[41]

Both rural and suburban resettlement efforts were wracked with problems. Most of the grief in the greenbelt program emanated from Congress. In the case of the farm communities, the problems were often of the RA's own making. Despite the large and multifaceted organization that the master planner put together, the execution of these rural experiments did not go according to plan. A thorough survey of land parcels to be acquired could not be done quickly, so RA administrators depended on local planning boards, which were subject to local politics, for advice. The land they got was sometimes a real challenge to make productive. The RA consistently underestimated the amount of land that would be necessary to make the farms profitable. The cost of preparing and irrigating the land was also underestimated. They overestimated the amount of livestock, furnishings, and equipment the farmers would be bringing with them; thus many families had to borrow more than was anticipated to get started, incurring worrisome debt. The RA farm managers were often both messianic and condescending. The communities that Tugwell hoped would be models of a more rational use of land and human resources were born of miscalculation and lived their lives under considerable stress.[42]

One of Tugwell's greatest hopes was that the farming communities would be showcases for producer, consumer, and service cooperatives. Farming cooperatives were not unknown in American agriculture. Many were organized in the early part of the century following successful European models that the Americans saw as practical, not political. They had attracted the attention of Theodore Roosevelt, who established a U.S. Country Life Commission in 1909 to promote a sense of community among the isolated and individualistic farmers and reorganize agriculture along cooperative lines. Marketing cooperatives were most successful and flourished in the 1920s but soon became centrally controlled, big-business enterprises beyond the control of individual farmers.[43]

Tugwell had a Cooperative Unit within his Economic Development Section to nurture co-ops. Many were established, but "an alarmingly large number failed because of poor management, resentment of government control, lack of understanding of the co-operative idea, non-businesslike practices, factionalism in the associations, and outside competition or opposition."[44] This seems true of the larger purchasing and marketing co-ops. Overall, however, their record was "no

Fig. 9.9. Greenbelt, Maryland, one of the greenbelt cities. The school/community building is center left, the swimming pool above it, and the business/shopping complex is in the center. Photograph by Farm Security Administration, uncredited

Fig. 9.10. Underpass allowing residents to get from housing to shopping without crossing the street. Photograph by Marion Post Walcott, Farm Security Administration

worse than the prevalence of failure and bankruptcy among private manufacturing enterprises." The smaller co-ops, where farmers teamed up to share breeding stock or machinery, were quite successful. By 1942 only 16 percent of 25,543 cooperative groups had failed and 63 percent of the loans were repaid.[45]

Medical cooperatives, where community members paid an annual fee to support a local clinic, were also quite successful. By 1942 the countywide plans were providing affordable health care to over six hundred thousand people in forty-three states. Physicians and medical societies gave full cooperation initially. This changed in the 1940s as the fear of "socialized medicine" increased. Thus these premature health maintenance organizations were soon forced out of existence.[46]

Unfortunately, failures of the cooperative spirit got more attention than successes. Stories of feuds and schisms within communities were widely reported and even repeated by later evaluations sponsored by the Farm Security Administration, the RA's successor. The consensus formed that most of the failure resided in the individuals. Those resettled from submarginal lands, the FSA concluded, were irreparably scarred by their failure and may not have been the brightest of farmers to begin with. They were greatly disappointed when their high expectations for a better life (which the RA bore some responsibility for inflating) were not realized, and they wanted someone to blame. They were rigidly independent, even "mule-headed," and resisted authority and new ideas. More recent historians, including Conkin, Baldwin, and Arthur Schlesinger Jr., have echoed the complaints.[47]

One historian, however, has challenged this conclusion. Using interviews, diaries, and community records of ten western RA projects, Brian Q. Cannon found considerable neighborliness and community spirit, even in Casa Grande, which had been characterized as split by bitter rivalries. He found an array of clubs, organizations, and community events sufficient to make up "a richly textured community life that coalesced despite the hardships faced by the relocatees." More evidence for community stability is found in the fact that the annual turnover was 5 to 10 percent. Compared with an image of traditional farm communities where people stay in one place for generations, this may seem high. Compared with any other living arrangement, particularly an experimental one, it is impressively low. By 1942 there had been a total turnover of only 18 percent, much of which can be attributed to new employment opportunities.[48]

A good deal of the conflict and some of the suppression of community life originated not with the ornery farmers but with the RA managers. In Casa Grande, the manager decided that community softball games were disrupting work schedules, so he dug up the ball field. At Bosque Farms the manager wanted to ban dances on the theory that they would lead to drinking and violence. To gain support, he invited the RA state director to visit on the morning after a Presidents' Day ball, then dumped empty liquor bottles and let loose a pack of dogs in the community building prior to the inspection. This ought to have provoked outright rebellion, but Cannon concluded that challenges by the settlers to such managerial policies were usually rational and well organized.[49]

The Suburban Resettlement Division originally envisioned twenty-five greenbelt towns. These were the RA's and, next to the TVA, perhaps the whole New Deal's most ambitious undertakings. According to Conkin, they were also "closest to Tugwell's heart" and his "grandest monument." In Tugwell's vision, the greenbelt cities would welcome families with low incomes. These hopes were compromised almost immediately. The Suburban Resettlement Division was in a budget squeeze from its inception. It was born in the midst of the development of the 1935 works program and had to share resources with the established PWA and the emergent WPA. The towns had to be built entirely with relief labor. The whole program had to be completed by June 30, 1936. The tight schedule was due partly to the desire to get people to work as quickly as possible but probably also to Roosevelt's perception of a small window of opportunity. He did not plan to go back to Congress for further appropriations.[50]

The greenbelt program, conceived in the shadow of the 1935 works bill, also paid homage to self-liquidation and included disavowals of competition with the private sector, a fundamental contradiction. Self-liquidation had already proved impractical for many desirable projects, as Hoover had discovered. Nonetheless, it was still in 1935 a chimera that required some placation. Housing could be rented, therefore the greenbelt project was potentially self-liquidating. It was not, however, possible if rents were low enough to be affordable by people on relief or with very low incomes. And if rents were high enough to be self-liquidating, the project *would* be in competition with private developers.[51]

Four sites had been selected for greenbelt cities, narrowed down from one hundred to twenty-five to five. The fifth, near St. Louis, was dropped at the last minute,

Fig. 9.11. Inexpensive furniture designed for Greenbelt residents. *House Beautiful* called it simple but dignified and not "theoristic." Photograph by Paul Carter, Farm Security Administration

Fig. 9.12. School and community building at Greenhills near Cincinnati, Ohio. Photograph by John Vachon, Farm Security Administration

because there was no time to acquire land. This left one in Maryland northeast of Washington, called Greenbelt; one north of Cincinnati, called Greenhills; one southwest of Milwaukee, called Greendale; and one in southern New Jersey, called Greenbrook.

The head of the Suburban Resettlement Division was John S. Lansill, a college friend of Tugwell's who had become wealthy on Wall Street. Being rich and a Republican did not prevent him from becoming an enthusiastic New Dealer. He was also a southern gentleman from Kentucky and was known to invite disputatious staff members to his home, ply them with mint juleps, and charm them into consensus. He enlisted the cream of the garden city movement, including planners Clarence Stein and Henry Wright. He got TVA's Roland Wank and housing expert Catherine Bauer. They set to work with great energy.[52]

With an appropriation of only thirty-one million dollars, savings would be essential. The planners soon accepted the fact that they could not build the five thousand units they wanted. They scaled back to thirty-five hundred but doubted they could do even this. Roland Wank, who had managed bigger budgets for TVA, thought they might make it "if nothing unforeseen arises." He added, however, "that it would be an unforeseen circumstance if nothing unforeseen occurs."[53]

The unforeseen occurrences were already arriving. The WPA commissioner for the District of Columbia area sent fifteen hundred relief workers to Greenbelt the day after the program was announced. The workers were transients. They were "unskilled, diseased, and hopeless." There were no blueprints ready yet, so they were put to work making a lake. This was hardly a key part of the town, but it was something that unskilled workers could undertake. With a workforce of fifteen hundred on the payroll, work under way, and hardly any plans to guide it, C. B. "Beanie" Baldwin, Tugwell's deputy and eventual successor, admitted he was "scared to death."[54]

The weather refused to cooperate. The winter of 1935–36 was one of the worst in history, freezing the ground to a depth of fourteen inches and obscuring the topography with ten-foot snow drifts. The following winter and spring brought heavy rains and a devastating flood. Then there were legal problems. Greenbrook had to be cancelled, because local property owners not only got a court injunction against the project but were trying to mount a challenge against the whole constitutionality of the Resettlement Administration. The RA understandably beat a hasty retreat from that fight in order not to jeopardize the whole program.[55]

The tight budget required cuts in the number of houses, but the utilities and other amenities like schools had to be constructed based on the original plan so that when the other units were built later, there would be infrastructure to support them. However, this raised the unit cost of the housing considerably.[56]

Despite all of this, work got under way. Blueprints were whisked off drawing boards and sent to the sites. Morale improved greatly in the transient work camps

Fig. 9.13. The houses and city layout at Greendale, Wisconsin, were more traditional, with pitched roofs and street grids. Photograph by John Vachon, Farm Security Administration

once building was started. Because of the need to absorb a lot of unskilled relief workers, use of machinery was purposively limited. Basements were dug by hand. An earthen ramp was used instead of cranes to get material to the roof of the Greenbelt theater. Horse-drawn wagons were used in Greendale. Tugwell expected they might next be ordered to dig with spoons. This made progress slow and also more expensive. It was estimated that five million dollars could have been saved by using more machinery. They could not meet the completion date the president had originally set, but the cities were built. Greenbelt was finished in the fall of 1937 and the other two in early 1938.[57]

The RA was able to construct 885 of the revised goal of 1,000 housing units in Greenbelt, in Greenhills 676 of 1,000, and in Greendale 572 of the planned 750. They were laid out following garden-city principles, the roads following the curves of the land contour with many of the residential streets ending in cul-de-sacs. Greendale compromised in retaining the grid plan in some areas. In general automobile traffic was kept to the periphery, and buildings faced inward to parks or play areas for children. In Greenbelt pedestrian underpasses allowed families and children to walk to the shopping center or school without crossing the major traffic artery. The Greenbelt community center doubled as an elementary school and included a swimming pool and athletic field. The shopping center had a movie theater. An inn and restaurant were planned but had to be cut from the budget. Community facilities in the other green towns were similar. Greendale included farms, and its shopping area was more like a traditional small town with a main street rather than a pedestrian mall. All were surrounded by the namesake belt of forest or farmland.[58]

There was considerable variety to the floor plans of the interiors. There were units with one, two, or three bedrooms. Greendale had fourteen basic house types; Greenbelt had seventy-one different floor plans. Provision was also made for furnishings. The RA hired artists to design simple, low-cost oak furniture for purchase by residents. An entire house could be equipped for as little as three hundred dollars. *House Beautiful* approved, praising the "simple yet dignified lines of the pieces." One caption declared that "the pieces tend toward modern design, but with a sturdy simplicity which displays nothing theoristic."[59]

There was no problem finding residents. As with the subsistence homesteads and rural resettlement communities, there were plenty of people who wanted to live in the greenbelt towns. Like the applicants for the other programs, they had to fill out applications and be screened by social workers. Minimum and maximum incomes were important qualifications. They had to be needy, to fit the RA's goals, but able to afford the higher rents that the congressional squeeze on the program had made necessary. Beyond that, however, one of the things being sought was a willingness to participate in the social and political life of a cooperative community. There might have been "nothing theoristic" in the RA's furniture, but

Fig. 9.14. A sharecropper's house with mud and wood chimney at left in Gee's Bend, Alabama, and a new house built by the Resettlement Administration. Photograph by Marion Post Walcott, Farm Security Administration

Fig. 9.15. The business and shopping center at Greenbelt, Maryland. Photograph by Marion Post Walcott, Farm Security Administration

Fig. 9.16. The Jeffrey King house in Phoenix Homesteads today. The neighborhood is listed on the National Register, enjoys high property values, and has an active community organization. Photograph by H. Anderson Photography

the expected social organization of the towns was theoristic heresy to New Deal critics. One newspaper announced, "First Communist Town in America Nears Completion."[60]

Community life in Greenbelt was indeed intense. The new residents plunged in with gusto. There were organizations and clubs for everything imaginable. Things got so bad that an official "stay-at-home week" had to be declared in December during which no meetings could be scheduled. This had nothing to do with socialism but attracted outside attention nonetheless.[61]

More threatening to critics were the consumer cooperatives set up in the greenbelt towns. Groceries, drugs, even haircuts were available through cooperative enterprises in which community members held stock. In Greenbelt 67 percent of residents were co-op members in 1940. Even elementary school students got into the act with a co-op for buying candy and school supplies. It became known as the "gum drop co-op." The economic fortunes of the co-ops waxed and waned. Many went out of business, and, after the war, all the greenbelt towns had private entrepreneurs operating in them. However, some co-ops prospered and extended their operations into the surrounding areas. The most recent study of Greenbelt reports that the spirit of cooperation and community involvement continues to survive. Greenbelt Homes Inc., which bought the row houses, is still in existence and still a cooperative.[62]

Fig. 9.17. Cumberland Homesteads when first built; it is now an upscale suburb. Photograph by Arthur Rothstein, Farm Security Administration

With the completion of the greenbelt towns in 1938, the Suburban Resettlement Division was abolished. In 1942 the towns were transferred to the U.S. Public Housing Authority. Always uncomfortable with this form of government landownership, Congress began pushing in earnest for a sell-off in 1947. Various nonprofit tenant and veterans groups managed to buy parts of the towns. Other parts were sold at auction to the highest bidder. The public facilities were sold to local governments. The liquidation was complete by 1954. The sheltering greenbelts themselves were soon devoured by private developers and highways.[63]

Rex Tugwell left the RA before his "grandest monument" was completed. Toward the end of 1937, he and his programs had come under increasingly intense attack, he had grown increasingly weary of it, and the president had become increasingly concerned that Tugwell's continuation in the administration was a liability. The election was approaching. The Resettlement Administration was transferred into the Department of Agriculture in September and renamed the Farm Security Administration (FSA). Tugwell resigned in December.[64]

Secretary Wallace was advised to dump the Resettlement Administration as soon as Tugwell left it. Before he left, however, Tugwell had challenged Wallace to make an inspection trip of RA projects and conditions in the rural South. Wallace accepted the challenge, covering two thousand miles and talking with many people along the back roads. He was stunned by the poverty. According to a reporter accompanying him, Wallace kept muttering, "It's incredible, incredible." The homes of Balkan peasants he had been in on trips to Europe "seem now like palaces compared with what we have seen here in the Cotton Belt." He concluded that the RA had done a "marvelous job" in its attempts to alleviate such conditions.[65]

Thus the FSA completed construction on the unfinished RA communities, including the greenbelt cities. It maintained and expanded support of farm cooperatives through loans and launched new efforts to help tenant farmers acquire their own land and farm it efficiently. The tenant purchase program was politically popular and provided the FSA some protection for its more controversial rehabilitation programs. It maintained a good repayment record, which it achieved by careful selection of clients, avoiding any who might need special supervision. The poorest and most desperate of the families Wallace had encountered were not therefore likely to be selected. Nor were African Americans. In eight southern states where they constituted, on average, 51 percent of the tenant population, blacks received 20 percent of the loans.[66]

Overall, the resettlement activities, including the cost of retiring submarginal land, were only 20 percent of FSA's budget. But it was a huge ideological irritation to Congress. Committed to the belief that the government did not belong in "the land business," it exerted strong pressure on FSA to sell the resettlement communities. When this was finally done, most projects showed a net loss on investment.

Fig. 9.18. Greenbelt today; some of it is still in cooperative hands. Photograph by R. D. Leighninger

The calculation, however, usually included a lot of factors not part of a normal real-estate transaction. The investment included community buildings and other physical and social infrastructure. The construction was usually done with relief labor, which was socially beneficial if not economically efficient. There were management and technical assistance costs. The fact that the families themselves would have been on relief if they had not been able to feed themselves was not considered, nor was the fact that their standard of living and eating was higher than it would have been on relief. Even more important, despite the fact that farm incomes were considerably lower than anticipated and borrowing was higher, many families were ultimately able to own their own farms.[67]

Another undertaking inherited and continued by the FSA was the program for migratory farm workers. The FERA and RA had provided emergency housing, subsistence, and medical care to some of the quarter million migrants who had trekked into California between 1935 and 1938 hoping for work. By the end of 1942, the FSA had built ninety-five camps accommodating seventy-five thousand people. Steinbeck's Joad family found a brief respite from misery in one of these camps that he called Weedpatch. He describes the joy of washtubs and hot running water, the magic of flush toilets, the privilege of being able to take a shower every day. He also describes the elected camp government, a picture of cooperation and democracy that might have come straight from Tugwell's dream. Most of all, Steinbeck illustrates the ability of these simple things to restore dignity. Ma says, after meeting with the camp manager and the three-woman Hygiene Committee: "An' now I ain't ashamed. These folks is our folks—is our folks. An' that manager, he come an' set an' drank coffee, an' he says, 'Mrs. Joad this, an' Mrs. Joad that—an' How you gettin' on, Mrs. Joad?' She stopped and sighed. 'Why I feel like people again.'" Steinbeck had firsthand experience with the camps and understood the importance of dignity. He had toured the state and written a pamphlet describing the problems of the migrants.[68]

The camp managers were not all as diplomatic as Steinbeck's Jim Rawley, however, and the system of self-government that the FSA tried to nurture was sometimes undermined by zealous and patronizing officials. In one California camp, the elected council decided to spend some funds they had managed to collect on an "ice cream feed." The manager lectured them on "momentary pleasure" and persuaded them to use the money for a new mimeograph machine.[69]

Some of the migrant camps were themselves migratory, with tents on platforms and showers, washtubs, and toilets in trailers. Others were permanent and included schools, clinics, stores, community buildings, and other amenities. All were humble structures built on budgets even tighter than the other FSA building programs, but they managed to attract considerable attention from the architectural press anyway. *Architectural Forum,* in a fifteen-page spread of photographs and drawings, found the FSA houses "of unusual interest for the quality achieved at phenomenally low prices." Talbott Hamlin, an influential architectural historian and critic, called the FSA work, "despite the necessary pressure of time, despite the tremendous need for unit economy, nonetheless true architecture." It is not surprising that some of the architects involved, including Vernon DeMars, Richard Neutra, and Gerrett Eckbo, went on to distinguished careers. Despite cheap construction, some camps survived long after the Depression and continued to provide housing for the rural poor.[70]

The Farm Security Administration, which had operated with considerable independence because its existence owed more to presidential fiat than legislative authorization, was finally reined in by Congress. In 1946 it was forced to liquidate its property, call in its loans, and be absorbed into the newly created Farmers Home Administration, an organization that would live comfortably with the American Farm Bureau Federation and the Cooperative Extension Service and stop worrying about the tenants and the croppers.

Politically, the FSA died a quiet death. In the visual arts, however, it became immortal. The photographs of Walker Evans, Dorothea Lange, Arthur Rothstein, Russell Lee, Gordon Parks, and others continue to this day to communicate the grim struggles and helpless despair of the exhausted croppers and dust bowl refugees of the Great Depression. For decades, and probably centuries, Lange's portrait of the "Migrant Mother" and Rothstein's shot of the father and sons running from the dust storm will be revered icons of the Great Depression. They were designed not just to document poverty but to communicate the experience to middle-class Americans. They did that well but not enough to make much difference to the support of the FSA. Ironically, the project director Roy Stryker, a young economics graduate who had worked with Tugwell at Columbia, chose to avoid trying to portray Tugwell's most cherished values, cooperation and community, focusing instead on individuals and family groups.[71]

The two driving concerns of the programs discussed here, a rational resettlement of the uprooted American population and the alleviation of rural poverty, were boldly addressed and doggedly pursued despite considerable opposition. Though many at the time saw the principal actors in these programs as misguided utopians, and many still do, their views of the world and its problems have proved more accurate than not. Business and industry have decentralized. Huge segments of the population have sought to live in places that promise a combination of rural health and urban stimulation. Farming has become a corporate enterprise, and family farmers, whether they held on or were forced out, needed special support to survive. Those that prosper today do so through a combination of farm and nonfarm income just like the subsistence homesteads.[72] The resettlement officials, in their different ways, saw the present and the future clearly and accurately. They thought they might be able to soften or deflect the force of the more harmful aspects of these trends. It seems cynical to call this utopian.

The practicality of subsistence homesteads as a suburban minifarm was only temporary, but that was harder to foresee. Having a buffer during economic downturns might have been something of long-term use. Orthodox economists in the 1930s were convinced that business cycles were inevitable and unstoppable, and unorthodox economists hoped only to iron them out, not eliminate them. Thus being able to grow your own food during tough times was not utopian but hard-nosed practicality from this perspective. What was utopian was predicting that a family would never again need a kitchen garden but would be able to get fresh produce year-round at a nearby supermarket.

The utopian label fits Rex Tugwell better. Believing that the management of agriculture, the conservation of the land, and the mass migration to the suburbs could be carried out in an orderly fashion that would achieve a harmonious integration of work, commerce, recreation, and residence was expecting a lot of America. Instead, these movements worked themselves out without the benefit of planning, producing considerable waste, pollution, and stress in the process. A half a century of urban sprawl destroyed the green areas and scattered the bases of life that have to be touched every day so far apart that we must spend a good part of that day on packed highways, consuming gasoline, producing smog, and wondering what kind of armament the driver in the next lane may be packing. Yet, the ideal of a more harmonious integration was not lost.

Attempts continued to reunite housing, workplaces, shopping, and schools. Even Levitt and Sons, who became eponymous for postwar suburbanization by putting up cookie-cutter housing at blinding speed, made some attempt to provide neighborhood shopping, schools, and even "village greens." Columbia, Maryland, and Reston, Virginia, were more carefully planned private developments that included green space and made attempts to provide housing for different income levels. The contemporary movement known as new urbanism encourages planning of whole communities with integrated facilities. Even the greenbelt has been resurrected and has made Portland, Oregon, one of the most desired residences in the nation. Tugwell's utopia has, in fact, been widely shared and may yet be built, though with fee-simple ownership, chain-store shopping, and a Starbucks in walking distance.[73]

The FSA's attempts to alleviate rural poverty have also been seen as having little effect. The loan programs focused on applicants who seemed most likely to be able to repay them. As we have seen, many New Deal programs were designed to help a broad spectrum of the distressed population but eventually abandoned the victims worst off or became two-tiered programs, as in housing where the poor got one kind of assistance while those better off got another, usually better, form of aid. Yet there is some evidence that FSA did manage, despite opposition from those who wanted to preserve a docile labor force of tenant farmers and sharecroppers, to reach some of those hardest hit by the Depression—African Americans.

In 1973 Lester M. Salamon looked at black participants of one of the RA's rural resettlement efforts to see what long-range results they may have had. Tracing land titles and interviewing original participants in eight of the thirteen black resettlement communities, Salamon found that over half of them, or their heirs, still possessed thirty years later the farms they had been able to buy through the FSA. They managed this in a period of great technological change when many families were forced out of farming, including two-thirds of the white resettlement participants. The black farm owners were also healthier than a comparison group of black nonowners, more confident about the future, and more likely to be participants in local social and political activities. In fact they were in some places the backbone of the civil rights movement that had recently emerged. This was exactly the sort of thing Rex Tugwell dreamed of—fostering economic stability and grassroots democracy among the most impoverished people in the country.[74]

One of the most enduring criticisms of the resettlement building programs is that they cost too much and did not return what was invested in them. In simple real-estate terms this is true. The question that must be asked then is, were they real-estate programs? Land was bought, buildings were built, and both were sold. In almost all cases the sales price was lower than the investment. If one builds a school and sells it thirty years later for less than it cost to build it, is that a bad investment? If we thought of education in such terms, would there be any school buildings?

Did the federal government get anything out of these programs besides real estate? What would it have cost to have these families on relief for six or eight years? If the thousands of relief workers who built the greenbelt cities had not had those jobs, they would have absorbed public relief funds without tangible return. Without improved nutrition, what kind of health problems would the resettled farm families have had in later years, and what would they have cost? How many of them would have become homeowners otherwise? What was the value of the rehabilitation of the submarginal land they were moved from? What is this worth to the economic health of the country?

Another problem with looking at these programs in real-estate terms is the time frame involved. Many members of Congress, upset from the beginning with the idea that government should own farms or build housing, put constant pressure on the FSA to sell. Thus in the interest of ideology, they violated conservative business practice. The wise investor does not sell out quickly. The bottom line would have been far better if these various properties had not been liquidated so soon. The Phoenix Homesteads, undoubtedly modernized and perhaps expanded, now sell for several hundred thousand dollars apiece. Cumberland Homesteads is now a "high-class suburb" of Crossville, Tennessee, called Homestead. It would be interesting to conduct an inventory of the current real-estate value of all these properties once owned by the FSA.[75]

Looking back on his experience with the RA, Tugwell wrote: "My advice to those who are thus moved by injustices and human needs, and who think they perceive better possibilities through social organization, is to go ahead. Fail as gloriously as some of your predecessors have. If you do not succeed in bringing about permanent change, you may at least have stirred some slow consciences so that in time they will give support to action. And you will have the satisfaction, which is not to be discounted, of having annoyed a good many miscreants who had it coming to them."[76] Tugwell was certainly annoying to many people. As a college student in 1915 he wrote a poem, which itself annoyed many people when it was later discovered, containing the lines: "I see the great plan already / And the keen joy of the work will be mine. . . . / I shall roll up my sleeves—make / America over."[77] In this he may not have been such a glorious failure as he thought.

This overview of New Deal public building programs, lengthy though it is, is nonetheless not exhaustive. One could add the National Youth Administration (NYA), originally part of the Works Progress Administration and later spun off on its own. It was mostly about keeping young people in school rather than letting them join the ranks of the unemployed riding the rails in search of work. But the NYA did build things and might merit a chapter of its own. The public power efforts of the PWA in the west that produced the monumental dams—Boulder, Bonneville, Fort Peck, Grand Coulee, Big Thompson, Parker, Buchanan, Austin, Imperial, Alcova—still vital to our hydroelectric, flood control, and irrigation systems, could support further scrutiny. The murals, paintings, and sculptures that enhanced public buildings produced by a variety of programs under the aegis of the CWA, WPA, and the Fine Arts Section of the Treasury department could also be considered, though, unlike New Deal architecture and engineering, they have already received some of the attention they deserve. There is more work to be done.

Yet we must now attend to the second purpose of the book. Part 2 is a consideration of public policy issues that the New Deal public building experience can illuminate. Part 1 was grounded in the material products of these programs. It takes no great imagination to discover them once one knows where to look. Part 2 requires more. It involves the interweaving of economics, political science, sociology, public administration, and law as well as history. It is more speculative and addresses four issues: the possibility of economic stimulus, the continuing need for public jobs, the necessity of infrastructure, and the paradox of pork.

Part Two

ISSUES

Chapter 10

ECONOMIC STIMULUS

The argument that consumption can revive a sagging economy goes back at least to the 1920s and got its first test during the New Deal by the Civil Works Administration (CWA) in the winter of 1933–34. Later, the underconsumption theory became a major defense in the continuation of the Works Progress Administration (WPA) and the Public Works Administration (PWA) in 1938. Whether or not it worked is still being debated. It is always difficult to evaluate social policies, because too much else is happening in the world at the same time a particular policy is being implemented. There is, however, evidence to be considered in this and later periods of economic crisis.

Economic stimulus is anything that causes investors to invest, producers to produce, and consumers to consume, increasing economic activity and growth. It can come from the "supply side" in the form of tax cuts or from the "demand side" in government spending. The idea of using government spending to stimulate the economy in times of depression is usually associated with the English economist John Maynard Keynes; however, its influence in America came earlier, and its most vigorous proponents were domestic. Herbert Hoover and others saw countercyclic public works as a way to smooth business cycles by maintaining production. Later in the decade, another group, led by former college president William T. Foster and investment banker Waddill Catchings, also advocated public works but for different reasons. They saw the cause of the growing depression as underconsumption and viewed public works not as a way to maintain production but as a way to enable citizens to buy things.

Production and consumption are intimately entwined, as are production and investment. As John Kenneth Galbraith put it wryly, "under-consumption and under-investment are the same side of the same coin."[1] They are, nonetheless, separable activities. One can have production without consumption and, at least briefly, consumption without production. And one can have both disjunctions simultaneously in different places. In the case of a stalled economy, reviving production is generally seen as the first order of business, because production provides employment and employment makes it possible to consume. Production is stimulated by investment. Hoover tried to stimulate production by reasoning with or exhorting the business community. He and others, including Henry Morgenthau, later Franklin Roosevelt's Treasury secretary, were focused on restoring "business confidence." That meant, among other things, balancing the federal budget, the traditional symbol of economic rectitude and safety.[2]

There are a number of reasons why investors might not want to invest and producers might not want to produce. One is that they lack capital. Another is that they fear the economy is unstable. They do not see clear opportunities to make profits, only opportunities to get hurt. They may prefer to hang on to their capital. Haranguing them might not work, and trying to reassure them might be a challenge beyond the capacity of either policy makers or psychoanalysts.

But one could start with consumers rather than producers. Consumption can be enabled simply by giving consumers money or by providing employment. The government could do this through public works projects. Foster and Catchings saw there was no lack of industrial capacity. Nor was there a lack of willing workers. Furthermore, there seemed to be a good deal of savings available in the hands of businesses and individuals to invest in production. But why should anyone use their savings to invest in production? No one was buying the goods being produced; why produce more?[3]

In their widely read book *The Road to Plenty,* published in 1928 before the crash but well into the Depression, Foster and Catchings laid out the underconsumption argument in the form of a dialogue among a group of men in the smoking car of a train going from Boston to Chicago. Two hundred and thirty pages and several hundred miles later, they have overcome their disagreements and formed a plan to save the economy. It involves creation of a government agency to do for consumption what the Federal Reserve Board does for production, collecting information and triggering intervention, most likely in the form of public works.[4]

Foster and Catchings saw their perspective as a radical departure from classical economics. It was, insofar as it rejected Say's Law of Markets, which asserted that one need not worry about consumption because production would always lead to demand. It was also a radical departure from the classic remedy for downturns: do nothing. Simply wait until deflation liquidated the surplus, cleansed inefficiency from the market, and forced individuals to tighten their belts and governments to balance their budgets.[5] But Foster and Catchings did not mention that the theory of underconsumption actually began with Malthus, who believed that the economy needed "parasites" who consumed but did not produce. Perhaps they thought this historical precedent might not win them friends in the Hoover administration, because Malthus's favorite examples of the parasite class were landlords.[6] Nor did they endorse the part of underconsumption theory that emphasizes maldistribution of income.[7]

The solution Foster and Catchings proposed, however, was not radical. Public works had already been endorsed by Hoover. Nonetheless, their program did not win the popular or professional support its advocates hoped. Hoover's commitment to public works was far too hesitant.[8] Another problem, perhaps, was Foster and Catchings's relaxed attitude toward public debt. "It means scarcely more than that the people of the United States collectively owe themselves more money," they said. "The country does not lose thereby." More time would have to pass before that conviction ceased being heresy. But they had made one important convert, a Utah banker named Marriner Eccles, soon to be head of the Federal Reserve Board.[9]

The orthodoxy of the balanced budget was the downfall of the Hooverite anticyclic theorists. Their idea was that public works projects would be financed by saving from more prosperous times. The projects would be planned and waiting, and they would be cheaper to build in the recession. It sounded good, but it did not work as an anticyclic tool. There were no savings from more prosperous times. If financing by borrowing was either improper, illegal, or both, they had nowhere to turn. The anticyclic theorists, however, in conjunction with the underconsumptionists, had at least established the idea in conventional thinking that public works could stimulate the economy, whether through production or consumption.[10]

What was needed was permission to borrow and tools to borrow with. Hard-pressed communities, bound by legal restrictions on borrowing, found the latter in the revenue bond and the public authority. These instruments signaled to communities a blinking yellow light rather than a bright red one and were being experimented with prior to the New Deal. But they had to wait for a new administration to change the light from yellow to green and allow traffic to surge ahead. The New Deal not only enabled other levels of government to borrow to meet their needs; it was going to set the example.[11]

Though the Civil Works Administration was conceived before consumption had become important in New Deal thinking, it served as a retrospective validation for the thesis. As we have seen, it put four million people to work. The CWA was hugely successful at what it was supposed to do. But it was also hugely expensive and scary to both its supporters and its enemies. Roosevelt was not willing to face the possibility that ending the Depression might take this level of commitment of national resources. So he pulled the plug, and CWA ceased operation at the end of March 1934.[12]

The CWA put a lot of people to work, filled a lot of empty stomachs, and brightened the Christmas celebrations of many Americans. But did it stimulate the economy? The *Wall Street Journal* thought so. It announced at the center of its front page, "Merchandisers' December Sales Big; Aided by Heavy Holiday Buying; Woolworth Tops 1932." Not just the retail economy, it said, but "all sectors of the economy are participating in the upturn." It attributed this to the "general revival in purchasing power" but said nothing about what might have caused this revival. However, in its story three weeks later headlined "January Setting Retail Records," it was willing to give some credit to "the government's payroll expenditures on public works programs."[13] *Business Week* also gave CWA credit in January, and it noted in the following month that mail-order sales were up 80 percent over the previous year. It also reported an increase in automobile production, with factories again working three shifts and "sales good all over . . . now with government payments coming through."[14]

If one looks at sales figures for department stores, variety stores, and food, apparel, and drug chain stores during the period when CWA payrolls were being delivered, one can see this spurt followed by a drop after the program closed. One can also see auto sales rise and fall at a lag of several months, propelled not by CWA employees but more likely by store owners seeing their inventories move.[15]

The CWA was a vitamin shot but not the hoped-for recovery. Therefore a year later a new works program was put together with the WPA as its centerpiece. At the same time, Harold Ickes's PWA was finally getting out of first gear and beginning to roll out traditional, heavy-duty public works projects and, together with the WPA, the CCC, and other New Deal jobs programs, was stimulating consumption.

By 1937 things were finally looking up. Roosevelt was still at heart a believer in economic orthodoxy and its chief tenet, the balanced budget, despite the fact that his flexibility and willingness to experiment had required him to flirt with heresy and that those flirtations had been rewarded. He was now encouraged by his much more doctrinaire Treasury secretary to attempt to restore the elusive "business confidence" and nail down the recovery by balancing the budget. On April 20, 1937, he told Congress he would cut back on all the public works programs. In the words of Alan Brinkley, "disaster followed."[16]

Six months later, a recession began. By the end of the year, the stock market, industrial production, corporate profits, and employment had fallen so far that comparisons with 1929 were being made. In fact, given the speed with which it developed, it was worse than 1929. Morgenthau was still counseling Roosevelt to return to a balanced budget and thereby restore business confidence. But business was in no mood to be reassured.[17]

During this period, a new challenge to orthodoxy was emerging. A new appreciation of the power of consumption was being used by advocates of public works programs to argue for restoration of their shrunken appropriations. Marriner Eccles, a disciple of Foster and Catchings, was now chairman of the Federal Reserve Board. He was joined by Lauchlin Currie, a young Harvard economist who was brought to Treasury by Morgenthau because of his expertise in monetary policy. He was also, however, someone who had read John Maynard Keynes's *General Theory of Employment, Interest, and Money* and had developed thereby an appreciation of the powers of deficit spending and public works. At the Fed he found a kindred spirit in Eccles.[18]

Private investment, according to Keynes and his American disciple, had been stimulated throughout history by three forces: geographic expansion, population growth, and technological change. The first two were now at a standstill, and the third was insufficient to keep the economy healthy on its own. A "fourth pillar" would have to be found, and that was public investment. It would provide the necessary stability to encourage private investment to come out of its bunkers and back into the economy. Consumption would provide that encouragement. Community consumption—investment in education, health, housing, social services—would begin the process. Private consumption would follow. Public works were the key to both.[19]

Leon Henderson, another apostate economist and Keynesian convert with an appreciation for the power of consumption, added his support to the arguments of Eccles and Currie in favor of stimulating consumption through public works. He was a New Deal insider who had worked with Hopkins at the WPA. His intellect and writing ability gave him considerable influence with other New Dealers. He helped turn the president in favor of public works spending by furnishing him with a history of federal activity to promote the economy, such as land grants for railroads. This shaped the argument in terms of continuity with tradition, not a radical departure from it. It liberated Roosevelt from his qualms about the risks of the deficit. With the intellectual weaponry from Eccles, Currie, and Henderson and the political encouragement of Hopkins and Ickes behind him, Roosevelt announced a broad, new package of public works spending.[20]

The recession was stopped but not reversed. Public works might be given the credit for this. The other things now going on in the economy, however, make assigning responsibility to any one policy extremely difficult. One major complication is the fact that the New Deal was now taking out of the economy about as much or more than it was putting in. The Economy Act cut government salaries and veterans' benefits. The new Social Security tax had taken effect, and some state taxes were being raised as well. The fact that matters were at least not getting worse after the return to public works might be another bit of evidence for the efficacy of consumption. Alvin Hansen, another Keynesian convert, gave public works credit for the recovery in a 1938 analysis. In 1954 economist Kenneth Roose accorded the works program "the major if not the exclusive responsibility for stimulating the revival."[21]

The most recent assessment of the issue by economists Price Fishback, William Horrace, and Shawn Kantor focused on spending and retail sales in three thousand counties over six years, from 1933 to 1939. They conclude that "for every dollar of

New Deal grant spending, income increased between one and two dollars." The effects grew over time.[22]

Since the Depression, tax cuts have become the stimulus delivery system of choice.[23] Some large public works—cold-war projects beginning with Truman and modeled on PWA, the Eisenhower interstate highway program of the 1950s, and Kennedy's space program in the 1960s—were undertaken. However, they were justified on other grounds and not made part of a national program to stimulate the economy. The GI bill was also an economic stimulus, also not defined as such.[24]

In three presidential administrations since the New Deal, economic stimulus has been attempted by tax cuts. John F. Kennedy's goal was to return the economy to full employment. He was willing to use both increased federal spending and tax cuts to boost consumption. However, because of business antagonism to increased federal spending, he chose tax cuts as the chief instrument of stimulus.[25]

Enacted in 1964, after Kennedy's death, this tax cut is widely credited with stimulating economic recovery through the rest of the decade. It had both demand and supply sides, but the focus was on influencing the ordinary taxpayer rather than the business investor. Like Foster and Catchings, the Kennedy/Johnson economists believed that the economy was operating below capacity and that putting more money in consumers' hands would increase demand and bring out increased production. It worked. Spending and output increased, and unemployment fell.[26]

Ronald Reagan made tax cuts his top priority and concentrated on production, the supply side, rather than consumption. Supply-side economics is in some ways the conservative answer to underconsumption theory. Here the emphasis is on business investment and production and its stimulation by reducing taxes and regulation. Supply siders believe tax cuts can actually increase government revenue by encouraging investment, which will create jobs, multiplying taxpayers, increasing their incomes, and hence their tax contributions.[27]

The success of the Kennedy tax cuts, however, was not due to investment. They operated, as expected, on the consumer side. Herbert Stein concludes that "the weight of evidence is against the idea that the supply-side effects of the tax cut were dominant." Output per worker did not increase, evidence that employers were not investing in research or technology that would have made productivity increase.[28]

Ronald Reagan's tax cuts, enacted in 1981, were much more famous and, like the Kennedy/Johnson cuts of 1964, are often cited as the cause of prosperity during the rest of the decade. Supply-side partisans see them as a thorough vindication of their theory.[29] According to subsequent economic analyses, they are partly right and partly wrong. The tax cuts, along with other factors, helped stimulate the economy. But the important stimulation was, like the 1964 cuts, on the demand side, not the supply side.

Partisans of the supply side include Lawrence Lindsey, a George W. Bush advisor, and Herman Liebling. Liebling saw recovery as being led by business investment that was responding to tax incentives. He saw no role for consumption. Charles Garrison, however, argues that one must track the individual components of the gross national product as they declined and advanced. He finds that personal consumption expenses and residential fixed investment hit bottom and rebounded before fixed business expenses and inventory investment. Consumption was stimulated by lower personal income tax rates, and residential investment was stimulated by a 1982 drop in Federal Reserve interest rates. *Newsweek* and *Washington Post* economic columnist Robert Samuelson goes even farther, calling the positive effects of the Reagan tax cut a "myth" and dating recovery at the Fed's relaxation of interest rates.[30]

Garrison's analysis leaves "no room for a supply side argument that tax incentives [to businesses] either sparked or sustained the expansion which began in 1983." When business' fixed investment did recover, it occurred in some areas such as office equipment, where taxes had actually risen. It is largely forgotten that Reagan supported tax increases in 1982 and 1983 to combat the deficit his 1981 tax cuts and defense spending had produced. Overall, the prosperity of the 1980s was led by consumption, not business investment. In fact economists Barry Bosworth and Gary Burtless report that "net investment fell as a share of national income over the decade." Brookings economist Henry Aaron adds that net domestic investment was 5 percent of net domestic product. The average for the three previous decades was 8 percent. "In short," he says, "the 1980s looked good primarily because the nation climbed painfully from the pits of the 1982 recession and because inflation was brought down to rates that would have been considered onerous in any prior post–World War II decade. Some transformation!"[31]

Whatever new tax revenues were stimulated by Reagan's tax cuts on individual incomes, they were not nearly enough to balance his spending increases. Record budget deficits resulted. Ironically, this may have provided more stimulus than tax cuts. Military spending has less of a multiplier effect than other kinds. Build a tank, and it just sits there waiting for a war; build a road or a school, and it immediately aids further production and consumption. Still, the initial defense production effort paid workers and consumed raw materials.

Of course, a ballooning deficit eventually sucks too much out of the economy in interest payments, leaving less for further public investment and upsetting private investment. This may take some time to do any damage. Deficits were an ideological embarrassment to the Reagan administration but seem to have done the economy no great harm.[32] Reagan, followed by the first George Bush, continued to allow deficits to increase. They finally reached the point where they could no longer be ignored.

So, Bush worked with the Democratic Congress to construct the 1990 Deficit Reduction Bill. Since it involved tax increases, it may have cost him reelection. And since it did not slow the growth of the deficit, Bill Clinton had to make a similar effort in 1993. This involved another tax increase, which Republicans predicted would ruin the economy. It did not. Instead, Clinton and some economists argue, it convinced private investors that the government was on a responsible and stable course, bringing prosperity to the rest of the decade.[33]

This particular business cycle seems, at last, to be led by business investment. In fact the rate of capital spending was double that of the 1980s. Businesses bought computers, fiber optic cables, and other technological goodies, allowing greater productivity, which increased profits without increasing prices. And, because it was accompanied by a tax increase rather than a cut, this investment boosted revenues high enough to create a budget surplus. The prospect of eliminating the deficit was on the horizon. But the investment spree stopped when the technology bubble burst in early 2000, and the economy was now back in the hands of consumers.[34]

At the same time, the White House was back in the hands of the Republicans, and the tax cut mantra was about to become policy again. The second George Bush preached the gospel of tax cutting at every opportunity—as an antidote to recession, as compensation for higher gasoline prices, as a solution to energy shortages, as a response to the outbreak of hoof-and-mouth disease, and finally as a counteroffensive against terrorism.[35]

The tax cut was passed, and most of it went to businesses and upper-income citizens. More important, most of it was to phase in over a period of years. Thus it was hardly a solution to any immediate problem. But Democrats, who doubted the wisdom of such massive cuts but refused to oppose them, did manage to persuade the administration to send out rebates in three-hundred-dollar and six-hundred-dollar amounts to ordinary taxpayers immediately. Unfortunately, it did not have the hoped-for stimulus. Most taxpayers saved the money.[36]

Why this difference from past consumption stimuli? One explanation is that household savings were low and debt was high; therefore saving was a more sensible act than consumption. The CWA workers had no savings and probably a lot of debt, but they were far more desperate for new shoes and coats than current middle-class consumers. The Bush money did not go to the people most likely to spend it. People who pay no income taxes were, of course, not eligible for tax rebates. A decrease in payroll taxes and an increase in the earned income tax credit (EITC) might be more to the point. Increased and extended unemployment compensation for those who lost their jobs in the recession or the aftermath of the terrorist attacks would also have helped this group of potential consumers.[37]

We should also look at the supply side. Corporations, even with the promise of large tax cuts coming along in the future, did not hold back—patriotism or no—from layoffs. Thus those who had jobs and might continue buying things had an added reason for not doing so—they could be in the next round of layoffs. Even those not worrying about losing their jobs—people with large stock portfolios benefiting from cuts in dividend taxes—did not put their gains back into the market. Richard Bernstein, Merrill Lynch's chief market strategist, concluded that these tax cuts "had no effect at all on the market." Business was also not desperate for capital. As Paul Krugman notes, giving eight hundred million dollars to General Motors is unlikely to stimulate investment when they already have eight billion dollars to play with. The same thing was true during the Depression.[38]

The corollary argument that high taxes inhibit growth is also questionable. It is assumed that if taxes are higher, people do not work as hard and investors do not invest as much. Yet from 1950 to 2002, productivity grew most during periods when top tax rates were highest. In other industrialized countries, high tax rates coexist with strong economies. This does not mean that high taxes cause growth, only that they do not prevent it.[39]

Finally, there is the one part of government action guaranteed to stimulate the economy: public works. Even conservatives are aware of this recourse and are actually advocating its use. George Will wants to build not only more B-2 bombers but also a new high-speed train from Boston to Washington. William Safire not only endorses more government spending for education as well as defense but also boldly embraces Keynesianism by name.[40] Both couple their endorsement of public works with an affirmation of the worthiness of corporate tax cuts. Still, this is a very interesting development.

Several conclusions emerge from this history of economic stimulus. First, restoring business confidence through persuasion, which Hoover tried assiduously and Roosevelt sporadically, does not seem to have been at all successful. During the New Deal, businesspeople had reason to be uncertain about what Roosevelt was up to. He often did not know himself. It was not irrational of them to doubt that what he advocated was in their best interests or the country's.

Second, supply-side carrots do not seem to be very effective either. Tax cuts for businesses during the Kennedy and Reagan eras and now under George W. Bush were not the major engines of prosperity they are commonly believed to be. They were useful only after consumption had already kicked off a recovery. If businesspeople are scared, or if they already have capital at hand, tax cuts are not important to their decision making.

Third, consumption seems to come first. The CWA put money into the hands of consumers, and they used it eagerly and to good effect. Kennedy- and Reagan-era consumers led the way in their decades, and current consumers have kept the current recession from being worse than it might have been. But there are limits here too. Tax cuts to middle-income citizens with no savings and some debt are not likely to result in consumption.

Fourth, those most likely to consume are those with the greatest needs. Income taxes do not reach them, though reduction of payroll taxes or increases in the EITC might. Public jobs programs, like the CWA, that put money in their hands could also be an economic stimulus.

Fifth, the only sure way of getting money into the demand-side multiplier is for the government to spend it itself, preferably on useful public works projects. Some materials are bought, which stimulates some parts of the economy. Some money gets into the hands of ordinary consumers. If they are low-income citizens, they are likely to spend it. If they are middle-income citizens, they may not. But the country is no worse off than it would be using tax rebates. And it is assured of having something to show for the effort, a contribution to our physical and cultural infrastructure that can be used this year, and next year, and for decades to come.

Chapter 11

· PUBLIC JOBS ·

One thing that all the programs discussed in this book had in common, however varied they might be otherwise, was the creation of jobs in the public sector for unemployed people. They were part of an attempted reversal of an economic depression that had caused mass unemployment. Whether they achieved such a reversal or not, it is undeniable that many people were employed and remained employed until the government provided a different kind of public employment —military service—and the private economy recovered. Many people thought that this experience demonstrated that public jobs should remain a standard part of the federal tool kit to respond to economic downturns and that it was a government responsibility to provide jobs to anyone who wanted to work when the private sector could not. Others continued to see public job creation as a flawed and inappropriate instrument to be avoided.

Many New Deal programs began as "universal" programs, ones available to all citizens. Most devolved into two-tiered programs with one kind of remedy available to one class of people and an entirely different one for another group. Housing policy split between a subsidy for the middle and upper class—the mortgage tax credit—and an accommodation that only the poorest citizens would want to use—public housing. Even the old-age pension, Title 1 of the Social Security Act, which was more universal than most and continues to enjoy broad support, was not a truly universal program; it had two tiers from the beginning. Its Title 4, Aid to Dependent Children, was a program for the poor—the beginning of "welfare." Also it left out sharecroppers and domestic workers entirely.[1]

Employment policy and the role of public jobs in it followed a similar path. During the New Deal, unemployment was clearly a problem for the whole society; it could happen to anyone. In later decades it began to appear as a problem only for some people. Increasingly, those people were not one's relatives and neighbors but people who lived somewhere else, like Appalachia or the inner city. They were more likely to be of ethnic minorities. Their problems were seen as individual failings or as products of the social environments in which they lived rather than structural problems in the economy. The challenge was no longer to get previously employed people back to work but to integrate into the economy people who had never held jobs. All of this made a national employment policy difficult to construct and even more difficult to find political support for.[2]

The New Deal brought both positive and negative forces to the effort to continue the experiment with public jobs. The Civilian Conservation Corps was its most popular building program and inspired a wide variety of youth employment programs that have been implemented since then with a variety of enrollment mixes and under a variety of economic conditions.[3] However, the negative associations of the other prominent public jobs program, the Works Progress Administration (WPA), were also strong. Policy historian Jean Weir believes that the WPA "generated sufficient animosity to be credited with taking public employment off the agenda for a generation."[4]

The Second World War solved the Depression's unemployment problem, but even before it was over many people were worrying about the postwar economy and the job opportunities it might provide for returning veterans. Amidst plans for the reconversion of war industries to peacetime production were plans for ensuring "full employment." The National Resources Planning Board (NRPB), which had originally been created by Harold Ickes to advise the PWA, was particularly industrious in this cause. It prepared a sweeping six-hundred-page report, released in 1943, that linked employment with social insurance for the unemployed, disabled, and elderly; public works; public jobs; and assistance for those not covered by any of the above. Alvin Hansen, regarded by Alan Brinkley as "the single most important economist in Washington," published a book the same year called *After the War—Full Employment,* which stressed the role of government in making all this happen.[5]

Roosevelt himself, in his state of the union message in 1944, outlined an "economic bill of rights" that included "the right to a useful and remunerative job" that would provide "adequate food, clothing, and recreation" and protection against "the economic fears of old age, sickness, accident and unemployment."[6] These sentiments were embodied in the Full Employment Bill of 1945, which would have established federal machinery for achieving these lofty goals. But when finally passed as the Employment Act of 1946, it had been gutted. It created the Council of Economic Advisors but otherwise provided only vague rhetorical support for any of the bold proposals offered by the NRPB or Hansen.[7] This deprived the federal government of an institutional capacity for carrying out an employment policy, a lack that would have long-term effects.[8]

Other aspects of the package were problematic. To keep employment at maximum levels, government spending—and possibly borrowing—might be necessary.

Full-employment advocates saw no problem with federal deficits as long as they kept the economy pulsing and as long as debt service did not get high enough to interfere with investment. Others continued to adhere to the orthodox belief that deficits were harmful if not immoral. Ideological preferences were already turning toward supply-side interventions. Maximum employment was not an appealing enough idea by itself to survive its association with all of these liabilities.[9]

Another very important piece of legislation drove a wedge into a potential national employment policy. The Servicemen's Readjustment Act of 1944, known from its inception by its American Legion label "GI Bill of Rights," swept through Congress. It included most of the benefits the NRPB had proposed but not for all citizens, only veterans. The act had a tremendous impact on American society, extending higher education opportunities to citizens who would never have had them otherwise and probably never dreamed of having them. It added considerable force to the postwar housing boom, alongside the Federal Housing Administration, by giving veterans mortgage loan guarantees. It thus added many new members to the American middle class. No one doubted that veterans deserved these things, but once they got them there was less interest in the conditions of nonveterans.[10]

After the war, unemployment was less than feared. Instead of the expected recession, the economy was doing just fine.[11] The G.I. bill, the Marshall Plan, and continued cold-war defense spending provided plenty of economic stimulus, including support for consumption. Maintaining maximum employment, it seemed, would not require the massive government programs of the 1930s and perhaps no programs at all. It might simply be a matter of keeping an eye on the economy as it changed, then training or retraining workers to fit into its changing demands. Adjustments in fiscal and monetary policy could be made to iron out the business cycles. Because these kinds of interventions were now more widely accepted than they had been before the Depression, it seemed reasonable that they could be administered in a timely fashion before disaster could strike again.[12]

The interventions of choice shifted from spending by the government to providing tax incentives to private businesses. It seemed better to have the private sector create the jobs and help people find them rather than to have the government do it. Those who were unemployed in the postwar period were not evenly distributed across the population, as they had been during the Depression. They were more likely to be in special segments of the economy, workers in a depressed region like Appalachia, victims of structural shifts in the economy, or, somewhat later, young African American men trapped in urban ghettos with few jobs that were not related to the drug trade. This seemed to call for different approaches to the problem.

It also involved a separation of concerns for the general health of the economy from concerns about the lives of unemployed individuals. The CCC, which began as an integrated effort to reclaim both ravaged land and wasting youth, lost some of its popularity once it became seen only as a relief program. The WPA, which was identified from its inception as a relief program, was never very popular with anyone other than those whose lives it saved. The PWA, always known as an economic program, earned the retrospective praise even of the anti–New Deal *Life* magazine.[13] Employment issues, notes Weir, "became partitioned into an 'economic' component and a 'social' component, each cast into a distinct orbit of politics and administration." There was a "politics of economic policy and a politics of poverty; no broader politics of employment united them."[14]

In the 1960s and 1970s, unemployment policy was swallowed up by a "war" on poverty and a crusade for civil rights. Large segments of the nation supported these efforts, but more out of a concern for fairness and justice than a sense that their economic interests were at stake. "Labor market policy became identified as a 'social' policy that offered assistance to needy individuals; it was rarely defended or promoted as a corrective for deficiencies in the private economy or as a potential contributor to broad economic goals."[15] Unemployment became a problem associated with the poor, and the poor became seen as racial minorities. As this conceptual horizon contracted, so did popular understanding and political support. The result was a series of stopgap programs that came and went in the following decades.

In this context, the attempted revival of the CCC was an uphill fight. It was considered in Congress in 1949–50, but the Korean War cut off the discussion. During the Eisenhower administration, Sen. Hubert Humphrey led two efforts, in 1958 and in 1959, to establish a Youth Conservation Corps (YCC). Both failed. Another attempt was organized in the new Kennedy administration. The president put forth a bill of his own. These failed too.[16]

In 1963 a further Humphrey proposal was stopped. However, a clue appeared to indicate that the forces that had defeated all these bills were not grounded solely in fiscal conservatism and anti–New Deal sentiment alone. Many opponents were, in fact, southern Democrats who had solidly supported the old CCC. Attorney General Robert Kennedy had been asked if the new YCC would be racially integrated. He said it would be. The issue was no longer conservation or the economy or employment. For some members of Congress, the issue was now race.[17]

Lyndon Johnson had been head of the National Youth Administration in Texas. He was also active in acquiring and promoting CCC camps in the state. As president, he presided over the Economic Opportunity Act (EOA) of 1964. The EOA and the larger "War on Poverty" were a response to the realization, prompted by the civil rights movement, that a major segment of American society had been left out of the prosperity of the postwar period. It was not focused wholly on blacks, however. Appalachian whites were receiving national attention as well. Walter

Heller, a member of both the Kennedy and Johnson Council of Economic Advisors, recommended a focus on getting young people into the labor market.[18]

It was appropriate therefore that the EOA offered programs similar to the CCC. One was the Neighborhood Youth Corps (NYC), which provided subsidized work experience in public and private nonprofit agencies to young people while in school and over the summer. It also included school dropouts. The other was the Job Corps, which, like the CCC, took youth to residential settings away from home. Unlike the CCC, however, it concentrated on vocational training and basic education, not work in the forests and fields.

The NYC was run by the Department of Labor (DOL). The jobs provided were mostly menial—cleanup and custodial. This was in part due to the unpredictability of congressional appropriations that might come through at the last moment, varying the number of available jobs and providing only short notice to create them. This fed the appearance, and sometimes the reality, of "make-work." Enrollees were 45 percent black, 40 percent white, and 15 percent Hispanic. Almost half were women. It was the largest youth employment program in the 1960s, with an average annual enrollment of almost six hundred thousand. Johnson's "War on Poverty" embodied the total shift of unemployment policy toward low-income groups and away from broader issues like countercyclic employment or even more limited ones of structural unemployment.[19]

The Job Corps came closest of all the youth employment programs to the CCC. It shipped enrollees off to camps away from home, though not all were in the forests. Like the CCC, it paid thirty dollars a month, but it put an additional fifty dollars a month aside to be paid at the end of the one-year enlistment. Of the thirty dollars, the enrollee could choose to send up to twenty-five dollars home, just like the CCC, but it would be matched by the corps. Unlike the old corps, it was mostly a training program, not one devoted to conservation work. It was not run by the army but by corporations, labor unions, and nonprofit organizations. It also had a much higher minority enrollment than the NYC or the old CCC. And, unlike the CCC, it was open to women.[20]

The Neighborhood Youth Corps was fairly popular with Congress, sometimes enjoying increases in appropriations at the same time as the Job Corps was being cut. It recruited from a broad population, was inexpensive, provided cheap labor to those who needed it, and, as urban unrest heated up in the '70s, came to be seen as "riot insurance." Because the quality of the individual programs and the work they provided varied greatly, it was difficult to evaluate them. Most studies failed to find much of a reduction in the school dropout rate, though some found that participants got better jobs after leaving. One justification for the program was the "aging vat" theory that keeping youth in school would allow them to mature and thus be more marketable when they got out. The problem with the theory was that job opportunities in central cities remained bad, particularly for minorities, regardless of the age and maturity of the applicant. One consistent finding of evaluations was that the quality of supervision was central to success. The NYC was terminated in 1974 but left behind the lesson of the importance of summer jobs for urban kids.[21]

The Job Corps was far more controversial than the NYC, enduring intense criticism in Congress and terrible publicity across the country in its early years due to incidents of violence and drug use at the camps, and yet it survived. Over the course of its first decade, it gradually acquired enough political support to outlive the NYC. More remarkably, when the Reagan administration entered office and cut all youth programs, it left the Job Corps largely untouched. This may have had something to do with better evaluations. It may also have had something to do with a single individual.

World heavyweight boxing champion, Olympic gold medal winner, and later barbeque entrepreneur George Foreman was a Job Corps alumnus. When Reagan was governor of California, he introduced Foreman at an award ceremony with these words: "I'm probably in the forefront of people complaining about government programs that don't succeed. . . . In Foreman's case it was a government program that changed the course of his life."[22] For Reagan, a single George Foreman may have been more persuasive than a file drawer of evaluation studies.

Because Job Corps enrollment was predominantly black and Hispanic, it was never popular with southern Democrats. In opposing its transfer from the Office of Economic Opportunity to Department of Health, Education, and Welfare, one representative explained that it was better "to keep all the trash in one pile."[23] Racism also contributed to poor relationships between the camps and their neighbors. Enrollees exacerbated this with outbreaks of violence both in the camps and outside them. Over time, recruitment policies for both enrollees and staff changed, discipline was tightened, camp conditions were improved, and administrators took more care with public relations. But, as with the CCC, community relationships were also greatly improved once the locals began to experience the economic benefits of the camps.[24]

The fact that most Job Corps camps were not run by government agencies but by corporations, unions, and nonprofit entities like universities provides an opportunity for considering varying kinds of public-private interaction. Corporations undertook sponsorship of Job Corps camps for financial reasons. One executive said frankly, "We got into the poverty business as a hedge against a decline in our defense work."[25] Their hopes for big profits were not realized, however. Running the camps was more difficult and expensive than anticipated. One of the benefits of enrollment was medical and dental care. Lacking affordable insurance or a national health system, enrollees needed a lot of it. Four out of five had never seen a doctor or a dentist. Interestingly, many corporations persevered and shared the satisfaction and good public relations as the program increased in popularity. Their involvement, particularly their sophistication in public relations, no doubt aided this change in attitude.[26]

Labor unions also became a vital part of Job Corps development. Carpenters, bricklayers, plasterers, painters, and operating engineers all developed apprenticeship relationships with the Corps. In 1972 the Carpenters' Union agreed to train 600 enrollees a month. Here was a clear avenue to good-paying jobs. The relationship also had a large payoff in political support. The arrival of the union programs, most of which operated in the conservation centers, probably saved these centers from extinction. Union oversight tightened entrance requirements and also added a push to complete a high school equivalency, which was a requirement of entry to the building trades.[27]

Part of the initial strategy of the Job Corps was to pull enrollees out of poverty by getting them away from their "debilitating" urban environments.[28] Enrollees could escape the influence of gangs, drugs, and the lack of positive role models and be taught to become productive members of mainstream society. This "culture of poverty" theory loomed over most of the programs of the time. It placed the focus on rescuing the individual enrollee and not on changing the nature of the labor market, which might prove equally debilitating.

The Job Corps is now recognized as a truly cost-effective program. A 2001 evaluation concluded that it provides a two-to-one return on investment. Almost seven thousand graduates were followed for four years and found to earn more, pay more taxes, use social services less, and be less involved in crime and substance abuse when compared with forty-five hundred members of a control group. Enrollees learn basic reading and calculating skills, as well as job-specific ones, which have the same long-range effects on earning power as an additional year of schooling.[29]

All other employment programs of the 1960s failed to survive beyond the decade. But they were soon replaced by other, more varied efforts. There were at least nine youth-oriented programs that came and went during the 1970s. Most of them emerged from the Comprehensive Employment and Training Act of 1973 (CETA).[30]

The economic downturn of the 1970s brought unemployment back into a more comprehensive policy framework, because, once again, a broader spectrum of the workforce needed jobs. Advocates for public jobs reemerged in Congress. There was a growing need for public jobs in cities whose revenues were being strangled by new limitations on property taxes. As in the 1890s, cities faced new problems without the resources to deal with them.[31]

The original idea behind CETA was to consolidate multiple manpower programs, dissolving "categorical" programs with specific federal mandates into block grants made to state and local governments who would decide what kinds of services suited local needs. Consortia of local agencies, known as prime sponsors, would call the shots. To some, the idea was to "put the money on the stump and run." This devolution was only partially successful, and the successes brought their own problems. Congress created further categorical programs, continuing to complicate local administration. Local administration also proved vulnerable, not surprisingly, to local political pressure in defining needs.[32]

Though training and education were supposed to be the main purpose of CETA, Public Service Employment (PSE) was soon its largest component. It made local politicians very happy, because benefits could be distributed more widely. Recipients of PSE were more likely to be white, male, less economically disadvantaged, and older than participants in other programs.[33] The kinds of jobs filled by CETA workers varied widely. The most common were building and grounds maintenance and repair. Next most popular were (1) social services—staffing programs for children, battered women, elders, and mental patients; and (2) education—teachers' aides, tutors, and school maintenance. Parks, hospitals, and public housing were common job sites. Some CETA workers did service as security guards. Some were even employed as outreach workers to improve police-community relations.[34]

CETA funds were given to local authorities to spend with little or no federal oversight or assistance, one of Nixon's ideological goals. They were eagerly seized by financially strained localities as a way to keep operations and services alive. The situation was made-to-order for the displacement of public workers. The Carter administration greatly expanded the program in 1976. This was made-to-order for corruption. Large amounts of unplanned-for money had to be allocated quickly. Local inexperience could not be compensated for by federal guidance, because the Department of Labor budget had also been cut. This also meant there was no outside check on corruption. It was a situation not unlike that faced by the WPA. Public reaction was quicker, however. The perception of mismanagement and corruption was widespread even though, like the WPA, actual abuses were far fewer than alleged. CETA was reauthorized in 1978 but cut back. Federal restrictions and DOL monitoring were belatedly imposed.[35] It was too late to save the reputation of public jobs, which were now, once again, associated with waste, inefficiency, and corruption. The PSE component of CETA was eliminated in 1981.

Though the political outcome was the same, there were some contrasts between the CETA and WPA experiences. The WPA retained a core of popular support throughout its nine years of existence despite the unending abuse of its critics. First, the issue of the displacement of public workers was less acute. By 1935 public services had already been bled dry, and it was obvious that if anything but a skeleton operation was to be maintained, the WPA had to do it. Second, there was at least some attempt at federal oversight. Harry Hopkins and his lieutenants worked hard to cut out corruption where they found it, direct pork to worthwhile ends, and distribute funds as equally as possible. Most people could tell that allegations of abuse were far greater than the actual abuse. Third, there was a mix of ephemeral and enduring output. People might see leaves being raked and wonder if it was necessary. But they could also see schools being built or repaired and know that something of lasting benefit was being accomplished. The output of CETA jobs tended much more toward the ephemeral than the enduring.

Though it got most of the money and all the attention, PSE was by no means all there was to CETA. A Youth Conservation Corps (YCC) became part of CETA in 1978. Being strictly rural and focused on conservation, it assumed the mantle of the old CCC and the residual political popularity that went with it. Unlike the other youth programs, it retained a diverse membership. Under 30 percent of enrollment was minority. and only 40 percent were from disadvantaged backgrounds. It did work generally recognized as useful. When both houses of Congress, with broad bipartisan support, passed a bill in 1984 continuing the program for three years, President Reagan vetoed it.[36] Unfortunately, the YCC had not produced a George Foreman; or if it had, Ronald Reagan had not met him yet.

Another irony in Reagan's veto was the existence of the California Conservation Corps, which was an expanded version of the Ecology Corps begun in 1971 when Reagan was California's governor. Gov. Jerry Brown, who undertook the expansion and renaming in 1976, pictured it as a combination "Jesuit seminary, Israeli kibbutz, and Marine boot camp." It had a troubled infancy but matured into a very popular program. It was noted for tough discipline, and the work was apparently every bit as arduous as that engaged in by the original corps. In fact its motto became "Hard Work, Low Pay, Miserable Conditions." Apparently, the Marines won out over the Jesuits.[37] The majority of California enrollees are white and come from all economic backgrounds. The program is considered cost effective. It was made a permanent state department by Gov. George Deukmejian, a Republican, in 1983.

In fact, there are now 118 service and conservation corps operating around the country, some statewide, some in cities. Many of them were started in the early eighties as Reagan was eliminating the federal programs. Minnesota started its program in 1981, Wisconsin in 1983, and Vermont in 1985. Federal funding reentered the picture in 1990, doubling the number of corps programs. President Clinton's AmeriCorps program, created by the National and Community Service Trust Act of 1993, continued federal support to these projects. The National Association of Service and Conservation Corps reports that in 2000, year-round and summer youth corps programs were operating in thirty-two states involving twenty-three thousand participants.[38]

Yet another CCC-type program, this one combining a WPA emphasis on construction with an NYA concern for high-school completion, is an enterprise called Youth Build. Initiated by private foundations and now also funded by the U.S. Department of Housing and Urban Development, Youth Build recruits small groups of urban high schoolers and pays them ten dollars a day for attending academic classes and minimum wage for learning construction trades. When they graduate from high school, they enter an apprenticeship sponsored by local contractors. Their on-the-job training often involves rehabilitating inner-city structures.[39]

Evaluating the effects of these many and varied public jobs programs is exceedingly difficult. Some of them were only in business a few years, and those that survived longer changed considerably over time. The economies they existed in also changed considerably. The case of the Job Corps suggests that it may take quite a while for a program to find out what really works. This is true for participants as well. One common finding is that the longer one stayed in a program the more favorable the impact was likely to be. Another was that programs that can make real connections for participants with real jobs were more effective than ones that operate mainly in the classroom or teach skills and provide work experiences that are not well connected with the job market. For this reason programs where business or unions could open a direct pathway to employment tended to work well, though the corporations discovered that providing the necessary supports along the way was expensive. Work that involved a visible product got more support both from the participants and from the public. Basic skills were more useful than job-specific ones. Local initiative is fine in principle, but some federal direction and oversight is necessary. Finally, the best training in the world is useless if the market is not ready to employ the trainee.[40]

In 1976, while the various CETA programs were working out their troubled destinies, Sen. Hubert Humphrey and Rep. Augustus Hawkins reopened the debate on full employment and reasserted governmental responsibility to provide jobs if the private market could not. Like its predecessors, the Humphrey-Hawkins Bill was eventually stripped of any meaningful capacity to achieve its goals. Congressional preference was to deal with unemployment by extending "passive" policies like unemployment compensation and trade expansion assistance benefits. This worked for people already part of the economy but not for those still unattached to it. It also perpetuated a racial divide and a fear of active government involvement.[41]

In the late 1980s and early 1990s, the economy moved slowly, and the gap between rich and poor widened. Manufacturing jobs were disappearing or moving overseas. New jobs were in the high-technology or service sectors. More people slipped below the poverty level. The Family Support Act of 1988 was intended to help by creating the Job Opportunities and Basic Skills program (JOBS). It included transitional Medicaid and child-care support. The program depended on state matching funds, which were meager because of the recession. And it featured job training for largely nonexistent jobs. Participation in JOBS was voluntary, but pressure to make workfare compulsory increased with each passing year. President

Clinton's effort to "end welfare as we know it," the Personal Responsibility and Work Opportunity Reconciliation Act of 1996, completed the process. Once the economy picked up and workfare sanctions began to operate, the welfare population dwindled, and the program was declared a success. Poverty had decreased far less than welfare expenditures, however.[42]

Seeing public jobs as part of a broad policy of responsibility for keeping the economy stable has been difficult. Repeated attempts at an integrated approach have failed. The New Deal, the Full Employment Act 1945, Humphrey-Hawkins Bill, and the Kennedy and Carter economic stimulus efforts all ended in fragments. A basic problem is the interweaving of social and economic problems in public jobs. When unemployment is seen as everyone's problem, its economic aspects take prominence even though it remains a social problem as well. The widespread concern that unemployment would destroy self-confidence, erode work habits, increase family conflict, and encourage excessive drinking was behind the preference among New Deal planners for work relief over the dole. These were social problems, but people saw their solution as economic. When unemployment is seen as a problem for certain groups only, and when those groups seem different from the rest of us in race, class, or gender, the economic aspect gets submerged in the social. Individual behavior, education, and "debilitating" environments gain prominence; the economy is not seen as part of their solution. Yet most people who have jobs that pay a living wage are buying consumer goods, making mortgage payments, paying taxes, and not committing crimes or taking drugs.

The Job Corps, the many state conservation corps, and some of the many other shorter-lived youth unemployment programs of the 1960s and 1970s demonstrate that such efforts are quite worthwhile and can produce positive results both intangible and cost effective if we take the time to develop a proper structure for running them. That development took a decade in some cases. In political life the patience for that kind of development is rare.

The broader public jobs programs like the WPA and CETA taught a similar lesson. Moving large amounts of money and large numbers of people quickly into programs that have not built an institutional capacity for handling either is going to be messy. Harry Hopkins tolerated the mess, got things moving, raked leaves, built schools, met payrolls, and paid the price of a certain amount of inefficiency, graft, and political favoritism. Harold Ickes had no tolerance for mess; he built schools and met payrolls in his own good time, with very little graft or waste. Robert Fechner juggled the demands of four bureaucracies, organized thousands of unruly young men, fought fires, and built parks quickly and with surprisingly little mess. All this makes clear that haste has costs, and institutions that promote efficiency and inhibit graft take time to build. It also leaves no doubt that the economic and social problems of unemployment can be tackled and that public jobs can play a role.

During the New Deal there were four common criticisms of public jobs programs. All are still relevant. First, they are inefficient. Second, they displace public workers already employed. Third, they compete with private jobs. Fourth, they are make-work; that is, they involve work that would not otherwise be done.

The response to the first charge must be immediate agreement. The CWA and WPA were *created* to be inefficient; they were designed to be labor intensive, which meant they could not do the efficient thing and use machinery. They involved training and retraining, which is less efficient than using workers already trained. As the private sector revived, it was supposed to pull workers out of public projects. This meant more retraining. It also meant that projects would be losing the more experienced workers, including supervisors. Inefficiency goes with the territory of a public jobs program.[43] It is also disingenuous to charge a project with doing something inefficiently if it is something that needs doing and the alternative is not doing it at all.

The charge of displacement was largely irrelevant during the New Deal but a more serious concern in the present. During the Depression, it was obvious that state and local governments were simply unable to do routine maintenance, much less undertake new construction. The Comprehensive Employment and Training Act, which used clerical and maintenance workers, could, and in some cases did, allow public agencies to replace regular salaried employees with free or subsidized training-program workers.[44]

Complaints about competition with private jobs during the New Deal were also largely baseless, because, until the early 1940s, there were few new private jobs to compete with. Where projects were shut down or workers laid off to answer critics, follow-up studies found the workers on other public jobs, on relief, or unemployed without relief.[45] Where stable, as opposed to temporary, private jobs actually existed, WPA workers took them.[46] Public jobs were truly competitive only where employers who were accustomed to paying meager wages for domestic service or farm labor and could no longer find people desperate enough to work for them. This was common in the South and Southwest, where black and Hispanic workers now had an alternative to peonage.[47]

In more recent times, as in the case of public displacement, the problem of private competition is more tangible. This leads to the fourth criticism: make-work. The nature of the job itself is now the focus. One way to move the work off the turf of private competition is to define it as not part of "normal government operations." This declares it to be, at best, unimportant and at worst, useless. If the job is not something that would be undertaken in the private market or by public bodies apart from the jobs program, then it is no threat to anyone. The more useful it is, the more it is a threat.[48]

To some extent this becomes a manipulation of the varied impressions of what a government should and should not be doing under normal circumstances. The conservation work of the CCC was enormously useful, but it was no threat to either public or private jobs, because no one was doing it at the time. The fact that it was not is a powerful indictment of the national ignorance and irresponsibility in the 1920s. There are similar tasks today in conservation, education, public health, and the arts that might seem to some as unnecessary or useless and therefore no threat to private enterprise or normal government. Not doing them, however, may be a similar dereliction of public responsibility.

The vast majority of the work projects undertaken by the New Deal public jobs programs were useful. Even leaf raking is useful "if there are leaves to be raked," said economist Garth Mangam.[49] That is assuming one composts them rather than let them blow away again. If the work involves the construction of something enduring, the charge of uselessness is harder to make. Yet this is usually overlooked in both historical and contemporary discussions of public jobs. One economist, while accusing another of exaggerating the lack of productive output of New Deal work relief, nonetheless agrees that it is "easy to say that what was done in the thirties was not productive."[50] It is easy only if one does not look at the actual products.

So the question of make-work boils down to beliefs about what normal government operations should consist of. The critic looks at the efforts of the public jobs program and asks, why are you doing this? Or rather, why are we spending public money to do this? However, one might also ask, why hasn't it been done already? Planting trees, building sidewalks, cleaning up parks and playgrounds, weatherizing homes, painting murals in public buildings, repairing leaky school roofs, supervising playgrounds, performing Shakespeare in the park, making public facilities more accessible, preserving historic records or property, building picnic tables, or teaching art and music may be make-work to some. They may be a normal part of public life to others. The very schools, parks, bridges, museums, rose gardens, clinics, stadiums, police stations, and other public facilities now in need of repair and maintenance were themselves seen as make-work decades ago. Now they are basic components of public life that we use and take for granted.[51]

A public jobs program is thus caught in an impossible position. If it does useful work, it threatens those who themselves would like to be paid for doing it. If it does useless work, it earns the public's righteous scorn. If it tries to do useful work while hiding behind public ambivalence about its usefulness, it undermines the possibility of our ever having a fully realized and properly funded public life.

The questions of what government ought and ought not to do can be infinitely debated, but the debate can be moved from defining the bare minimum of existence to describing some sense of adequacy. The debate may get beyond adequacy to excellence someday, but just debating adequacy would be a decided improvement. Fix the leaks in the school roof? Of course. Provide hot meals and warm apartments for elders? Definitely. Plant flowers in the courthouse square? Perhaps. Teach music and drawing? Well, are the arts a luxury or an everyday necessity?

Could this exploration of a fuller public life get out of hand? How about building a Lawrence Welk museum? Classical music lovers would see no need to use public money to memorialize schmaltz. The Cato Institute declared it "not in the public interest." George F. Will agreed. But some citizens of North Dakota thought otherwise.[52]

However, this may lead into a corner. A fuller conception of what public life ought to be, backed by a willingness to fund it through tax dollars, might mean that all the things that public jobs programs do would already be done. There would be nothing to do.[53] Is a cheap public life necessary in order to give public workers the periodic chance to enlarge it?

The answer is to accept that such a utopian public life is unattainable and yet maintain hope that public life can at least be improved. A functioning economy without the extremes of rich and poor we currently see has existed in the past. "Full" employment without finding a job for everyone with a pulse is attainable. A "normal" public life that is more abundant than the current bargain-basement vision and yet subject to improvement by countercyclic public employment or regular job training programs is hardly impossible.

If we could resuscitate the idea of a national unemployment policy that dealt both with those temporarily dislodged from the labor market and those yet to enter it, such as the New Deal was working towards, we might heal the racial and gender splits in our current jobs programs. If we could come to terms with the utility of a countercyclic public jobs option, institutionalized in some part of the federal bureaucracy such as the Department of Labor, we might be able to see the connections between our fear of losing a job and the Job Corps member's anxiety of finding one. If we could imagine a legitimate public life less circumscribed than our current one, we might be willing to pay for it with our tax dollars in prosperous times and welcome public workers funded by temporarily borrowed federal dollars to maintain it during recessions.[54] In so doing, we might restore our faith in government's ability to get things done, extend the benefits of a more smoothly functioning economy to more corners of the population, and even discover greater potential within ourselves as we move out from our private spaces into the public realm.

Chapter 12

FEERALISM

The kinds of public works projects that are necessary to meet the basic needs of all communities—drinkable water, treated sewage, roads without potholes, safe schools—have been referred to since the 1980s as infrastructure. Public works that are unique to one community or congressional district have, since the nineteenth century, been referred to as "pork."[1]

A federal system of government has multiple units or levels with some powers constitutionally granted to a central authority and others reserved. The U.S. system has three levels: a central or federal government, geographically bounded states, and local city and county governments. Infrastructure is built by all levels of government, but what is built and who pays for it at each level has varied considerably. The variation depends on three main factors: the revenue each level can generate, the geographic area being served, and ideological debates over the proper roles of each level of government. The levels can cooperate or not. The New Deal set up a new form of federalism characterized by cooperation, particularly between central and local levels. This has gradually broken down.

Governments have three principal sources of revenue. They levy taxes, charge fees, and issue bonds (that is, borrow). All three levels of government can do all three things, but there are limits, particularly in the kinds of taxes they can collect. Property taxes are primarily local. State and local governments assess sales taxes. The federal government and most states levy personal and corporate income taxes.[2]

The property tax has advantages and disadvantages. The governmental unit decides what a piece of land and the improvements made to it (for example, buildings) are worth and taxes a portion of that worth. Since the amount of tax paid is related to the value of the property, as the tax burden increases, the assets of the property owner are also increasing. However, for persons on fixed incomes—retirees or people with disabilities—this can be a problem. They may not wish to, or be able to, sell their homes, so the increased value is of no use in paying the bills. For them the tax is "regressive." It is not based on ability to pay. Assessment often lags behind increases in property values, limiting the government's ability to keep up with maintenance or respond to new problems. The advantage, however, is that the revenue is dependable. It comes in even in bad times. Other taxes (for example, income and sales taxes) will decline when the economy dips.[3]

The sales tax is regressive for all, not just some. It is tied to purchases. It can be avoided simply by not buying things. However, purchases of food and some clothing cannot be avoided. In areas lacking public transportation, cars are also a necessity. Some places counteract regressiveness by exempting food and clothing from taxation. Overall, however, the lower one's income, the higher a percentage of it one is paying in sales taxes.

The income tax is generally seen as "progressive." It is related to one's ability to pay. Those with higher earnings pay a greater percentage on their incomes. However, the great reductions in the upper income brackets and the resulting increase of the proportion of the tax that is for Social Security has washed out much of this progressiveness.

In addition to levying taxes, all units of government can assess fees. Licenses to drive a car or hunt a turkey, admissions to a park or museum, tolls for a bridge, and other assessments where the payee is getting some direct benefit are all in this category. In cases where it is in the public interest for everyone to use public facilities, fees may be detrimental. Public schools are not funded by user fees, because it is in the public interest to have a well-educated citizenry. Fees for museums and libraries could be opposed on the same principle. Fees for parks, swimming pools, and other athletic and recreational facilities work against public health and will extract costs elsewhere.[4] Overall, user fees seem fair and are also less noticeable than taxes.

User fees may cover maintenance costs, but they are usually not high enough to finance capital construction—that is, new infrastructure. For this, borrowing is a common recourse. The choices are "general obligation" (GO) bonds or revenue bonds. One is paid back through taxes, the other through billing citizens for the cost of services, such as sewage treatment. Usually, GO bonds are used for maintenance and revenue bonds for new construction. Interest rates are higher on revenue bonds, because there is always a risk that the revenues will not materialize. General obligation bonds have less risk and lower interest, because they are backed by the "full faith and credit" of the government issuing them.[5]

Issuing bonds usually requires voter approval. Most of PWA's projects were financed by local bond issues. Voters usually approved, often overwhelmingly. In those days only a simple majority was required. More recently, resistance to taxes has brought legislation requiring not just a majority but a "supermajority," 60 or 75 percent. Urban Institute policy analysts have observed that this "has been devastating to general obligation bond funding," effectively rendering it impossible in most places. Revenue-bond financing has fared better, but officials are often quite wary of putting proposals to a vote even where there is a potential for public support. One way around this is the certificate of participation, a public-private leasing arrangement that does not require public approval.[6]

Cities found ways to escape the limitations on borrowing that had been imposed upon them in the nineteenth century by creating special-purpose "authorities" that had their own taxing and bonding powers. The authority was invented also because many of the problems facing cities—water pollution, for example—crossed political jurisdictions. Moreover, authorities are a way around the roadblock of the supermajority.

Authorities cover the needed service area, and their budgets are not tied to local politics. This makes their funding base more stable and allows longer-range planning. There are, however, disadvantages. The boundary-spanning, and sometimes overlapping, nature of authorities obscures accountability. This, amidst the general confusion of multiple levels of government trying to cooperate, produces a feeling of "government by blob." The separation of authority from state and local budgeting also separates it from any regional planning. The comparative "merits of providing an additional toll collection lane on the Mass Pike as compared to a new trolley car for the [Metro Boston Transit Authority]" cannot be debated. The authority's stable revenue and insulation from politics may also reduce its need to search for maximum cost effectiveness. To centralize all capital spending might gain comprehensive planning and cheaper operation but at the cost of less professional management and more political deal making.[7]

Geographic impact is the second factor that influences which level of government should build which kind of infrastructure. In general projects are supported by those who are going to use them. Schools are usually planned by local school boards and financed by local property taxes, sometimes with state support. Interstate highways are federal undertakings. An arterial highway or beltway in a large city may be supported by all levels, because it will be used not just by city residents but by others passing through. States spend much of their money on noninterstate highways. Local roads are covered by local governments. Airports are a combination of federal, local, and private investment. Dams, dredging, and water navigation projects are federal; ports, water, and sewage systems are local.[8]

The third factor that influences what is built at what level is ideology—convictions on the proper role of government in the lives of its citizens. Two areas that contribute most to infrastructure policy are attitudes toward taxation and beliefs about the division of authority in political and economic decision making, particularly the widely held conviction that the locals know best what their problems are and should be left alone to deal with them.

The first question is whether taxation should be "progressive," based on ability to pay. This was until recently a widely accepted belief. An early supporter of progressive taxation was laissez-faire icon Adam Smith. The first of his four maxims on taxes asserts that "the subjects of every state ought to contribute towards the support of the government, as nearly as possible, in proportion to their respective abilities; that is, in proportion to the revenue which they respectively enjoy under the protection of the state." In recent years, this obligation has been increasingly repudiated.[9]

For some, taxes—particularly the income tax—have become symbols of government oppression, and tax cutting has become a near-universal platform for politicians. State legislators, faced with the decision to raise taxes or cut popular and essential services, often acknowledge that it would be more practical and fair to impose or raise an income tax. However, they turn to sales taxes and fee increases, which are less unpopular or less visible. As state and local taxes were cut through the 1980s and '90s, miscellaneous fees and charges grew.[10]

The second ideological issue that influences infrastructure spending is local superiority. Thomas Jefferson and Andrew Jackson were early believers that government should be small and, as much as possible, administered locally. The belief that people in faraway Washington cannot understand local problems continues to make sense to many.[11]

The resources available for infrastructure, the geographic dimensions of infrastructure projects, and the ideological reasons for undertaking or not undertaking them have changed over time. As we have seen, action shifted from the federal level in the early republic to the states in the first half of the nineteenth century and to the cities in the second half. The federal government initially did little, but state and local governments pushed their construction dreams hard and were slapped down by economic reversals. In reaction state and local legislatures imposed limitations on borrowing that not only prevented the reappearance of exuberant building but also made it very difficult even to keep up with the normal needs of a growing population.

Prior to the New Deal, each level of government went its own way. Federal lands were granted to the states for schools or railroads. In 1887 the Hatch Act provided annual cash grants for agricultural experiment stations, and in 1890 the second Morrill Act did the same for land-grant colleges. Overall, however, grants-in-aid amounted to only 1 percent of the federal budget in 1890. With the introduction of the federal income tax in 1913, other activities such as highway construction, vocational education, and some aid to mothers and children were initiated. By 1930 cash grants to states were up to 5 percent of federal spending, much of it for highways. Mostly, however, this "dual federalism" kept the states distant from the federal government and ignored the cities entirely.[12]

The New Deal introduced a "cooperative federalism" whereby the federal government took a direct responsibility for solving problems in the states and cities. Between 1931 and 1938 the number of federal grant programs was doubled, including the public works programs we have reviewed. The billion dollars being spent annually was five times the investment at the beginning of the decade. Many of these grants went directly to local governments. It was a turning point, a defining moment, in American history. And, though it brought a major expansion of the federal government, it was also a decentralizing effort. It was truly cooperative, usually combining fiscal centralization with administrative decentralization.[13]

The New Deal is often seen as the point at which "big government" emerged and smaller units were eclipsed. In fact the federal involvement encouraged them to enlarge their responsibilities as well. "The New Deal legacy," say economists John Wallis and Wallace Oates, "has arguably been stronger governments at all levels, not just central government. This is a result of national government programs that encourage, even demand, state and local participation in nationally funded programs. . . . The New Deal was clearly the time during which the national government came into prominence in the domestic sphere, but the way in which this took place has led to a cooperative form of federalism involving active roles for all three levels of government."[14]

After the New Deal, this cooperative federalism took several different forms. The amount of federal support rose and fell, and the degree of federal control varied also. New Deal public works, as we have seen, gave many communities a solid core of infrastructure that solved, or went a long way toward solving, their health and safety problems. For example in 1930 a full third of the urban population was drinking untreated water; by 1940 it was down to 1 percent. In 1930 only 30 percent of the sewage in cities was being treated; by 1940 treatment had doubled.[15]

As prodigious as these efforts were, they would soon be strained by the growing postwar population. Restrictions on borrowing limited the abilities of communities to provide these services. Some states had introduced taxes on individual and corporate income and some now had sales taxes, but the infrastructure needs were greater still. The federal government stepped in with grants in such areas as education and housing. Federal grants-in-aid increased 400 percent from 1945 to 1972. But grants were "categorical," restricted to special purposes, and problems grew faster than categories.[16] Many of these new problems were necessarily federal as well as local. Mass transit took its place alongside highways as national energy and pollution concerns escalated. Environmental protection of all kinds was a federal concern since most such problems cross state lines.

In the mid-1960s, economists in the Johnson administration observed these problems compounding. At the same time, they saw the federal income tax bringing in more money as the economy expanded. Property taxes were not nearly as responsive. This "fiscal mismatch," the economists thought, could be solved by putting federal revenue at the disposal of the lower units. These grants would be unconditional.[17] Walter Heller, a Kennedy/Johnson advisor, in making his argument for revenue sharing added the ideological rationale that local people understood their problems best. He said that there was enough money in the federal government to finance national programs, but there was "not enough wisdom to *administer* them centrally."[18]

The plans for revenue sharing did not emerge from Congress until the Nixon administration. Nixon added that there was not just a fiscal mismatch but also a political one. "The time has come . . . ," he said, " to reverse the flow of power and resources from the States and communities to Washington and start power and resources flowing back from Washington to the States and communities and, more important, to the people all across America."[19]

However, Congress was not ready to surrender control. It attached high-priority categories and allocation formulae to the legislation. A Seattle mayor complained that while he could get all the latest radio equipment he needed, he was unable to find any support for fixing the plumbing in his nineteenth-century police stations. Still, what emerged gave state and local government some freedom to move money around.[20]

Next, revenue sharing metamorphosed into block grants, where federal funds were sent to the states with general problem areas targeted but less control over how the money was spent. Block grants had been advocated by Walter Heller and Charles Shultz during the Johnson administration as ways to consolidate the confusing multiplicity of federal grants. Grants to states for health planning were made in 1966 and crime control 1968.[21] With their emphasis on local control of spending, block grants suited the Nixon, and later Reagan, ideology well.

However, there was less for the locals to spend in the 1980s. It was a growing Republican conviction that domestic spending should be drastically curtailed. Comparatively, the states were now in better financial shape than the federal government, so the argument of a mismatch no longer held. By late 1980s, locals did almost half of all public works spending.[22]

A lot of this was managed through authorities. In 1986, 40 percent of all infrastructure financing was through bonds, and half of the bonds were issued by authorities. The kinds of things covered by authorities greatly expanded from physical infrastructure, like bridges and sewers, to cultural infrastructure, like museums and zoos. They even covered such entities as "antinoxious weed districts and television improvement districts." Some authorities required public votes; others could issue debt without public awareness. In 1990 in Massachusetts, only 25 percent of capital spending went through the state budget. This was not just because it was easier to develop capital projects through authorities but also because it was much harder for the state to invest. Such projects were squeezed out of state budgets by current service needs.[23]

During this time, the rationale for public works was also changing. Early federal public works carried some symbolism of national unity but were largely commercial. Local public works in the late nineteenth century focused on health and safety. The New Deal brought economic purposes together with health and safety concerns: a new waterworks not only decreased disease and increased fire protection, it also reduced unemployment and stimulated the economy.[24]

In the postwar period, the economic development rationale receded again. Interstate highways were justified more for defense reasons than commercial ones. Clean air and water were worthy ends in themselves. But in the 1990s, the economic justifications returned. Investment in infrastructure was good, some began to argue, because it would stimulate economic development. Whether true or not, the interesting thing is that the rationale was seen as necessary to justify doing something that was once worth doing for its own sake. Finally, economic development projects began to be undertaken *instead* of infrastructure maintenance. They are seen as the only way to bring revenue back to the city.[25]

Despite a growing infrastructure crisis, alarmingly portrayed in the title of one book as *America in Ruins,* cities began to spend less on maintenance or construction of traditional public works and move instead into projects promising "economic development." They hoped athletic stadiums, convention centers, arts complexes, and other "tourist destinations" would attract free-spending outsiders who would keep local businesses afloat and enhance tax revenues.[26]

This was particularly salient to cities that had lost much of their tax base to suburbs and edge cities and were stuck with a population disproportionately in need of social services and disproportionately less able to pay for them. A related strategy was to try to attract businesses and industries to come or return to the city by offering tax breaks. Taking further blows to the tax base was regarded as acceptable if new jobs could be added to the local economy. States also entered this "tax competition." Tax experts usually regard such targeted tax incentives as "inequitable, inefficient, and largely unnecessary." They advance an alternate strategy of keeping taxes comparable to other states while providing better services. Tax incentives, however, remain more politically popular, perhaps because they are easier to sell than quality of life.[27]

The fact that economic development projects are now being pursued instead of infrastructure repair is interpreted by some as evidence that the infrastructure needs are not as pressing as assumed. Others argue that it is evidence of triage. Governmental units have to defer maintenance and put the health and safety of their citizens at risk in order to attend to the failing health of the local economy.[28] These public "choices" are tied up in increasing federal disinvestment and the general unwillingness of everyone to pay more taxes.

This puts still more pressure on cities to fund capital projects through authorities, thus both avoiding taxes and evading state-imposed debt limits. The fact that municipal bonds were tax-free meant that their increased use decreased federal revenue. In an attempt to plug this revenue drain, the Tax Reform Act of 1986 made bonds that funded "private activity" projects, like industrial parks and other economic development efforts, taxable, while preserving the tax-free status of traditional government infrastructure bonds. When this was challenged by South Carolina in 1988, the Supreme Court upheld the act but went a step further, declaring that no municipal bonds were constitutionally entitled to tax immunity. Congress could thus tax all municipal bonds, which would make infrastructure construction harder still. So far it has chosen not to.[29]

In the 1990s, the economy improved for both states and the nation. Personal income increased, inflated by stock market investments, and state treasuries were in a position to offset federal withdrawal. However, the costs of education, health, and welfare were also escalating, particularly because they are wage intensive. So infrastructure still got less attention than it needed. Some have accused the states of "reckless spending" in this period, but state and local spending as a percentage of gross domestic product changed little over the decade. States did, however, follow the federal lead by persistently cutting taxes. When the stock market bubble finally burst, state revenues deflated with it, and even those with "rainy day funds" were soon facing huge deficits. States again raised fees and sales taxes, deferred maintenance, and used accounting gimmicks to fend off disaster one more term.[30]

Cooperative federalism now seems to have come completely apart. The current crisis, however, may force its reconstitution. Resources, geography, and ideology could all be reconsidered. A quarter century of aversion to taxes, particularly personal and corporate income taxes, may soon be overwhelmed by the reality of infrastructure needs. Resistance to property tax increases remains strong, but different balances of sales and income taxes are appearing. In Virginia a bipartisan coalition passed a two-year, four-billion-dollar package of both sales and income tax increases. Its direction is mostly progressive; taxes on low incomes and food would be lowered. Republican governors in Colorado, Indiana, Nevada, Georgia, and Ohio have also turned from cutting to raising taxes.[31]

New geographic ideas are also available. William Barnes and Larry Ledebur argue that the cities-versus-suburbs argument leads to a dead end. The United States is not a single economy but a complex of regional economies sometimes encompassing multiple cities and suburbs. Land and labor markets are not coterminous with city and county limits. Efforts at economic development must take this into account, which requires new means of political cooperation and policy making. A regional focus would not only assist economic growth and eliminate ruinous tax competition but also reduce class and racial polarizations. Income levels in cities and their suburbs covary, and economic development increases as income disparities decline. This consciousness would take cooperative federalism to a new level.[32]

The supremacy of local democracy is also due for reconsideration. Is it possible that state and local governments are actually less democratic and less responsive to local problems than the federal government? A smaller percentage of the electorate votes in local elections. State and local governments may also pay less attention to certain segments of the electorate, particularly urban dwellers and minorities. They may be less concerned about national and regional problems like environmental pollution. This is partly because they lack the jurisdiction, but also because they may not bear the consequences as much as those downstream and are not under any pressure to recognize the problem. Local governments may lack technical expertise and professional management. Finally, we must remember that if solutions to civil rights problems were left to state and local governments, much of the nation would still be segregated.[33]

One political scientist has investigated a number of our assumptions about democracy in suburban government. J. Eric Oliver compared civic activity in over sixteen hundred municipalities across the country. He found that civic participation was indeed greater in smaller suburbs, but it declined the more economically and racially homogeneous the municipality was. Citizens had identical interests. Most conflicts were between other units with different demographics. Because the differences are not encompassed within the unit, the democratic process of articulation, conciliation, and problem solving did not work there. He concluded that in order to develop effective democracies, ones with the civic capacity to solve serious problems, one would either have to redraw the boundaries of suburbs—an unlikely prospect—or bring them together in a larger metropolitan government.[34]

Another aspect of local democracy is the behavior of local newspapers. In order for citizens to make wise decisions and take appropriate actions, they must be well informed. However, local reporters often lack the training to write in-depth budget stories. They may be less critical, because they have personal relationships with participants. They may have little knowledge of or interest in minority issues.[35]

Questions about the proper size of a democratic government in America were raised in *The Federalist*. James Madison argued that a larger unit would offer a better choice of candidates, make manipulation of elections less likely, and help control factions. "Extend the sphere and you take in a greater variety of parties and interests; you make it less probable that a majority of the whole will have a common motive to invade the rights of other citizens." If the diversity of "interests, parties, and sects" in the polity is great, they are unlikely to unite "on any other principles than those of justice and the general good." Indeed, "the larger the society, provided it lie within a practical sphere, the more duly capable it will be of self-government." And "happily," federalism allows us to carry the practical sphere to "a very great extent."[36]

Obviously, one should not expect to find in *The Federalist* an exultation of localism and an advocacy of total devolution of powers. However, it is interesting to see that the arguments of those who opposed the Constitution need to be addressed again. Some need to be reminded, it seems, of why the Constitution exists.

The possibility that grassroots democracy may not be completely democratic is not an argument for trusting the infallibility and incorruptibility of the federal government. Rather, it is an argument to continuing to look for a balance of cooperative federalism that will optimize the advantages of all levels of government. In the search we should reconsider the New Deal experience.

The New Deal building programs varied widely in where they lodged initiative and administrative responsibilities. Civilian Conservation Corps projects were usually selected and designed at the federal level by staff of the National Park Service and the Forest Service. State foresters often played a major role. The army ran the camps, and the CCC coordinated the whole. There were few problems of corruption or mismanagement. The TVA was a centrally planned program but had good state and local cooperation. Some believe it was eventually co-opted by local interests. The WPA was willing to work through the political machines of big cities with minimal oversight. A certain amount of graft and inefficiency was expected and tolerated. The program that merits most attention, however, is the Public Works Administration.

Sociologist Benjamin Kleinberg asserts that "the federally decentralized administrative approach first associated with PWA has been found suited to the multi-interest distributive politics of urban redevelopment and even has been put to use as the delivery model for such explicitly redistributive programs as public housing."[37] In its nonfederal public works program, the PWA invited local communities, school boards, states, and other administrative units to submit proposals. They were designed by local architects and engineers and, if approved, built by local contractors with local labor. The cost was shared according to a standard formula. There was little attempt to tell communities what they should want. The legal, financial, and engineering aspects of each project were scrutinized by PWA staff in Washington. The books were audited by PWA staff. On the site of each project was a PWA engineer-inspector who monitored bidding, construction, and labor practices.

Complaints against the PWA centered on its slowness, not its honesty. There were attempts to defraud the government, cheat workers, blackmail contractors, cut corners, favor local politicians, and other shenanigans. Most were caught and corrected before legal action was necessary. No large-scale scandals were ever substantiated.

The PWA's Housing Division had to create an entire new aspect of local government, the housing authority, in order to accomplish its program. This required considerable political and legal inventiveness. The effort was so successful that all public housing operations were eventually turned over to local government. Though making no direct assault on segregation in southern states, PWA allocated significant resources to both races and built structures of equal quality for both. In so doing, it furthered a national interest that was not popular locally. Once the Housing Division was dissolved and the U.S. Housing Administration created in its place, federal funding was placed under local administrative control. With no oversight, some incredible scandals developed in later decades.[38]

There is another aspect of PWA infrastructure projects that is generally ignored. They usually were well designed and well built, which is why so many are still standing. Their aesthetic merits are part of that. These projects are being used as support for recent efforts to hire high-profile architects for water treatment plants and incinerators even if it costs more. Good design seems to ensure not only continued use and reuse but public support.[39]

Special-purpose authorities, given new prominence by the New Deal, have proven so successful that most infrastructure projects are now in their hands. They have, however, considerably stretched the bonds of cooperative federalism. They have become well insulated from local politics. This may avoid battles, but it disguises the extensive needs for public construction and maintenance and tends to make governmental efforts to meet these needs invisible. Support for government at all levels is undermined, and citizens are encouraged to believe that necessary services are being provided for free.[40]

Can infrastructure issues be brought back into the open and citizen participation restored? The states of New Jersey and Kentucky have developed capital planning commissions that include key state officials and representatives of both parties and both houses of government. The commissions review all capital requests, hold hearings, and weigh alternatives. The governor has a veto. Thus some comprehensive planning is possible. Citizen input is encouraged. One measure of the success of the system is that 94 percent of bond issues proposed by the commissions have passed in state elections.[41]

State and local revenues and federal aid may change considerably in the future. The need to repair and renew our physical and cultural infrastructure will remain.[42] We can continue to deal with this covertly or open it to public debate and struggle at all levels. We need a new era of cooperative federalism. There is no magic in either local improvisation or central fiat, though there is demonstrated wisdom in local initiative and central oversight. The federal ideal that grounds our Constitution is sufficiently resilient to inspire new means of cooperation.

Chapter 13

THE PARADOX OF PORK

While infrastructure projects provide the public works improvements that every community needs, other projects that are proposed for a single community or political jurisdiction may or may not be needed. Such things have come to be known as "pork-barrel" projects. The metaphor connotes both waste and hunger. The kind of pork cured in salt and stored in barrels was notably fatty, often referred to as "fatback." There was a tradition of the periodic distribution of pork barrels by plantation owners to slaves. Depending on their degree of malnourishment, slaves were likely to scramble to get something to feed themselves and their families. Thus public projects are pictured as political nourishment for hungry politicians. The reference to slavery is generally ignored; therein lies some irony.[1]

Public works were regarded by many of our first leaders as a means of strengthening the nation. However, to some, public works had a dark side. They have been seen as bad things in themselves, symbolic of bad things, and leading to other bad things. This has been true even when neither taxation nor borrowing were necessary to build them, as in the days when they were financed by protective tariffs paid by noncitizens.

Thomas Jefferson and Andrew Jackson feared that internal improvements undertaken by a central government, and those who invested in them, would undermine state and local democracy. They wanted to avoid precisely what Hamilton hoped to encourage—a financial elite with an interest in government operations. They also feared that the politicians who enabled government spending would be corrupted by their association with large sums of money and those who loaned them. They would be tempted to line their own pockets and to favor the wants of their own constituents over the national interest. Jefferson was not a fanatic about this, however. He cut taxes, but less than expenditures; so he achieved a surplus, which he spent along Hamiltonian lines.[2]

Up through the New Deal, public works always had two purposes. They were internal *improvements,* good for their own sake. They also served a larger good: physically and symbolically uniting the colonies, gaining the support of the financial elite, establishing international credit, smoothing business cycles, stimulating the economy, and providing emergency employment. Since the New Deal, this connection between the intrinsic merits of public works and their larger role in the national economy and psyche has been weakened, if not dissolved.

During the New Deal there was no lack of doubters of the intrinsic worth of public works projects. Nonetheless, the New Deal builders could argue that they were making contributions, immediately and in the long range, to local communities, as well as contributing to the public good of the nation as a whole through the revival of its economy. As such, the building programs were debated in Congress and followed in the national as well as the local press. Their vocal critics and supporters could be heard throughout the country.

The criticisms leveled at New Deal building programs were manifold but not usually directed toward particular projects. There were arguments on the policy level: whether the federal government should be doing anything like this at all, whether such efforts were alleviating or worsening the Depression, and whether work relief was superior to the dole. If the programs were accepted as legitimate, there were then questions about who should execute them: the private contractors used by the PWA or government itself, as in the WPA? Should projects be restricted to those on relief? Should preferences be given to given to veterans, to local workers, to union members? There was criticism about how the programs were run: were they efficient or wasteful, did they take too long, should they be labor intensive or use machinery, should they be carefully planned or started immediately? There were endless charges of political favoritism. There does not seem, however, to have been much argument over whether a particular school, bridge, or courthouse was really useful.

There were constant complaints about "boondoggles," the word closest to "pork" in the New Deal lexicon, but they were usually made in general. The outside appraisers of PWA and WPA report no specifics. Williams concludes, "While the federal public works agency has received adverse criticism from those who oppose federal spending and from other persons who doubt the efficacy of public works as an economic stabilizers, the charge of 'boondoggling' has not been made against PWA." Though the WPA was more vulnerable, MacMahon, Millett, and Ogden's discussion of popular reactions also concentrates on policy and process, not products. They note that one of WPA's constant public relations defects was that the local sponsor got all the credit once a project was completed.[3] Thus a pattern emerges that will be followed in later decades: concerns about boondoggles or pork are expressed more in the abstract than in the concrete. True boondoggles are always in someone else's district.

The in-house assessment of PWA projects had its own criticisms. The original edition of the Short and Stanley-Brown report to the president, eight volumes in length, includes a final section illustrating poorly designed projects. The designers, however, were all locals, so the criticism is directed at PWA's engineers for approving them.[4] There were also projects that, in comparison with schools, courthouses, or bridges, might seem have seemed superfluous—for example, huge war memorials in Indianapolis and St. Louis. However, the former stands as the focal point of the city's civic plaza around which much municipal activity takes place. The latter, a soldier's memorial devoted to veterans of all wars, is still a free museum and on the Convention and Visitors' Center's list of "must-see" attractions.

One could argue that all that was built was not immediately used. Some took a while to be discovered. The CCC structures in state and national parks were not enjoyed to full capacity until the mid-1950s. The ski trails that are now economic engines for Stowe, Vermont, and other skiing centers were probably not used much until after the war. The amphitheater on Manhattan's Lower East Side did not become the venue of free summer Shakespeare festivals until 1956. Timberline Lodge did not begin to make money until the 1960s.[5] However, this only confirms Herbert Hoover's maxim that it is better to engage in public works during depressions, because materials and labor will cost less. It is an example of true long-range public investment.

Since the 1930s, there have been only two comparable public works programs of national scope: the interstate highways program of the Eisenhower administration and the space program launched by John F. Kennedy. Both of these received broad support. Both were justified as matters of national defense. No other program of public building since then has involved the nation as a whole and taken place in the public eye.[6]

As local public works were split from a sense of national purpose, another division developed—a political one. Conservative leaders, while continuing to support defense spending, became increasingly hostile to domestic spending. Without a larger public purpose to justify them, public works were prey to the old fears of extravagance, waste, and corruption. A proper conservative, even a Jeffersonian Democrat, should not be associated with them. However, public works did not disappear. Politicians of both parties remained proponents of federal spending in their own districts. They could advocate fiscal responsibility at the national level while keeping the locals well fed on bacon. The debate about public spending could be carried on in the abstract; the concrete spending was local.

It is not uncommon to find champions of fiscal restraint and relentless enemies of pork not only beaming with approval at federal projects in their districts but fighting fiercely for the necessary appropriations. Sen. Larry Craig, an Idaho conservative, was eager to secure funding for a national Sheep Industry Improvement Center. Former senate majority leader Trent Lott of Mississippi, whose state includes the Gulf Coast shipyards, worked doggedly for the $350 million appropriation necessary to build a helicopter carrier that the navy had not asked for. Some are willing to risk unpopularity to maintain their principles. Reps. John Shadegg and Jeff Flake of Arizona refused a fourteen-million-dollar earmark for highway repairs. But such examples of consistency are extremely rare. For most, principles are suspended at home. This local exceptionalism was once satirized in a congressional debate over public power in which a doctrinaire opponent voted for a power project in his home state. An indignant public power advocate concluded, "The Congressman from Nebraska would support the second coming of Christ only if he came to Nebraska."[7]

Hypocrisy is not the only explanation for this. The contradiction may arise because activities close to home are easier to evaluate. The project in another district is easier to label "pork," because all that is known about it is the cost. The project at home has more visible virtues.

A fragmented budgetary process that allows "earmarks" and "riders" indulges the district-specific project. Earmarks are devices that require a specific amount of money out of a general appropriations bill to be spent on specific projects. The projects usually belong to members of the committee administering the appropriation. The metaphor is also pork related. It comes from the practice of farmers tagging the ears of their pigs for identification purposes. Representatives do not usually debate these projects in the committee or on the floor of either house. They do not criticize the projects of other representatives. Projects rarely come to the attention of the general public outside the affected district. "Earmarks are like mushrooms," said one House committee chair. "They grow best in the dark."[8] If other inducements are needed for a favorable vote, there is "log-rolling." Representatives agree to vote for each other's projects.

Riders are projects or programs attached, often at the last minute, to an omnibus spending bill. They may have nothing to do with the purpose of the bill. These, too, are rarely debated unless the president threatens to veto the bill because of the riders. If the president wants the bill badly enough, the riders will trot to funding. The bill is held hostage to the attached pork.[9]

A further problem is that not all public works projects start out in the public domain. Some are back-door public works, inherited from the private sector. The multibillion-dollar federal bailout of the savings-and-loan industry in 1990 gave the government unrented office buildings, empty shopping malls, and undersubscribed country clubs. Few voters would have supported adding these things to the federal inventory, but they got them anyway. They also acquired the hulls of two cruise ships, thanks to federal loan guarantees that Senator Lott was able to secure for shipbuilders in his district. The builders went bankrupt. The hulls are rusting in Pascagoula, Mississippi, and the government still owns them.[10]

Thus pork-barrel spending could thrive while at the same time being widely deplored. This may be called the paradox of pork. What keeps this curious dual-personality syndrome going? Why does pork proliferate if it is such a bad thing? And if it is not such a bad thing, why is it necessary to continue to condemn it?

Three explanations might be offered. They are not mutually exclusive but overlap to varying degrees. They are matters of emphasis. First, pork-barrel projects may be necessary for reelection. Second, there may be structural arrangements that develop between elected officials, federal agencies, and constituencies of voters that ensure that the agencies continue to exist and to sponsor local projects. They are sometimes known as "iron triangles." Finally, there is the possibility, hardly ever articulated on the national level, that projects might actually have some intrinsic merit. They may be useful, even necessary.

Politicians and the political scientists who study them believe that rational self-interest is the best explanation. They see pork as a necessary means to reelection. There is considerable lore about the political benefits of pork and an abundance of horror stories about expensive projects built, not because of local need, but because a politician felt it would help him or her be reelected. Investigations into the actual efficacy of pork in producing reelection have led scholars to doubt that there is any strong relationship, but that may make no difference to political behavior. As David Mayhew observed, it may be difficult to know how much federal benefits contribute to voting, "but it would be hard to find a Congressman who thinks he can afford to wait around until precise information is available. The lore is that they count."[11]

Backing this theory of pork as a rational calculation is a considerable literature, emanating from economics but with numerous supporters in other disciplines, that tries to explain all political behavior as a matter of rational maximization. It applies the basic assumption of classical economics—that people act primarily in terms of profit and loss—to the political realm. It began with Anthony Downs's *An Economic Theory of Democracy* and gained considerable momentum from Mancur Olson's *The Logic of Collective Action.* Downs spent a lot of time defining the circumstances under which it would be irrational to vote. He also asserted that politicians "never seek office as a means of carrying out particular policies" and are interested only in winning elections, not in making society better. Ideology is a tool for recruiting supporters and should be consistent in order to retain them but can be abandoned if it gets in the way of winning elections. Olson analyzed interest group politics in terms of whether it made sense to unite with others for a common cause. He concluded that usually it did not. If they did it anyway, it was because they were either small, homogeneous groups or were coerced.[12]

This approach to politics is known variously as "social choice," "public choice," "rational choice," or, by some critics who saw a connection to behavioral psychology, "rat choice." Public-choice theorists worry a lot about some people being "free riders" at the expense of others. They concentrate on individuals and tend to ignore larger "actors" like corporations, agencies, and parties. They downplay the role of ideas and ideology in political motivation. The theory depends on a lot of "surreptitious postulates" and "heroic assumptions." It requires very flexible definitions of rationality and self-interest in order to explain complex situations. Even with these maneuvers, there is still a lot that happens in political life that cannot be explained by self-interest alone. Nevertheless, it has had considerable influence on political science, law, and even history.[13]

When rational maximization is applied to the behavior of elected officials, it is operationalized as a desire for reelection. This seems reasonable and is often the first recourse for attempts to explain political behavior used even by people with no interest in an economic frame of reference. There may be politicians who do what they think is right regardless of how it affects their chances for reelection. David Mayhew calls them "saints" and believes them to be in short supply. He also notes that if they have goals that require more than one term to achieve, reelection is a necessary means. Reelection is also the principal way in which politicians are held accountable to the people they represent.[14]

Closer scrutiny of the relationship between pork and reelection by Robert Stein and Kenneth Bickers led them to conclude that there was a relationship, but it obtains only under certain conditions. It is most commonly found in districts where the incumbent is feeling vulnerable. However, in these days of polarized parties and partisan redistricting, there are fewer vulnerable incumbents. This may be expected to lead to less pork, but that does not seem to be the case. In 1989 Morris Fiorina documented the decline of marginal districts and the increasing power of incumbency. He concluded, however, that representatives remain just as responsive to their districts as earlier politicians. "No matter how electorally secure they may seem to outside observers, today's members run scared and take nothing for granted." If this is true, the tight association of pork with elections remains strong.[15]

However, it seems to be stretching the argument to apply it across the board. Some of the more secure politicians in Congress persist in fighting for large projects for their states and districts. House speaker Dennis Hastert of Illinois from 2001 to 2005 brought twenty-four million dollars to his district in health facilities alone. Ernest Hollings, not only the occupant of a safe seat in the Senate but also the coauthor of balanced budget legislation, had no problems taking a sizable piece of what the Citizens Against Government Waste labeled a landmark pork bill.[16]

The second explanation, the iron triangle theory, attributes the resilience of pork to relationships between elected officials, government agencies, and groups of constituents who benefit from the programs that particular agencies offer. Iron triangles are most apparent in defense contracting, but they can be constructed in less likely areas as well. Federal support of the arts is maintained, despite constant attack, because artists, arts educators, audience members, wealthy patrons, and businesses who supply artists or who have stores and restaurants near arts venues can be mobilized to tell their representatives how important the arts are to them. Arts patrons are often wealthy and politically well connected. Representatives may get campaign contributions as well as useful publicity in return for their support for the tiny ballerinas in a *Nutcracker* production. The National Endowment for the Arts tells the representatives how much money in grants and other supports have come into their districts. They or the local chamber of commerce can fund studies on how much audience members spend in the community when they attend an exhibit or performance and how much a new auditorium or museum will increase this. Like defense contracts, support for the arts cuts across party and class lines.[17]

A testimony to the resilience of iron triangles can be found in Ronald Reagan's effort to cut back or wipe out thirty-one federal agencies. Six years later they were not only still around but had prospered more than agencies that had not been threatened. Apparently, the threat had mobilized the agencies and their constituencies to fight back. They managed to increase their programs, reach more districts, and involve a more diverse population. In 1994 House Republicans campaigned on a "Contract with America" that pledged to cut two cabinet departments and $75.3 billion worth of spending. In 1999 both departments still existed and had larger budgets. The total budget for these and other programs targeted for extinction was seventy-seven billion dollars. Republicans controlled the House during this period.[18]

This is not to say that all federal agencies are immortal, as is commonly believed. Some are closed down. A Brookings Institution study of 421 government organizations documented the demise of twenty-seven of them. The very high mortality rate of public jobs programs seen in chapter 11 is another example. However, while they last, these structural relationships can certainly be useful in keeping incumbents in office.[19]

The third theory of the resilience of district-specific public works and the federal agencies that facilitate them is that they are actually useful, and the people supporting them genuinely believe in them. The Brookings study noted that in most cases, the functions of the defunct agencies were continued somewhere else, testimony to the possibility that they were needed. Also politicians who are secure in their incumbency may still want to do what they can to help their constituents. Steven Kelman argues that despite current widespread cynicism, this is an observable fact of political life. Politicians and those who elect them are capable of concern for others and cognizant of the possibility that pursuit of their own self-interest, which may be appropriate in the marketplace, may not always be appropriate in civic life. Or they might see it as Alexis de Tocqueville did, that making a better society is really "self-interest, rightly understood." The norms and institutions of American politics are constructed to reinforce this concern for others.[20]

Not all public works since the New Deal are things of beauty and utility. The two-hundred-million-dollar bridge to Gravina Island, Alaska, serving fifty people would probably head the list of anyone's dubious investments. However, under present circumstances it is very difficult to know just how bad or good things are. Public-works funding now happens much more in the dark than in the light. Riders and earmarks are slipped into spending bills in committees or on the floor at the last minute. If there is any public awareness of them at all, it is local. The only opportunity to see them all together is provided by the annual *Pig Book* published by the Citizens against Government Waste, and this is available only after the legislation is passed. It is then too late for debate. Nor, since this organization's main purpose is to stop these projects, are details provided that might allow us to assess their merit. It is sufficient for a project to be defined as "pork" by this organization if it is proposed by only one congressman, which, because of the current nature of public-works budgeting, is a highly likely occurrence.[21]

In order to make any reasonable assessment of the current utility, or lack thereof, of public works, they must be brought into the open, putting the *public* back in public works. If the entire roster of public works proposals, all the earmarks and riders, could somehow be viewed together, it might be possible to see what they were contributing to the common good, how responsibly they were budgeted, who they were benefiting, and how broad their support was and compare them on any number of criteria. If the opponents of domestic spending are correct, they would be exposed as waste and repudiated. Some might be recognized as useful and worthy of public expenditure.

Would it help to outlaw all earmarks and riders and try to collect public works projects all in one place? Could a "capital" budget representing long-range investment projects conferring long-range benefits be separated from an operations budget comprised of short-term operating expenses?[22] Could all public works be lumped into several omnibus spending bills rather than being tacked on or smuggled into many separate bills? This would allow representatives to face openly the dilemma of wanting to curtail domestic spending in general but not deprive their districts of needed benefits. It would challenge them to reach some agreement on an acceptable amount of spending and then argue about what should be included in it. The bottom line would be out in the open. Individuals could explain to their constituents their decisions to sacrifice projects or accept lower levels of funding as necessary for the common good of national fiscal responsibility. This is the kind of bargaining that used to go on in the days when a balanced budget was still a shared ideal and party polarization had not reached its current extreme.[23]

Might a nonpartisan review panel of experts be given the responsibility of reviewing projects? This is in fact how federal grants for scientific research were once awarded. The result was that most of the money was channeled to elite institutions. Those with less stellar reputations and those just becoming established were usually left out. As a result, such institutions have worked with their legislators to place earmarks in spending for their projects. Advocates of the old system worry that this dilutes the quality of research. Others believe that it will promote creativity.[24]

In the arts, experts are viewed with even more suspicion. The National Endowment for the Arts came under vociferous attack because grants were made to artists whose work offended members of Congress. Advisory panels that were intended to provide political insulation by defining excellence in the arts found themselves trying to reconcile conflicts between popular and elite arts and balance competing geographic and ethnic claims for support. The system, however, survives, and the public debates over "good" art are usually both healthy and entertaining.[25]

One standard that could be imposed on all district-specific public-works projects is a minimum of local participation. The PWA required that 70 percent, and later 55 percent, of each project be covered by local resources. The WPA also expected local participation but was much more flexible about how much. Such a requirement would test the degree of local commitment. During the New Deal, local communities frequently had to approve bond issues by elections in order to participate in federally funded projects, just as they do now for infrastructure projects proposed by special-purpose authorities. This in itself might bring the restraint on pork that fiscal conservatives yearn for.[26]

Perhaps there is a model from our recent political history that is applicable. Commissions are a time-honored way of undertaking independent research on an important problem and/or insulating important decision making from partisan influence. Some have long and useful lives, like the Federal Reserve banking system, the Federal Trade Commission, and the Social Security Commission. Others, like the Kerner Commission on Civil Disorders, were ignored.[27]

A public works commission could, at the very least, bring the politics of pork into the open. The general legitimacy of domestic spending as well as the merit of individual projects could be debated in public. A very modest step in this direction was made in the handling of the 2003 defense spending bill. The chair of the Senate Appropriations Committee agreed to explain projects attached to the bill that had been labeled "pork" by Sen. John McCain. As summarized, they certainly smelled of pork. What did Shakespeare, canola oil, and brown tree snakes have to do with defense? And why were repairs being made to a closed base? Sen. Ted Stevens explained a program to bring the arts to military personnel and their families, a research project to develop a new fuel cell using canola, and an attempt to prevent snakes from migrating on military planes from Guam to Hawaii, where they disrupt farming. The closed base was being used as an Air Force research lab. Senator McCain had a chance to criticize the programs, although the bill had already passed, ninety-five to zero. The Associated Press called the discussion "refried pork." It was unusual, however, to have any cooking done in daylight.[28]

One recent commission seems particularly worth considering as a structure for addressing the paradox of pork. As the structure and needs of the armed forces changed in the evolving cold war, the Defense department made repeated attempts to cut its overhead costs by closing bases it no longer needed. These facilities were spread across the country, and elected officials fought fiercely to keep their local bases. The resistance was usually successful. Between 1978 and 1988, no bases were closed at all. In 1988 the secretary of Defense created a Commission on Base Realignment and Closure (BRAC). It was charged with developing criteria for deciding whether facilities should be closed and ranking them according to those criteria.

In 1990 Congress agreed to delegate authority for deciding on base closure to the commission. It would conduct hearings where a base's constituents could make the case for keeping it open. It could conduct independent research. The president would have fifteen days to approve or disapprove the BRAC report, and then Congress would have forty-five days to do likewise. However, it was an up-or-down vote on the whole package with no amendments allowed.[29]

Military bases are recognized as a kind of pork. They provide employment and stimulate the local economy that borders them. They also present another example of the paradox of pork: taking one position in the abstract on the national level and the opposite one locally. In principle no one would oppose the closing of expensive and outdated military bases if the Defense department declared it in the interest of national security. But citizens of the base's hometown might find reasons to betray that principle.[30]

The BRAC went through three cycles of base closing, in 1991, 1993, and 1995. Both Presidents Bush and Carter approved its reports as did Congress, despite much argument and arm twisting. Some bases were saved or had their lives extended. In the end, however, most bases on the list were closed. That which had been impossible previously was accomplished. Generally, neither party nor seniority influenced decisions. The cuts followed military priorities rather than political ones. David Sorenson, who studied all three closing cycles, concludes that "most politicians . . . stayed on the political high road." Most important, Congress proved that it could give up power "when the collective interest of the institution and the nation are threatened by the individual interests of members."[31]

The fact that the final BRAC recommendation was a package and not scattered bills, earmarks, and riders not only allowed full public scrutiny but also shielded individual representatives from the sole responsibility of keeping their bases open. The structure gave elected officials a chance to fight for local interests within the context of national interest. There is no evidence that anyone lost an election because of a base closing. This can be studied further as a new round of base closings began in 2005.[32]

There is no getting around the fact that there are public works that must be built, repaired, and maintained. Health, education, the administration of justice, transportation, recreation, and all the other parts of public life require investment. The nature and extent of this investment should be a matter of public debate, as should the means of paying for it. None of the principal means—taxes, fees, and borrowing—enjoy great popularity, but they are necessary considerations if we are to have a public life at all.

Long-range public investment is real. It is not a luxury to be postponed until it is "affordable." It is a necessity that needs to be discussed openly, planned for carefully, and paid for fairly. To neglect it is to risk long-range peril to health, education, science, art, and economic development. To do it covertly is to risk waste. To do it haphazardly is to risk inefficiency. To do it unfairly is to risk political rebellion or the impoverishment of future generations.

The New Deal, in a very short period of time, contributed a tremendous amount to the nation's public life in the form of physical and cultural infrastructure. That investment paid dividends for many decades thereafter and in many cases is still paying back. That should be remembered in times when commitment to public life ebbs and belief rises that we simply cannot afford to invest. There was a time in our history when people found ways to combat despair by building for the future. The evidence is all around us.

Notes

Chapter 1: Public Works in American History

1. Udo Sautter, *Three Cheers for the Unemployed* (New York: Cambridge University Press, 1991), 344.

2. William J. Shultz and M. R. Caine, *Financial Development of the United States* (New York: Prentice-Hall, 1937), 98; Aaron Wildavsky, *The New Politics of the Budgetary Process* (Glenview, Ill.: Scott, Foresman, 1988), 38–42.

3. Alberta M. Sbragia, *Debt Wish: Entrepreneurial Cities, U.S. Federalism, and Economic Development* (Pittsburgh: University of Pittsburgh Press, 1996), 21–22.

4. David C. Perry, "Building the City through the Back Door: The Politics of Debt, Law, and Public Infrastructure," in *Building the Public City,* ed. David C. Perry (Thousand Oaks, Calif.: Sage, 1995), 203–4; Sbragia, *Debt Wish,* 23–24.

5. Perry, "Building the City," 203–7.

6. George F. Will, "Start Your Steamrollers," *Newsweek,* 1 March 2004, 68.

7. Perry, "Building the City," 208–10; Sbragia, *Debt Wish,* 35–42.

8. Sbragia, *Debt Wish,* 62–79; Gail Radford, "From Municipal Socialism to Public Authorities: Institutional Factors in the Shaping of American Public Enterprise," *Journal of American History* 90, no. 3 (December 2003): 872.

9. Perry, "Building the City," 210–14; Sbragia, *Debt Wish,* 59–60.

10. Laurence S. Knappen, *Revenue Bonds and the Investor* (New York: Prentice-Hall, 1939), 8–14; Perry, "Building the City," 214–16; Gail Radford, "Public Authorities and the Dilemma of New Deal Statebuilding" (paper presented at the annual meeting of the Organization of American Historians, Los Angeles, 2001); Sbragia, *Debt Wish,* 112–16.

11. Herbert Spencer, *The Man Versus the State,* ed. Donald Macrae (1884; repr., Baltimore: Penguin, 1969), 149–50, 195–233.

12. William J. Barber, *From New Era to New Deal: Herbert Hoover, the Economists, and American Economic Policy, 1921–1933* (New York: Cambridge University Press, 1985), 7–8, 13–16; Sautter, *Three Cheers,* 107–8.

13. Barber, *From New Era to New Deal,* 1–2.

14. Joan Waugh, "'Give This Man Work!' Josephine Shaw Lowell, the Charity Organization Society, and the Depression of 1893," *Social Science History* 24, no. 2 (Summer 2001): 217–46; Sautter, *Three Cheers,* 4–7, 18, 344.

15. Sautter, *Three Cheers,* 94–99.

16. Barber, *From New Era to New Deal,* 16–19.

17. John Kenneth Galbraith, *The Great Crash, 1929* (Boston: Houghton Mifflin, 1979), 128–30, 179–80.

18. Sautter, *Three Cheers,* 272.

19. J. Kerwin Williams, *Grants-in-Aid under the Public Works Administration* (1939; repr., New York: AMS Press, 1968), 11, 17–18.

20. Williams, *Grants-in-Aid,* 20.

21. *Emergency Relief and Reconstruction Act of 1933,* Public Law 302, *U.S. Statutes at Large* 47 (1933): 709; Sautter, *Three Cheers,* 308–11; Williams, *Grants-in-Aid,* 22–29.

22. *Reconstruction Finance Corporation,* Public Law 2, *U.S. Statutes at Large* 47 (1933): 5; Sbragia, *Debt Wish,* 129.

23. Williams, *Grants-in-Aid,* 232–36; Barber, *From New Era to New Deal,* 177–78; James Stuart Olson, *Herbert Hoover and the Reconstruction Finance Corporation, 1931–1933* (Ames: University of Iowa Press, 1977), 77.

24. Olson, *Herbert Hoover,* 78.

25. Williams, *Grants-in-Aid,* 33; Sautter, *Three Cheers,* 314; Olson, *Herbert Hoover,* 79; Arthur Gayner, *Public Works in Prosperity and Depression* (New York: National Bureau of Economic Research, 1935), 88.

26. Knappen, *Revenue Bonds,* 175–76.

27. Barber, *From New Era to New Deal,* 198n9.

Chapter 2: The Civilian Conservation Corps, 1933–42

1. James Russell Woods, "The Legend and Legacy of FDR and the CCC" (Ph.D. diss., Syracuse University, 1964), 22.

2. In one interesting example of the latter, the author cannot remember the name of CCC director Robert Fechner but does not bother to go look it up. He pauses in the narrative to insert a paragraph on reincarnation because "this is as good a place as any." He thoughtfully provides an index but leaves out the page numbers. However, like all the CCC memoirs, it is a wonder and a delight to read. It is also unique because the author was a camp army officer, not an enrollee. Gerald H. Reynalds, *The Woodpecker War* (Clearwater, Fla.: Gerald H. Reynalds, 1977).

3. John A. Salmond, *The Civilian Conservation Corps, 1933–1942: A New Deal Case Study* (Durham, N.C.: Duke University Press, 1967), 3.

4. Kenneth Holland and Frank Ernest Hill, *Youth in the CCC* (Washington, D.C.: American Council on Education, 1942), 12; Phoebe Cutler, *The Public Landscape of the New Deal* (New Haven, Conn.: Yale University Press, 1985), 106; Perry H. Merrill, *Roosevelt's Forest Army: A History of the Civilian Conservation Corps* (Montpelier, Vt.: Perry H. Merrill, 1981), 11, 36.

5. Salmond, *Civilian Conservation Corps,* 4.

6. Alison T. Otis, William D. Honey, Thomas C. Hogg, and Kimberly K. Larkin, *The Forest Service and the Civilian Conservation Corps* (Washington, D.C.: U.S. Department of Agriculture, 1986), 5–6; Salmond, *Civilian Conservation Corps,* 6–9; Woods, "Legend and Legacy," 4, 23–26.

7. Salmond, *Civilian Conservation Corps,* 6, 30; Woods, "Legend and Legacy," 2, 85–90.

8. *Relief of Unemployment through the Performance of Useful Public Works,* Public Law 5, *U.S. Statues at Large* 48 (1933): 22; "The Civilian Conservation Corps Is Started," Executive Order 6101, 5 April 1933," in *The Public Papers and Addresses of Franklin D. Roosevelt,* ed. Samuel I. Rosenman (New York: Random House, 1938), 2:107–8; *Civilian Conservation Corps,* Public Law 163, *U.S. Statues at Large* 50 (1937): 319; Ray Hoyt, *We Can Take It: A*

Short History of the C.C.C. (New York: American Book Company, 1935), 7–9; Salmond, *Civilian Conservation Corps,* 10, 26n1; Woods, "Legend and Legacy," 59.

9. Woods, "Legend and Legacy," 104.

10. Merrill, *Roosevelt's Forest Army,* 4; Salmond, *Civilian Conservation Corps,* 32–33.

11. Hoyt, *We Can Take It,* 29; Woods, "Legend and Legacy," 137.

12. Edwin G. Hill, *In the Shadow of the Mountain: The Spirit of the CCC* (Pullman: Washington State University Press, 1990), xvi; Salmond, *Civilian Conservation Corps,* 86; Frank Ernest Hill, *The School in the Camps: The Educational Program of the Civilian Conservation Corps* (New York: American Association for Adult Education, 1935), 66.

13. Ray Hoyt, *Your CCC: A Handbook for Enrollees* (Washington, D.C.: Happy Days Publishing, n.d.), 26, 40; Richard Melzer, *Coming of Age in the Great Depression: The Civilian Conservation Corps Experience in New Mexico, 1933–1942* (Las Cruces, N.M.: Yucca Tree Press, 2000), 25.

14. Salmond, *Civilian Conservation Corps,* 14–22; Woods, "Legend and Legacy," 71–78.

15. Conrad L. Wirth, *Parks, Politics, and People* (Norman: University of Oklahoma Press, 1980), 80–81; Salmond, *Civilian Conservation Corps,* 27–28; Woods, "Legend and Legacy," 96–101.

16. Salmond, *Civilian Conservation Corps,* 29, 73–77.

17. Ibid., 35–37.

18. Ibid., 34–35; Reed L. Engle, *Everything Was Wonderful: A Pictorial History of the Civilian Conservation Corps in Shenandoah National Park* (Luray, Va.: Shenandoah Natural History Association, 1999), 27; E. G. Hill, *In the Shadow of the Mountain,* 109.

19. Donald L. Parmam, *The Navajos and the New Deal* (New Haven, Conn.: Yale University Press, 1976), 32–37, 124, 265, 282; Salmond, *Civilian Conservation Corps,* 33–34; Garrick Bailey and Robert Glenn Bailey, *A History of the Navajos: The Reservation Years* (Santa Fe: School of American Research Press, 1986), 192.

20. Olen Cole Jr., *The African-American Experience in the Civilian Conservation Corps* (Gainesville: University Press of Florida, 1999), 14; Salmond, *Civilian Conservation Corps,* 90–91.

21. Salmond, *Civilian Conservation Corps,* 95–96; Cole, *African-American Experience,* 14–18; see Melzer, *Coming of Age,* 249–53, on Hispanics.

22. Cole, *African-American Experience,* 20–22, 42.

23. Ibid., 22; Frederick W. Stetson, "The Civilian Conservation Corps in Vermont," *Vermont History* 46, no. 1 (Winter 1978): 36; E. Kay Kiefer and Paul E. Fellows, *Hobnail Boots and Khaki Suits* (Chicago: Adams Press, 1983), 78, 108, 123; E. G. Hill, *In the Shadow of the Mountain,* 159; Reynalds, *Woodpecker War,* 36; Merrill, *Roosevelt's Forest Army,* 56.

24. Holland and Hill, *Youth in the CCC,* 112; Otis et al. *Forest Service and the CCC,* 118.

25. Michael Sherradan, "The Local Impact of the Civilian Conservation Corps, 1933–1942," *Journal of Sociology and Social Welfare* 10, no. 3 (September 1983): 519; Salmond, *Civilian Conservation Corps,* 93.

26. Cole, *African-American Experience,* 25–26; Salmond, *Civilian Conservation Corps,* 91–99.

27. Sherradan, "Local Impact," 515–18.

28. Otis et al., *Forest Service and the CCC,* 38.

29. Sherradan, "Local Impact," 519; Salmond, *Civilian Conservation Corps,* 93–94.

30. Donald Dale Jackson, "They Were Poor, Hungry, and They Built to Last," *Smithsonian* 25, no. 9 (December 1994): 66–78; Merrill, *Roosevelt's Forest Army*, 77, 101; Kiefer and Fellows, *Hobnail Boots*, 175; E. G. Hill, *In the Shadow of the Mountain*, 83, 85; Hoyt, *We Can Take It*, 82–84; Paul A. Lawrence, *Remembering the CCC* (San Anselmo, Calif.: PAL Press), 1983; Melzer, *Coming of Age*, 151–52.

31. Tamara K. Hareven, *Eleanor Roosevelt: An American Conscience* (Chicago: Quadrangle, 1968), 66–68; F. E. Hill, *School in the Camps*, 83; Dan K. Utley and James W. Steely, *Guided with a Steady Hand: The Cultural Landscape of a Rural Texas Park* (Waco, Tex.: Baylor University Press, 1998), 128; Otis et al., *Forest Service and the CCC*, 8.

32. Merrill, *Roosevelt's Forest Army*, 9.

33. Ibid., 24–28; Salmond, *Civilian Conservation Corps*, 127–28; Stetson, "CCC in Vermont," 25. Salmond reports a higher death toll: 120.

34. Salmond, *Civilian Conservation Corps*, 47; Woods, "Legend and Legacy," 98, 333–35; Harold Ickes, *The Secret Diary of Harold L. Ickes: The First Thousand Days, 1933–1936* (New York: Simon and Schuster, 1953), 79. One might think that this was a far from typical meal for the CCC boys, rather one enhanced in honor of the visiting dignitaries. However, steak appears more than once in the boys' memoirs. One said he ate a lot of steak, though it was often tough. Engle, *Everything Was Wonderful*, 49; Kiefer and Fellows, *Hobnail Boots*, 166; Louis Lester Purvis, *The Ace in the Hole: A Brief History of Company 818 of the Civilian Conservation Corps* (Columbus, Ga.: Brentwood Christian Press, 1989), 61; Roman Malach, *Home on the Range: Civilian Conservation Corps in the Kingman Area* (Kingman, Ariz.: Bureau of Land Management, 1984), 45; Melzer, *Coming of Age*, 102–7. Most thought the food was wonderful. Their praise must be considered in the context of their general malnourishment prior to enrollment. However, by most reports, the food was ample and varied in most camps.

35. Ickes, *Secret Diary*, 79–80.

36. F. E. Hill, *School in the Camps*, 8.

37. Salmond, *Civilian Conservation Corps*, 48; Merrill, *Roosevelt's Forest Army*, 19, ix; F. E. Hill, *School in the Camps*, 9.

38. Salmond, *Civilian Conservation Corps*, 48–53; F. E. Hill, *School in the Camps*, 10; Woods, "Legend and Legacy," 170.

39. F. E. Hill, *School in the Camps*, 30.

40. Salmond, *Civilian Conservation Corps*, 53.

41. Ibid.; Engle, *Everything Was Wonderful*, 52–64; Cole, *African-American Experience*, 48–50.

42. Salmond, *Civilian Conservation Corps*, 54; Woods, "Legend and Legacy," 80.

43. Salmond, *Civilian Conservation Corps*, 56.

44. Woods, "Legend and Legacy," 208–16; Salmond, *Civilian Conservation Corps*, 63.

45. Salmond, *Civilian Conservation Corps*, 64–65.

46. Ibid., 65–68.

47. Alan Brinkley, *The End of Reform: New Deal Liberalism in Recession and War* (New York: Random House, 1996), 25.

48. Salmond, *Civilian Conservation Corps*, 147–52; Woods, "Legend and Legacy," 243–50.

49. Brinkley, *End of Reform*, 19–20; Salmond, *Civilian Conservation Corps*, 157.

50. Cutler, *Public Landscape*, 96; John C. Paige, *The Civilian Construction Corps and the National Park Service* (Washington, D.C.: U.S. Department of the Interior, 1985), 34–35.

51. Brinkley, *End of Reform,* 23–28; Salmond, *Civilian Conservation Corps,* 170–71; Woods, "Legend and Legacy," 262.

52. Woods, "Legend and Legacy," 272; Salmond, *Civilian Conservation Corps,* 58–61.

53. Woods, "Legend and Legacy," 268–73; Salmond, *Civilian Conservation Corps,* 177–79.

54. Paige, *CCC and National Park Service,* 53–54, 58–59; Woods, "Legend and Legacy," 275–78; Salmond, *Civilian Conservation Corps,* 171–76; Wirth, *Parks, Politics, and People,* 138–41.

55. E. G. Hill, *In the Shadow of the Mountain,* xvi; Salmond, *Civilian Conservation Corps,* 172.

56. Salmond, *Civilian Conservation Corps,* 194–97, 209, 212.

57. E. G. Hill, *In the Shadow of the Mountain,* 136–37, 163; Merrill, *Roosevelt's Forest Army,* 64, 73, 75, 89; Kiefer and Fellows, *Hobnail Boots,* 103, 110, 162, 175, 177.

58. Jack J. Preiss, *Camp William James* (Norwich, Vt.: Argo Books, 1978); Calvin W. Gower, "Camp William James: A New Deal Blunder?" *New England Quarterly* 38, no. 1 (March 1965): 475–93; Salmond, *Civilian Conservation Corps,* 202–7.

59. Gower, "New Deal Blunder?" 487.

60. Salmond, *Civilian Conservation Corps,* 211–15; Woods, "Legend and Legacy," 329.

61. Salmond, *Civilian Conservation Corps,* 219; Woods, "Legend and Legacy," 345, 266.

62. Albert H. Good, *Park and Recreation Structures* (Washington, D.C.: Government Printing Office, 1938); W. Ellis Groben, *Acceptable Building Plans* (Washington, D.C.: USDA Forest Service, 1938).

63. Otis et al., *Forest Service and the CCC,* 119; Cutler, *Public Landscape,* 91–93.

64. Paige, *CCC and National Park Service,* 16; National Association of Civilian Conservation Corps Alumni, "Did You Know?" (St. Louis, Mo.: NACCCA, n.d.); Carroll Van West, *Tennessee's New Deal Landscape: A Guidebook* (Knoxville: University of Tennessee Press, 2001), 148–211.

65. Cutler, *Public Landscape,* 70–76; Linda McClelland, *Presenting Nature: The Historical Landscape Design of the National Park Service, 1912 to 1942* (Washington, D.C.: National Park Service, 1993), 47–251. The RDAs passed through several administrative hands. Emerging out of the FERA, they fit appropriately into the mission of the Resettlement Administration and were taken over by the NPS after the RA's demise. The WPA also provided labor to some of them.

66. Cutler, *Public Landscape,* 155; Joseph H. Engbeck Jr., *By the People, For the People: The Work of the Civilian Conservation Corps in California State Parks, 1933–1942* (Sacramento: California State Parks, 2002), 103–16.

67. Parmam, *The Navajos,* 265; Paige, *CCC and National Park Service,* 114.

68. Otis et al., *Forest Service and the CCC,* 68; Virgil Heath and John Clark Hunt, "Alaska CCC Days," *Alaska Journal* 2, no. 2 (Spring 1972): 55; Paige, *CCC and National Park Service,* 115.

69. Merrill, *Roosevelt's Forest Army,* 183; Valerie Rochon, Stowe Chamber of Commerce, telephone conversation, 26 August 2002; David D. Draves, "The Civilian Conservation Corps in New Hampshire," *Historical New Hampshire* 43, no. 2 (Summer 1988): 88–119; Paige, *CCC and National Park Service,* 118; Otis et al., *Forest Service and the CCC,* 26.

70. Jean B. Weir, "A WPA Experiment in Architecture and Crafts: Timberline Lodge" (Ph.D. diss., University of Michigan, 1977); Engle, *Everything Was Wonderful;* Harley E.

Jolley, *The Blue Ridge Parkway* (Knoxville: University of Tennessee Press, 1969); C. W. Short and R. Stanley-Brown, *Public Buildings: A Survey of Architecture Constructed by Federal and Other Public Bodies between the Years 1933 and 1939 with the Assistance of the Public Works Administration* (Washington, D.C.: Government Printing Office, 1939), 557, 338.

Chapter 3: The Public Works Administration, 1933–35

1. *National Industrial Recovery Act,* Public Law 67, *U.S. Statutes at Large* 48 (1934): 195.

2. Arthur Gayer, *Public Works in Prosperity and Depression* (1935; repr., Ann Arbor, Mich.: Xerox University Microfilms, 1976), 89; Harold Ickes, *Back to Work: The Story of the PWA* (New York: Macmillan, 1935), 56.

3. Arthur W. Macmahon, John D. Millett, and Gladys Ogden, *The Administration of Federal Work Relief* (Chicago: Public Administration Service, 1941), 21.

4. Public Works Administration, *America Builds: The Record of the PWA* (Washington, D.C.: Government Printing Office, 1939), 36–37; Jack F. Isakoff, "The Public Works Administration" (Ph.D. diss., University of Illinois, 1937), 198–99.

5. J. Kerwin Williams, *Grants-in-Aid under the Public Works Administration* (1939; repr., New York: AMS Press, 1968), 43, 49. This is the only full-length study of the PWA. It is invaluable. The Isakoff dissertation is also useful but concludes in 1937 before the last big spending program.

6. Williams, *Grants-in-Aid,* 60n5; Isakoff, "The PWA," 19; Public Works Administration, *America Builds,* 221, 26–27.

7. Williams, *Grants-in-Aid,* 61; Harold Ickes, *The Secret Diary of Harold L. Ickes: The First Thousand Days, 1933–1936* (New York: Simon and Schuster, 1953), 56.

8. There are several biographies of Harold Ickes. T. H. Watkins's *Righteous Pilgrim: The Life and Times of Harold L. Ickes, 1874–1952* (New York: Holt, 1990) is the most thorough and comprehensive. Jeanne Nienaber Clarke's *Roosevelt's Warrior: Harold L. Ickes and the New Deal* (Baltimore: Johns Hopkins University Press, 1996) is also useful. Linda J. Lear's *Harold L. Ickes: Aggressive Progressive, 1874–1933* (New York: Garland, 1980) concentrates on Ickes's pre–New Deal life. Least helpful is the Freudian psychoanalysis attempted by Graham White and John Maze, *Harold Ickes of the New Deal* (Cambridge, Mass.: Harvard University Press, 1985). I have relied most heavily here on Watkins.

9. Harold L. Ickes, *The Autobiography of a Curmudgeon* (New York: Reynal and Hitchcock, 1943), 260.

10. Raymond Moley, *After Seven Years* (New York: Harper and Bros., 1939), 127.

11. Jonathan Dembo, introduction to Arthur Goldschmidt, "The Curmudgeon: Harold Ickes," in *The Making of the New Deal: The Insiders Speak,* ed. Katie Louchheim (Cambridge, Mass.: Harvard University Press, 1983), 247.

12. Williams, *Grants-in-Aid,* 65–70; Isakoff, "The PWA," 46.

13. Williams, *Grants-in-Aid,* 71, 111; Ickes, *Back to Work,* 23–30.

14. Ickes, *Back to Work,* 47.

15. Ibid., 41–45.

16. Gayer, *Public Works in Prosperity and Depression,* 120–21; Williams, *Grants-in-Aid,* 124–26, 150.

17. Ickes, *Back to Work,* 34–35.

18. Williams, *Grants-in-Aid,* 88–90, 173–74, 188–93.

19. Public Works Administration, *America Builds,* 40.

20. Public Works Administration, "Bulletin for the Information of Staff," no. 20 (13 November 1933), Washington, D.C. (located in the Library of Congress).

21. I have read hundreds of project files in eight states and have yet to find an example of "she."

22. Ickes, *Back to Work,* 19, 66.

23. Ibid., 64–65.

24. Williams, *Grants-in-Aid,* 77.

25. Ibid., 76–81, 262; TRB, "New Year Stock-Taking," *New Republic,* 11 January 1939, 285.

26. Watkins, *Righteous Pilgrim,* 352; James McGregor Burns, *Roosevelt: The Lion and the Fox* (New York: Harcourt, Brace, 1956), 192.

27. Arthur Goldschmidt, "The Curmudgeon: Harold Ickes," in Louchheim, *The Making of the New Deal,* 248–49; Williams, *Grants-in-Aid,* 160–61.

28. Williams, *Grants-in-Aid,* 105–6.

29. Ibid., 41, 111–12; Laurence S. Knappen, *Revenue Bonds and the Investor* (New York: Prentice-Hall, 1939), 175–76.

30. Gayer, *Public Works in Prosperity and Depression,* 264–65.

31. Isakoff, "The PWA," 164; Williams, *Grants-in-Aid,* 126; Claire L. Felbinger, "Conditions of Confusion and Conflict: Rethinking the Infrastructure-Economic Development Linkage," in *Building the Public City: The Politics, Governance, and Finance of Public Infrastructure,* ed. David C. Perry, (Englewood Cliffs, N.J.: Sage, 1995), 111.

32. Williams, *Grants-in-Aid,* 231–246; Isakoff, "The PWA," 189.

33. Williams, *Grants-in-Aid,* 267–70.

Chapter 4: The Civil Works Administration, 1933–34

1. June Hopkins, *Harry Hopkins: Sudden Hero, Brash Reformer* (New York: St. Martin's Press, 1999), 15–19; Bonnie Fox Schwartz, *The Civil Works Administration, 1933–1934: The Business of Emergency Employment in the New Deal* (Princeton, N.J.: Princeton University Press, 1984), 24–25.

2. Hopkins, *Sudden Hero,* 152.

3. Schwartz, *Civil Works Administration,* 17; J. Kerwin Williams, *Grants-in-Aid under the Public Works Administration* (1939; repr., New York: AMS Press, 1968), 15n7.

4. Harry Hopkins, *Spending to Save* (New York: W. W. Norton, 1936), 87.

5. *Federal Emergency Relief Act of 1933,* Public Law 15, *U.S. Statutes at Large* 48 (1934): 55.

6. Schwartz, *Civil Works Administration,* 24; June Hopkins, *Sudden Hero,* 161.

7. Walter I. Trattner, *From Poor Law to Welfare State* (New York: Free Press, 1989), 11, 18, 273; James N. J. Henwood, "Experiment in Relief: The Civil Works Administration in Pennsylvania, 1933–1934," *Pennsylvania History* 39, no. 1 (Winter 1972): 50–51; Douglas L. Smith, *The New Deal in the Urban South* (Baton Rouge: Louisiana State University Press, 1988), 36–37; Harry Hopkins, *Spending to Save,* 66.

8. Henwood, "Experiment in Relief," 53–53; Harry Hopkins, *Spending to Save,* 76–77.

9. Arthur D. Gayer, *Public Works in Prosperity and Depression* (1935; repr., Ann Arbor, Mich.: Xerox University Microfilms, 1976), 88; Schwartz, *Civil Works Administration,* 18–22; June Hopkins, *Sudden Hero,* 159.

10. Schwartz, *Civil Works Administration,* 26–27.

11. E. Wright Bakke, *The Unemployed Worker* (New Haven, Conn.: Yale University Press, 1940); Harry Hopkins, *Spending to Save,* 100–101; Schwartz, *Civil Works Administration,* 130–31.

12. Harry Hopkins, *Spending to Save,* 104–5; George McJimsey, *Harry Hopkins: Ally of the Poor and Defender of Democracy* (Cambridge, Mass.: Harvard University Press, 1987), 56.

13. Schwartz, *Civil Works Administration,* 97; Forrest A. Walker, *The Civil Works Administration: An Experiment in Federal Work Relief* (New York: Garland Press, 1979), 27.

14. Corrington Gill, "The Civil Works Administration," in *Municipal Year Book, 1937* (Chicago: International City Managers Association, 1937), 420.

15. Harry Hopkins, "The Developing National Program of Relief," *Proceedings of the National Conference of Social Work* (Chicago: University of Chicago, 1933), 65.

16. Schwartz, *Civil Works Administration,* 34–36.

17. "White House Statement and Executive Order Creating the Civil Works Administration to Put 4,000,000 Unemployed to Work," 8 November 1933; Executive Order No. 6420B, 9 November 1933, in *The Public Papers and Addresses of Franklin D. Roosevelt,* ed. Samuel I. Rosenman (New York: Random House, 1938), 2:454–57; Walker, *Civil Works Administration: An Experiment,* 29–35.

18. Schwartz, *Civil Works Administration,* 38–42.

19. Ibid., 43; Merwin R. Swanson, "The Civil Works Administration in Idaho," *Idaho Yesterdays* 32, no. 4 (Winter 1989): 4.

20. Walker, *Civil Works Administration: An Experiment,* 72–74; Harry Hopkins, *Spending to Save,* 116–17; Schwartz, *Civil Works Administration,* 48–50.

21. Walker, *Civil Works Administration: An Experiment,* 56–57; Schwartz, *Civil Works Administration,* 46–47.

22. "Relief," *Time,* 5 February 1934, 16–17; "Relief," *Time,* 19 February 1934, 11–13.

23. Harry Hopkins, *Spending to Save,* 113–14.

24. Schwartz, *Civil Works Administration,* 132–42, 165–78; Walker, *Civil Works Administration: An Experiment,* 34, 97–103.

25. Schwartz, *Civil Works Administration,* 181.

26. "Merchandisers' Sales Big," *Wall Street Journal,* 5 January 1934; "January Setting Retail Records," *Wall Street Journal,* 27 January 1934.

27. Schwartz, *Civil Works Administration,* 214–17, 222–25; William S. Collins, *The New Deal in Arizona* (Phoenix: Arizona State Parks Board, 1999), 79; William S. Bremer, "Along the 'American Way': The New Deal's Work Relief Programs for the Unemployed," in *The New Deal: Conflicting Interpretations and Shifting Perspectives,* ed. Melvyn Dubofsky (New York: Garland, 1992), 201–19; Swanson, "Civil Works Administration in Idaho," 10.

28. Schwartz, *Civil Works Administration,* 86–95.

29. Walker, *Civil Works Administration: An Experiment,* 104–30; Schwartz, *Civil Works Administration,* 115; McJimsey, *Harry Hopkins,* 62.

30. Schwartz, *Civil Works Administration,* 219–20; June Hopkins, *Sudden Hero,* 171; Walker, *Civil Works Administration: An Experiment,* 149–54.

31. *FERA Additional Appropriation,* Public Law 93, *U.S. Statutes at Large* 48 (1934): 351.

32. Walker, *Civil Works Administration: An Experiment,* 131–35; Nancy E. Rose, *Put to Work: Relief Programs of the Great Depression* (New York: Monthly Review Press, 1994), 53–56.

33. Schwartz, *Civil Works Administration,* 243–44; Henwood, "Experiment in Relief," 62; Swanson, "Civil Works Administration in Idaho," 5.

34. Henry G. Alsberg, *America Fights the Depression* (New York: Coward-McCann, 1934).

35. Schwartz, *Civil Works Administration,* 185; Collins, *New Deal in Arizona,* 67; William Gannon, *The Civil Works Administration of Missouri: A Review,* 2d ed. (Jefferson City, Mo.: Missouri Relief and Reconstruction Commission, 1934), 36; Virgil L. Mitchell, *The Civil Works Administration in Louisiana: A Study in New Deal Relief, 1933–1934* (Lafayette: University of Southwest Louisiana, 1976), 71.

36. Mitchell, *Louisiana,* 15, 52, 57–58.

37. Margaret F. Maxwell, *A Passion for Freedom: The Life of Sharlot Hall* (Tucson: University of Arizona Press, 1982), 192–97; Marguerite Madison Aronowitz, *Art Treasures and Museums in and around Prescott, Arizona* (Prescott, Ariz.: Pine Castle Books, 2001), 105, 199–204.

38. Smoki Museum, *Annual Report, October 1, 1999 to September 30, 2000* (Prescott, Ariz.: Smoki Museum Press, 2000).

39. Arizona Hospitality Research Center, *The Economic Impact of Tourism in Prescott* (Flagstaff: Arizona State University, 1997); Jeb J. Rosebrook, "The Making of Junior Bonner," *Arizona Highways* 77, no. 6 (June 2001): 6–13.

40. Harry Hopkins, *Spending to Save,* 178.

41. Ibid., 120.

Chapter 5: The Works Progress Administration, 1935–43

1. Robert Sherwood admits to being confused himself despite the fact that he was a White House insider and knew the heads of both agencies, Harry Hopkins and Harold Ickes, well. Robert E. Sherwood, *Roosevelt and Hopkins: An Intimate Portrait* (New York: Harper and Bros., 1948), 70.

2. The term meant something quite different originally. It was coined by a scoutmaster to describe craft projects or the making of useful objects out of materials at hand. It was the opposite of waste. However, the colorful whimsy that the word conveyed overcame its practical substance and proved irresistible to the anti–New Deal forces. They successfully turned it into a widely used weapon, still popular today. Arthur Goldschmidt, "The Relief Programs and Harry Hopkins," in *The Making of the New Deal: The Insiders Speak,* ed. Katie Louchheim (Cambridge, Mass.: Harvard University Press, 1983), 192–93; John D. Millett, *The Works Progress Administration in New York City* (1938; repr., New York: Arno Press, 1978), 22n44.

3. "Engineer Group Hears Giragi," *Arizona Republic,* 9 September 1936. It is interesting to note that despite constant attacks on supposed boondoggling, *Fortune* magazine's survey in late 1936 found 54.2 percent of its respondents believed that WPA did useful work and another 22.2 percent found it "partly" useful. "The Fortune Quarterly Survey VI," *Fortune,* October 1936, 210.

4. Donald S. Howard, *The WPA and Federal Relief Policy* (New York: Russell Sage Foundation, 1943), 486–90; Searle F. Charles, *Minister of Relief: Harry Hopkins and the Depression* (Syracuse, N.Y.: Syracuse University Press, 1963), 148; "Unemployment in 1937," *Fortune,* October 1937, 188A.

5. George McJimsey, *Harry Hopkins: Ally of the Poor and Defender of Democracy* (Cambridge, Mass.: Harvard University Press, 1987), 76.

6. Ibid., 77–78.

7. Henry H. Adams, *Harry Hopkins* (New York: Putnam, 1977), 70–71.

8. Harold L. Ickes, *The Secret Diary of Harold L. Ickes: The First Thousand Days, 1933–1936* (New York: Simon and Schuster, 1953), 203; Edwin Amenta, *Bold Relief: Institutional Politics and the Origins of Modern American Social Policy* (Princeton, N.J.: Princeton University Press, 1998), xii.

9. "Annual Message to Congress," 4 January 1935, in *The Public Papers and Addresses of Franklin D. Roosevelt,* ed. Samuel I. Rosenman (New York: Random House, 1938), 4:19–20.

10. Arthur J. Altmeyer, *The Formative Years of Social Security* (Madison: University of Wisconsin Press, 1968), 12–13.

11. Arthur W. Macmahon, John D. Millett, and Gladys Ogden, *The Administration of Federal Work Relief* (1941; repr., New York: DeCapo Press, 1971), 21; June Hopkins, *Harry Hopkins: Sudden Hero, Brash Reformer* (New York: St. Martin's Press, 1999), 184; "Message to Congress Reviewing the Broad Objectives and Accomplishments of the Administration," 8 June 1934, in Rosenman, *Public Papers and Addresses,* 3:291.

12. Macmahon et al., *Administration of Federal Work Relief,* 69. Howard, *The WPA and Federal Relief Policy,* has more detail but less critical analysis.

13. Edwin Amenta and Drew Halfman, "Who Voted with Hopkins? Institutional Politics and the WPA," *Journal of Policy History* 13, no. 2 (2001).

14. Sherwood, *Roosevelt and Hopkins,* 65.

15. Adams, *Harry Hopkins,* 71–72.

16. Sherwood, *Roosevelt and Hopkins,* 1. It should be noted that he never had much of his own. His energetic public service made him poorer rather than richer: his salary throughout the New Deal and the war years was less than he had made before the Depression.

17. Sherwood, *Roosevelt and Hopkins,* 53.

18. Charles, *Minister of Relief,* 111–12; Adams, *Harry Hopkins,* 79; Macmahon et al., *Administration of Federal Work Relief,* 72.

19. *Emergency Relief Appropriations Act of 1935,* Public Resolution 11, *U.S. Statutes at Large* 49 (1936): 115.

20. *Congressional Record,* 74th Cong., 1st sess., 15 February 1935, pt. 2:2015.

21. Ibid., 2014.

22. Macmahon et al., *Administration of Federal Work Relief,* 30–34.

23. Ibid., 41–43.

24. Howard, *WPA and Federal Relief Policy,* 351–79.

25. Ickes, *Secret Diary,* 248; Howard, *WPA and Federal Relief Policy,* 490–513.

26. Howard, *WPA and Federal Relief Policy,* 150–53. The contractors were not frozen out entirely; they made money from WPA by renting equipment.

27. Macmahon et al., *Administration of Federal Work Relief,* 74; Sherwood, *Roosevelt and Hopkins,* 71; "Three White House Statements Outlining the Machinery for Handling the Four-Billion-Dollar Works Relief Appropriation," 23, 25, 26 April 1935, in Rosenman, *Public Papers and Addresses,* 4:128; "The Creation of Machinery for the Works Progress Administration," Executive Order 7034, 6 May 1935, in Rosenman, *Public Papers and Addresses,* 4:163–66.

28. In the earlier press conference, the language was "*very* small projects" that could be completed in a "very short space of time" (emphasis added).

29. Macmahon et al., *Administration of Federal Work Relief,* 76–77; Sherwood, *Roosevelt and Hopkins,* 69.

30. Macmahon et al., *Administration of Federal Work Relief,* 90–100. Fortunately, the experience was not fatal for Walker. He returned to public life, serving as postmaster general from 1940 to 1945 and head of the Democratic National Committee for two of those years. He died in 1959.

31. Charles, *Minister of Relief,* 123; Adams, *Harry Hopkins,* 82.

32. Sherwood, *Roosevelt and Hopkins,* 69.

33. Ickes, *Secret Diary,* 348; Macmahon et al., *Administration of Federal Work Relief,* 109–10.

34. Macmahon et al., *Administration of Federal Work Relief,* 114.

35. Ibid., 115–16; Ickes, *Secret Diary,* 222.

36. James S. Olson, ed., *Historical Dictionary of the New Deal* (Westport, Conn.: Greenwood Press, 1985), 254–55.

37. Macmahon et al., *Administration of Federal Work Relief,* 118–20; McJimsey, *Harry Hopkins: Ally,* 81.

38. Macmahon et al., *Administration of Federal Work Relief,* 211–15.

39. McJimsey, *Harry Hopkins: Ally,* 84; J. Kerwin Williams, *Grants-in-Aid under the Public Works Administration* (1939; repr., New York: AMS Press, 1968), 137–39; Sherwood, *Roosevelt and Hopkins,* 78; Adams, *Harry Hopkins,* 83.

40. McJimsey, *Harry Hopkins: Ally,* 85–86; Ickes, *Secret Diary,* 426–28, 434.

41. Macmahon et al., *Administration of Federal Work Relief,* 121–26.

42. Sherwood, *Roosevelt and Hopkins,* 78; Adams, *Harry Hopkins,* 85; McJimsey, *Harry Hopkins: Ally,* 85; Ickes, *Secret Diary,* 436–37.

43. Macmahon et al., *Administration of Federal Work Relief,* 313–14; Amenta, *Bold Relief,* 129; Federal Works Agency, *Final Report on the WPA Program, 1935–1943* (Washington, D.C.: Government Printing Office, 1946), 100; Howard, *WPA and Federal Relief Policy,* 145–50.

44. *First Deficiency Appropriations Act of 1936,* Public Law 739, *U.S. Statutes at Large* 49 (1936): 1599.

45. Macmahon et al., *Administration of Federal Work Relief,* 46, 170–71; Howard, *WPA and Federal Relief Policy,* 107–8.

46. *Congressional Record* 86 (14 June 1940): 12588.

47. Macmahon et al., *Administration of Federal Work Relief,* 168–71; Alan Brinkley, *The End of Reform: New Deal Liberalism in Recession and War* (New York: Vintage, 1999), 20.

48. Charles, *Minister of Relief,* 136; Sherwood, *Roosevelt and Hopkins,* 78; Adams, *Harry Hopkins,* 75; McJimsey, *Harry Hopkins: Ally,* 89–90.

49. McJimsey, *Harry Hopkins: Ally,* 89, places this feature in the ERRA of 1936, but it was in the original 1935 legislation. Macmahon et al., *Administration of Federal Work Relief,* 269; Adams, *Harry Hopkins,* 77–78; Howard, *WPA and Federal Relief Policy,* 113–14.

50. Adams, *Harry Hopkins,* 102–4; Howard, *WPA and Federal Relief Policy,* 116–18, 301–3.

51. Harnett T. Kane, *Louisiana Hayride: The American Rehearsal for Dictatorship, 1928–1940* (1941; repr., Gretna, La.: Pelican Press, 1971), 268–71.

52. Hodding Carter, "Kingfish to Crawfish," *New Republic,* 24 January 1934, 303.

53. Sherwood, *Roosevelt and Hopkins,* 68, 98.

54. Federal Works Agency, *Final Report,* 81, 83; Macmahon et al., *Administration of Federal Work Relief,* 238.

55. Elizabeth Wickenden, "The Relief Programs and Harry Hopkins," in Louchheim, *Making of the New Deal,* 180; Elizabeth Wickenden, oral history transcript, Wisconsin State Historical Society, box 16, folder 3, 1986–87, 19; Roger Biles, *A New Deal for the American People* (DeKalb: Northern Illinois University Press, 1991), 106; Macmahon et al., *Administration of Federal Work Relief,* 287.

56. Millett, *Works Progress Administration in New York City,* 49–51, 96.

57. Macmahon et al., *Administration of Federal Work Relief,* 282–87; Charles, *Minister of Relief,* 198.

58. Macmahon et al., *Administration of Federal Work Relief,* 290; Hallie Flanagan, *Arena: The Story of the Federal Theater* (1940; repr., New York: B. Blom, 1965); Howard, *WPA and Federal Relief Policy,* 119–20, 318–24.

59. Charles, *Minister of Relief,* 173; McJimsey, *Harry Hopkins: Ally,* 110–11; Howard, *WPA and Federal Relief Policy,* 587–93.

60. Harry Hopkins, *Spending to Save* (New York: W. W. Norton, 1936), 120.

61. Macmahon et al., *Administration of Federal Work Relief,* 273.

62. Ibid., 291.

63. Adams, *Harry Hopkins,* 117–19; Brinkley, *End of Reform,* 28.

64. Brinkley, *End of Reform,* 28–30.

65. Ibid., 75–77, 82.

66. "Recommendations to Congress Designed to Stimulate Further Recovery," 14 April 1938, in Rosenman, *Public Papers and Addresses,* 7:231–32; Amenta, *Bold Relief,* 125–26; Brinkley, *End of Reform,* 100.

67. Macmahon et al., *Administration of Federal Work Relief* (1941), 57–58, 128–29, 135.

68. "The President Presents Plan No. 1 to Carry Out the Provisions of the Reorganization Act," 25 April 1939, in Rosenman, *Public Papers and Addresses* (1941), 8:245–71.

69. Macmahon et al., *Administration of Federal Work Relief,* 59, 135–36.

70. Janet R. Daly Bednarek, *America's Airports: Airfield Development, 1918–1947* (College Park: Texas A&M Press, 2001).

71. Don Boxmeyer, "Pearl Harbor Counterstrike Was Aided Here," *St. Paul Pioneer Press,* 2 June 2001.

72. Noel E. Allard and Gerald N. Sandvick, *Minnesota Aviation History, 1857–1945* (Chaska, Minn.: MHAB Press, 1993), 127–28, 136–37, 227–31.

73. Amenta and Halfman, "Who Voted with Hopkins?" 263–64; McJimsey, *Harry Hopkins: Ally,* 114; Amenta, *Bold Relief,* 219–25.

74. Louis Lomax, *San Antonio River* (San Antonio, Tex.: Naylor, 1948); Green Peyton, *San Antonio: City in the Sun* (New York: McGraw-Hill, 1946), 188–89, 194–202; Charles Ramsdell, *San Antonio: A Historical and Pictorial Guide* (Austin: University of Texas Press, 1958).

75. *San Antonio: 2003–2004 Visitor Profile* (San Antonio, Tex.: San Antonio Convention and Visitors Bureau, 2005).

76. J. Lyles, *Direct Dollar Impact of Livestock Shows and Events* (Baton Rouge, La.: East Baton Rouge Parish Chamber of Commerce, 1995).

77. Jean B. Weir, "A WPA Experiment in Architecture and Crafts: Timberline Lodge" (Ph.D. diss., University of Michigan, 1977), viii–ix; Phoebe Cutler, *The Public Landscape of the New Deal* (New Haven, Conn.: Yale University Press, 1985), 153; Jon Tillis, Timberline Lodge Public Relations Department, personal communication, 3 January 2002.

78. Cutler, *Public Landscape,* 43.

79. Florence Christman, *The Romance of Balboa Park* (San Diego, Calif.: San Diego Historical Society, 1985).

80. *UTEC, University Technology Center: Where Businesses Start and Grow,* pamphlet, (Minneapolis: University Technology Center, n.d.).

81. Cutler, *Public Landscape,* 22.

82. Donald L. Parman, *The Navajos and the New Deal* (New Haven, Conn.: Yale University Press, 1976), 225.

83. Cutler, *Public Landscape,* 10–11; Dave Michaels, "City's Parks Have a Story to Tell," *Dallas Morning News,* 30 October 2001.

Chapter 6: The Public Works Administration, 1935–42

1. J. Kerwin Williams, *Grants-in-Aid under the Public Works Administration* (1939; repr., New York: AMS Press, 1968), 132; Harold L. Ickes, *The Secret Diary of Harold L. Ickes: The First Thousand Days, 1933–1936* (New York: Simon and Schuster, 1953), 383, 433–38.

2. Williams, *Grants-in-Aid,* 52–55.

3. Upjohn Institute for Employment Research, *Public Works and Employment from the Local Government Point of View* (Chicago: Public Administration Service, 1955), 98–99.

4. Williams, *Grants-in-Aid,* 133n60.

5. Ibid., 149n99.

6. Ibid., 99–100.

7. Ickes, *Secret Diary,* 27.

8. Ibid., 616.

9. Williams, *Grants-in-Aid,* 127–28, 270; Ickes, *Secret Diary,* 267–69, 291, 317.

10. Raymond A. Moley, *The First New Deal* (New York: Harcourt, Brace and World, 1966), 327; James A. Farley, *Behind the Ballots: The Personal History of a Politician* (New York: Harcourt, Brace, 1938), 250; Anthony J. Badger, "Huey Long and the New Deal," in *Nothing to Fear: New Perspectives on America in the Thirties,* ed. Stephen W. Baskerville and Ralph Willets (Manchester, Eng.: Manchester University Press, 1985), 83–86; Betty Marie Field, "The Politics of the New Deal in Louisiana, 1933–1939" (Ph. D. diss., Tulane University, 1973), 39, 114–15, 132–37.

11. Hodding Carter, "Kingfish to Crawfish," *New Republic,* 24 January 1934, 303; Robert D. Leighninger Jr., *Community Assets: The Legacy of the Public Works Administration in Louisiana* (Jackson: University Press of Mississippi, forthcoming 2007).

12. Williams, *Grants-in-Aid,* 260–61.

13. Ibid., 96n83; Jack F. Isakoff, "The Public Works Administration" (Ph.D. diss., University of Illinois, 1937), 107.

14. Isakoff, "The PWA," 297; C. W. Short and R. Stanley-Brown, *Public Buildings: A Survey of Architecture Constructed by Federal and Other Public Bodies between the Years 1933 and 1939 with the Assistance of the Public Works Administration* (Washington, D.C.:

Government Printing Office, 1939), 670. The number of questionnaires sent out was not reported.

15. Fred L. Hargett, Report to the Director, Inspections Division, 7 July 1937, reel 5958, docket 1008, RG 135, Microfilm Records of the Public Works Administration, National Archives II, College Park, Md. (referred to hereafter as PWA Microfilm).

16. Arthur J. Bulger, memo from the director of the PWA Engineering Division, 26 July 1937, reel 5960, docket 1030, PWA Microfilm.

17. Fred L. Hargett, special report, 18 July 1937, reel 5787, docket 1077, PWA Microfilm.

18. John M. Whitney to L. L. Kilgore, 20 December 1938, reel 5831, docket 1317, PWA Microfilm.

19. Public Works Administration, *America Builds: The Record of the PWA* (Washington, D.C.: Government Printing Office, 1939), 132–34.

20. "The President Presents Plan No. 1 to Carry Out the Provisions of the Reorganization Act," 25 April 1939, in *The Public Papers and Addresses of Franklin D. Roosevelt,* ed. Samuel I. Rosenman (New York: Random House, 1938), 8:245–71; Williams, *Grants-in-Aid,* 285–87.

21. Jason Scott Smith, "Public Works and the Postwar World: The Legacies of New Deal Public Works Programs, 1943–1956" (paper presented at the Policy History Conference, St. Louis, Mo., 2002), 8. See also Jason Scott Smith, *Building New Deal Liberalism: The Political Economy of Public Works, 1933–1956* (New York: Cambridge University Press, 2005).

22. "List of All Allotted Non-Federal Projects, All Programs, by State and Docket, as of May 30, 1942," Federal Works Agency, Public Works Administration, entry A1, no. 59, RG 135, National Archives II, College Park, Md. (referred to hereafter as 1942 Status Report), 109–18.

23. Ibid.

24. Ibid.

25. Ibid., 9–18.

26. Public Works Administration, *America Builds,* 25.

27. 1942 Status Report, 9–18.

28. Steven R. Strom, "A Legacy of Civic Pride: Houston's PWA Buildings," *Houston Review* 17, no. 2 (1995): 103–21; 1942 Status Report, 162–91.

29. 1942 Status Report, 4–6; Phyllis Ball, *A Photographic History of the University of Arizona, 1885–1985* (Tucson, Ariz.: privately printed, 1986), 171, 206–11; Short and Stanley-Brown, *Public Buildings,* 151, 322, 338–41, 644; see also William S. Collins, *The New Deal in Arizona* (Phoenix: Arizona State Parks Board, 1999).

30. Public Works Administration, *America Builds,* 252–55; 1942 Status Report, 181–87.

31. Leighninger, *Community Assets,* 122–40.

32. Leighninger, *Community Assets,* 97–121.

33. Incredibly, they seem unaware of any of the many New Deal contributions to their fair city. They conclude that "most of the new federal programs for municipalities involved relief and jobs for the distressed and left no physical mark on the city." Harold M. Mayer and Richard C. Wade, *Chicago: Growth of a Metropolis* (Chicago: University of Chicago Press, 1969), 364.

34. Ickes, *Secret Diary,* 37–38. It was, however, called "Hoover Dam" in the *Emergency Relief and Reconstruction Act of 1933,* Public Law 302, *U.S. Statutes at Large* 47 (1933): 717.

35. Gerald D. Nash, *The Federal Landscape: An Economic History of the Twentieth-Century West* (Tucson: University of Arizona Press, 1999), 24–26, 45, 146; Short and Stanley-Brown, *Public Buildings,* 507–26; Public Works Administration, *America Builds,* 116–20.

36. Public Works Administration, *America Builds,* 259–61.

37. Short and Stanley-Brown, *Public Buildings,* 610–11, 614–15, 622; Phoebe Cutler, *The Public Landscape of the New Deal* (New Haven, Conn.: Yale University Press, 1985), 22.

38. "Federal and Non-Federal Projects Approved during the Period from September 1 to September 8 Inclusive," 2 October 1933, box Y690, Publications of the U.S. Government, RG 287, National Archives II, College Park, Md.; memo, 10 April 1934, Navy Department, Bureau of Construction, Repairs, and Engineering, Washington, D.C., entry 35, Correspondence Relating to Federal Projects, 1934–1941, box 3, RG 135, National Archives II, College Park, Md.

39. Public Works Administration, *America Builds,* 8.

Chapter 7: The Tennessee Valley Authority, 1933–

1. C. Herman Pritchett, *The Tennessee Valley Authority: A Study in Public Administration* (Chapel Hill: University of North Carolina Press, 1943), 3.

2. David E. Lilienthal, *TVA: Democracy on the March* (New York: Pocket Books, 1945).

3. "TVA I: Work in the Valley," *Fortune,* May 1935, 93, reprinted in *James Agee: Selected Journalism,* ed. Paul Ashdown (Knoxville: University of Tennessee Press, 1985), 63–96.

4. *National Defense Act,* Public Law 85, *U.S. Statutes at Large* 39 (1917): 166; Paul K. Conkin, "Intellectual and Political Roots," in *TVA: Fifty Years of Grass-Roots Bureaucracy,* ed. Edwin C. Hargrove and Paul K. Conkin (Urbana: University of Illinois Press, 1983), 10–13; Pritchett, *TVA,* 13–14.

5. Walter L. Creese, *TVA's Public Planning: The Vision, the Reality* (Knoxville: University of Tennessee Press, 1990), 28–31; North Callahan, *TVA: Bridge over Troubled Waters* (New York: A. S. Barnes, 1980), 24–26; Pritchett, *TVA,* 8–9.

6. George W. Norris, *Fighting Liberal: The Autobiography of George W. Norris* (New York: Macmillan, 1945), 156–61; Richard Lowitt, "A Neglected Aspect of the Progressive Movement: George W. Norris and Public Control of Hydroelectric Power, 1913–1919," *The Historian* 27, no. 3 (May 1965): 350–65.

7. Norris, *Fighting Liberal,* 246.

8. Conkin, "Intellectual and Political Roots," 17. See also Preston J. Hubbard, *Origins of the TVA: The Muscle Shoals Controversy, 1920–1932* (Nashville: Vanderbilt University Press, 1961.

9. Carroll Van West, *Tennessee's New Deal Landscape: A Guidebook* (Knoxville: University of Tennessee Press, 2001), 213.

10. "TVA I," 148.

11. Pritchett, *TVA,* 34, 43.

12. Conkin, "Intellectual and Political Roots," 22–23.

13. "A Suggestion for Legislation to Create the Tennessee Valley Authority," 10 April 1933, in *The Public Papers and Addresses of Franklin D. Roosevelt,* ed. Samuel I. Rosenman (New York: Random House, 1938), 2:122.

14. Quoted in Callahan, *Bridge,* 61.

15. *Tennessee Valley Authority Act of 1933,* Public Law 14, *U.S. Statutes at Large* 48 (1934): 58.

16. Ibid., 69.

17. Conkin, "Intellectual and Political Roots," 30–31; Creese, *TVA's Public Planning,* 285.

18. Callahan, *Bridge,* 90–95; Edwin C. Hargrove, "The Task of Leadership: The Board Chairman," in Hargrove and Conkin, *TVA: Fifty Years,* 92. See also Roy Talbert, *FDR's Utopian: Arthur Morgan of the TVA* (Jackson: University Press of Mississippi, 1987).

19. Hargrove, "Task of Leadership," 90–93; Pritchett, *TVA,* 149–50; Conkin, "Intellectual and Political Roots," 31.

20. Hargrove, "Task of Leadership," 98–101; Richard Lowitt, "TVA, 1933–1945," in Hargrove and Conkin, *TVA: Fifty Years,* 39; Callahan, *Bridge,* 96–97. See also Steven M. Neuse, *David E. Lilienthal: The Journal of an American Liberal* (Knoxville: University of Tennessee Press, 1996).

21. Hargrove, "Task of Leadership," 95–98; Lowitt, "TVA, 1933–1945," 39–40; Callahan, *Bridge,* 40; Creese, *TVA's Public Planning,* 156–57.

22. Richard Lowitt and Maurine Beasley, eds., *One Third of a Nation: Lorena Hickok Reports the Great Depression* (Urbana: University of Illinois Press, 1983), 269.

23. "TVA I," 153.

24. Creese, *TVA's Public Planning,* 162–64; Cincinnati (Ohio) Chamber of Commerce and Merchants Exchange, *The Cincinnati Union Terminal Station: A Pictorial History* (Cincinnati: Chamber of Commerce, 1933). This glorious combination of art, architecture, craft, and engineering is still standing and now houses a complex of museums.

25. John H. Kyle, *The Building of TVA: An Illustrated History* (Baton Rouge: Louisiana State University Press, 1958), 58–59; Julian Huxley, *TVA: Adventure in Planning* (Cheam, Surrey, U.K.: Architectural Press, 1943), 74.

26. Huxley, *Adventure,* 76; Creese, *TVA's Public Planning,* 168–79, 237–38; Callahan, *Bridge,* 33; Kyle, *Illustrated History,* 23, 27, 31.

27. Lewis Mumford, "The Architecture of Power," *New Yorker,* 7 July 1941, 60.

28. Talbott Hamlin, "Architecture of the TVA," *Pencil Points,* November 1939, 721–22; Kenneth Reid, "Design in TVA Structures," *Pencil Points,* November 1939, 691.

29. Mumford, "Architecture of Power," 60; Reid, "Design in TVA Structures," 703; Hamlin, "Architecture of the TVA," 724.

30. West, *Tennessee's New Deal Landscape,* 222–23.

31. English Garden Cities, discussed in chapter 9, had twelve per acre.

32. Kyle, *Illustrated History,* 15–21; Creese, *TVA's Public Planning,* 240–63; Callahan, *Bridge,* 30–39; West, *Tennessee's New Deal Landscape,* 221–26.

33. "TVA I," 142; Callahan, *Bridge,* 31. This anecdote inspired a 1960 Hollywood movie, *Wild River,* directed by Elia Kazan with Montgomery Clift as the TVA agent and Jo Van Fleet as the widow.

34. Callahan, *Bridge,* 31, 49; "TVA I," 142; West, *Tennessee's New Deal Landscape,* 226; Phoebe Cutler, *The Public Landscape of the New Deal* (New Haven, Conn.: Yale University Press, 1985), 136.

35. Kyle, *Illustrated History,* 108–18; Elizabeth Mock, *The Architecture of Bridges* (New York: Museum of Modern Art, 1949).

36. Creese, *TVA's Public Planning,* 244–46; Callahan, *Bridge,* 43–44.

37. Cutler, *Public Landscape,* 138; Callahan, *Bridge,* 35; Creese, *TVA's Public Planning,* 258–59; "TVA I," 142.

38. Hargrove, "Task of Leadership," 93; Creese, *TVA's Public Planning,* 279.

39. Pritchett, *TVA,* 185–211; Callahan, *Bridge,* 90–112; Lowitt, "TVA, 1933–1945," 44–46; see also Arthur E. Morgan, *The Making of the TVA* (Buffalo, N.Y.: Prometheus Books, 1974); Thomas K. McCraw, *Morgan vs. Lilienthal: The Feud within the TVA* (Chicago: Loyola University Press, 1970).

40. "TVA II: The Power Issue," *Fortune* (May 1935): 154–59.

41. Lowitt, "TVA, 1933–1945," 36, 42; "TVA II," 98, 167.

42. "TVA II," 160; Lowitt, "TVA, 1933–1945," 41–44; Callahan, *Bridge,* 53–65, 139–40. See also Scott Henderson, *Power and the Public Interest: the Memoirs of Joseph C. Swidler* (Knoxville: University of Tennessee Press, 2002).

43. *U.S. v. Appalachian Electrical Power Co.,* 311 U.S. 377; *Oklahoma v. Atkinson Co.,* 311 U.S. 508.

44. Lowitt, "TVA, 1933–1945," 43–44, 61; Callahan, *Bridge,* 62–63; Dewey W. Grantham, "TVA and the Ambiguity of Reform," in Hargrove and Conkin, *TVA: Fifty Years,* 324.

45. Nancy J. Grant, *TVA and Black Americans: Planning for the Status Quo* (Philadelphia, Pa.: Temple University Press, 1990); "TVA I," 145–46; Lowitt, "TVA, 1933–1945," 58–61; Callahan, *Bridge,* 33, 94.

46. Callahan, *Bridge,* 33; Philip Selznick, *TVA and the Grass Roots* (New York: Harper and Row, 1966), 112–14.

47. Callahan, *Bridge,* quote from Morgan's unpublished 1910 diary, 94.

48. Cutler, *Public Landscape,* 143–44; Lowitt, "TVA, 1933–1945," 50; "TVA I," 148.

49. Callahan, *Bridge,* 327–29. Nancy L. Grant, *TVA and Black Americans: Planning for the Status Quo* (Philadelphia: Temple University Press, 1990), 37–44.

50. Lowitt, "TVA, 1933–1945," 50; Callahan, *Bridge,* 336–37.

51. Lowitt, "TVA, 1933–1945," 49; Callahan, *Bridge,* 82–83.

52. Lowitt, "TVA, 1933–1945," 53; Mumford, "Architecture of Power," 60.

53. Hamlin, "Architecture of the TVA," 732; Arthur M. Schlesinger Jr., "Sources of the New Deal: Reflections on the Temper of a Time," in *The New Deal: The Critical Issues,* ed. Otis L. Graham Jr. (Boston: Little, Brown, 1971), 108–21.

54. Grantham, "TVA and the Ambiguity of Reform," 316; Creese, *TVA's Public Planning,* 176; Lowitt, "The TVA, 1933–45," 53.

Chapter 8: Housing

1. Edith Elmer Wood, "The Cost of Bad Housing," in "Current Developments in Housing," ed. David T. Rowlands and Coleman Woodbury, *Annals of the American Academy of Political and Social Science* 190 (March 1937): 145; Catherine Bauer, *Modern Housing* (Boston: Houghton Mifflin, 1934), 79–80; 71–87; Mark Swenarton, *Homes Fit for Heroes: The Politics and Architecture of Early Estate Housing in Britain* (London: Heinemann, 1981), 27–28, 71–87.

2. Helen Searing, "Housing in Holland and the Amsterdam School" (Ph.D. diss., Yale University, 1971); Nancy Stieber, *Housing Design and Society in Amsterdam: Reconfiguring Urban Order and Identity, 1900–1920* (Chicago: University of Chicago Press, 1998); Barbara Lane Miller, *Architecture and Politics in Germany, 1918–1945* (Cambridge, Mass.: Harvard University Press, 1968), 88–124; Arie Keppler, "Housing in the Netherlands," in Rowlands and Woodbury, "Current Developments," 205–13; Judith Robinson, Laura Bobeczko, Paul

Lusignan, and Jeffrey Shrimpton, *Public Housing in the United States, 1933–1949: A Historic Context* (Washington, D.C.: National Register of Historic Places, 1999), 2:8–9.

3. Daniel T. Rogers, *Atlantic Crossings: Social Politics in a Progressive Age* (Cambridge, Mass.: Harvard University Press, 1998), 194–98. Two decades later, when Catherine Bauer, a young American, brought these ideas to the United States through magazine articles and the 1934 book *Modern Housing,* they would receive a warmer reception (ibid., 392–404).

4. Gwendolyn Wright, *Building the Dream: A Social History of Housing in America* (Cambridge, Mass.: MIT Press, 1981), 58–64, 177–84; Deveraux Bowley Jr., *The Poorhouse: Subsidized Housing in Chicago, 1895–1976* (Carbondale: Southern Illinois Press, 1978), 1–6; Rogers, *Atlantic Crossings,* 194; Jacob Riis, *How the Other Half Lives* (1890; repr., New York: Hill and Wang, 1957), 203–26; Gail Radford, *Modern Housing for America: Policy Struggles in the New Deal Era* (Chicago: University of Chicago Press, 1996), 23–24, 29–31.

5. Wright, *Building the Dream,* 58–66, 177–84; Swenarton, *Homes Fit for Heroes,* 5–9; Walter Stranz, *George Cadbury, 1839–1922* (Aylesbury, Eng.: Shire Publications, 1973); Stanley Buder, *Pullman: An Experiment in Industrial Order and Community Planning, 1880–1930* (New York: Oxford University Press, 1967). Seeing the company town as an extension of the industrialist's ego did not start with Pullman. English tycoons Titus Salt and George Cadbury also named their towns after themselves. Margaret Crawford, *Building the Workingman's Paradise: The Design of American Company Towns* (London: Verso, 1995).

6. Radford, *Modern Housing for America,* 14–15; *Federal Farm Loan Act,* Public Law 158, *U.S. Statutes at Large* 39 (1917): 360.

7. Rogers, *Atlantic Crossings,* 286–90.

8. Radford, *Modern Housing for America,* 8, 19–21; Robinson et al., *Public Housing in the U.S.,* 10–11; Rogers, *Atlantic Crossings,* 197.

9. Radford, *Modern Housing for America,* 24; Arnold R. Hirsh, *Making the Second Ghetto: Race and Housing in Chicago, 1940–1960* (New York: Cambridge University Press, 1983); Edgar O. Olsen, "A Competitive Theory of the Housing Market," in *Housing Urban America,* ed. Jon Pynoos, Robert Schafer, and Chester Hartman, 2d ed. (Chicago: Aldine, 1980), 234–44; Richard P. Applebaum and John I. Gilderbloom, "Supply-Side Economics and Rents: Are Rental Housing Markets Truly Competitive?" in *Critical Perspectives on Housing,* ed. Rachael G. Bratt, Chester Hartman, and Ann Meyerson (Philadelphia, Pa.: Temple University Press, 1986), 167.

10. Radford, *Modern Housing for America,* 47–53, 87; Michael W. Straus and Talbot Wegg, *Housing Comes of Age* (New York: Oxford University Press, 1938), 23; Federal Emergency Administration for Public Work, *Urban Housing: The Story of the PWA Housing Division, 1933–1936,* bulletin 2 (Washington, D.C: Government Printing Office, 1936), 14–15.

11. *National Industrial Recovery Act,* Public Law 67, title 2, sec. 202, *U.S. Statutes at Large* 48 (1934): 201.

12. Straus and Wegg, *Housing Comes of Age,* 33–34; Radford, *Modern Housing for America,* 89–91.

13. Roger Biles, "Nathan Straus and the Failure of U.S. Public Housing, 1937–1942," *The Historian* 53, no. 1 (Winter 1990): 35.

14. Straus and Wegg, *Housing Comes of Age,* 34; Radford, *Modern Housing for America,* 92.

15. Miles L. Colean, *American Housing: Problems and Prospects; The Factual Findings* (New York: Twentieth Century Fund, 1944), 276; Radford, *Modern Housing for America,* 92.

16. Warren Jay Vinton, "A Survey of Approaches to the Housing Problem," in Rowlands and Woodbury, "Current Developments," 11.

17. Federal Emergency Administration for Public Works, *Urban Housing,* 28–30.

18. Straus and Wegg, *Housing Comes of Age,* 35–36.

19. Ibid., 38–39.

20. Ibid., 40–47; Stieber, *Housing Design and Society,* appendix, "Housing Projects Approved by the Amsterdam Municipal Council from 1908 to 1919, 269–79"; Radford, *Modern Housing for America,* 93–95.

21. Straus and Wegg, *Housing Comes of Age,* 124–25.

22. Radford, *Modern Housing for America,* 101.

23. Ibid., 102.

24. Federal Emergency Administration for Public Works, *Urban Housing,* 47.

25. Straus and Wegg, *Housing Comes of Age,* 98–102.

26. Radford, *Modern Housing for America,* 102–3; Straus and Wegg, *Housing Comes of Age,* 62, 84–90.

27. Straus and Wegg, *Housing Comes of Age,* 115.

28. *Emergency Relief Appropriations Act of 1935,* Public Resolution 11, *U.S. Statutes at Large* 49 (1936): 115; Straus and Wegg, *Housing Comes of Age,* 122–23, 128–30; Harold L. Ickes, *The Secret Diary of Harold L. Ickes: The First Thousand Days, 1933–1936* (New York: Simon and Schuster, 1953), 436; Colean, *American Housing,* 277.

29. "U.S. Housing Manual," *Fortune,* June 1935, 79; Straus and Wegg, *Housing Comes of Age,* 121.

30. *Architectural Record* 77 (March 1935): 148–74.

31. Straus and Wegg, *Housing Comes of Age,* 74–75.

32. Ibid., 71; Richard Pommer, "The Architecture of the Urban United States in the Early 1930s," *Journal of Architecture History* 37 (December 1978): 262–63. Pommer singles out Mackley Houses, Lakeview Terrace, and Harlem River Houses for this accolade. He sees the housing division becoming too rigid in what it would approve by 1935 to allow truly creative designs toward the end of the program and is even more critical of USHA efforts like Red Hook, described later in this chapter.

33. Colean, *American Housing,* 277.

34. Radford, *Modern Housing for America,* 97.

35. Larry Keating and Carol A. Flores, "Sixty and Out: Techwood Homes Transformed by Enemies and Friends," *Journal of Urban History* 26, no. 3 (March 2000): 275; Julie Stoiber, "Historic Apartments' New Future: The Carl Mackley Houses, Popular for Many Decades, Have Undergone a Revival," *Philadelphia Inquirer,* 25 June 1999.

36. Simon Brienes, "Uncle Sam Clears a Slum: A Comparison of the Administration's Claims and Accomplishments in Slum Clearance and Re-Housing," *Social Work Today* 4 (March 1937): 7–8; Rev. Edward Roberts Moore, "Much Ado About Housing," *Saturday Evening Post,* 10 June 1939, 115, 118; "U.S. Housing Manual," 177–78.

37. Radford, *Modern Housing for America,* 104; Robert D. Leighninger Jr., *Community Assets: The Legacy of the Public Works Administration in Louisiana* (Jackson: University Press of Mississippi, forthcoming 2007).

38. Radford, *Modern Housing for America,* 104.

39. *National Housing Act,* Public Law 479, *U.S. Statutes at Large* 48 (1934): 1246; Straus and Wegg, *Housing Comes of Age,* 126–27; Radford, *Modern Housing for America,* 193.

40. Radford, *Modern Housing for America*, 184–86; Biles, "Nathan Straus," 35.

41. Radford, *Modern Housing for America*, 186–87; Biles, "Nathan Straus," 35–36.

42. *U.S. Housing Act of 1937*, Public Law 412, *U.S. Statutes at Large* 50 (1937): 888; David T. Rowlands, "Urban Housing Activities of the Federal Government," in Rowlands and Woodbury, "Current Developments," 87–88; Radford, *Modern Housing for America*, 190–93; Rachel G. Bratt, "Public Housing: The Controversy and Contribution," in Bratt, Hartman, and Meyerson, *Critical Perspectives*, 337. There are also those who believe that modernist architecture itself is inhumane and stigmatizing. This ignores the fact that many affluent families live by choice in high-rise modernist apartments. However, they have decent-sized rooms, functioning utilities, and doormen. See Peter Blake, *Form Follows Fiasco: Why Modern Architecture Hasn't Worked* (Boston: Little, Brown and Co., 1977), 79, 123–24; Robert D. Leighninger Jr., "Ornament and Amenity: The Role of Aesthetics in Housing Satisfaction," (paper presented at the International Research Conference on Housing, Policy, and Urban Innovation, Amsterdam, the Netherlands, 1988).

43. Wright, *Building the Dream*, 227.

44. Biles, "Nathan Straus," 36–38.

45. Radford, *Modern Housing for America*, 192; Biles, "Nathan Straus," 39–41, 45; Pommer, "Architecture of the Urban U.S.," 256. The skip-stop elevator idea was repeated in the notorious Pruitt-Igoe project built in St. Louis in 1954, where a combination of design, budget, and policy failures contributed to deterioration so devastating that the buildings had to be dynamited. Katherine G. Bristol, "The Pruitt-Igoe Myth," *Journal of Architectural Education* 44 (May 1991): 163–171.

46. Biles, "Nathan Straus," 33, 39; D. Bradford Hunt, "Re-Thinking the History of Public Housing: The 1937 Housing Act and Its Early Administration" (paper presented at the Policy History Conference, St. Louis, Mo., 2002); Robinson et al., *Public Housing in the U.S.*, 45.

47. Robinson et al., *Public Housing in the U.S.*, vol. 1, appendix 4, 1–19; 2:40.

48. Yvonne Wingett, "Phoenix Tenants Resist Housing Overhaul," *Arizona Republic*, 11 March 2003.

49. *National Defense Housing*, Public Law 849, *U.S. Statutes at Large* 54 (1941): 1125; Paul R. Lusignan, "Public Housing in the United States, 1933–1969," *Cultural Resources Management* 25, no. 1 (2002): 36–37.

50. Radford, *Modern Housing for America*, 194.

51. Dolores Hayden, *Redesigning the American Dream* (New York: W. W. Norton, 1984), 42–45; Herbert J. Gans, *The Levittowners: Ways of Life and Politics in a New Suburban Community* (New York: Pantheon, 1967); Kenneth T. Jackson, *Crabgrass Frontier: The Suburbanization of the United States* (New York: Oxford University Press, 1985), 236–37.

52. Citizens Commission on Civil Rights, "The Federal Government and Equal Housing Opportunity: A Continuing Failure," in Bratt, Hartman, and Meyerson, *Critical Perspectives*, 299–301; Jackson, *Crabgrass Frontier*, 203–18

53. Hayden, *Redesigning the American Dream*, 6–8; Wright, *Building the Dream*, 247–48.

54. Radford, *Modern Housing for America*, 105–6.

Chapter 9: Resettlement

1. Stanley Baldwin, *Poverty and Politics: The Rise and Decline of the Farm Security Administration* (Chapel Hill: University of North Carolina Press, 1968), 22.

2. Paul K. Conkin, *Tomorrow a New World: The New Deal Community Programs* (Ithaca, N.Y.: Cornell University Press, 1959), 13–18; Rosabeth Moss Kanter, *Commitment and Community: Communes and Utopias in Sociological Perspective* (Cambridge, Mass.: Harvard University Press, 1972); Paul Kagan, *New World Utopias* (New York: Penguin, 1975).

3. Conkin, *Tomorrow a New World*, 18–23.

4. Russell Lord, *The Wallaces of Iowa* (Cambridge, Mass.: Houghton Mifflin, 1947), 297.

5. Harry McDean, "Western Thought in Planning Rural America: The Subsistence Homesteads Program, 1933–1935," *Journal of the West* 31, no. 4 (October 1992): 16; Lord, *The Wallaces of Iowa*, 303.

6. John Steinbeck, *The Grapes of Wrath* (1939; repr., New York: Random House, 1993); James Agee and Walker Evans, *Let Us Now Praise Famous Men* (1941; repr., Boston: Houghton Mifflin, 1960); Dorothea Lange and Paul Schuster Taylor, *An American Exodus: A Record of Human Erosion* (1939; repr., New York: Arno Press, 1975).

7. Lord, *The Wallaces of Iowa*, 304.

8. Ibid.; M. L. Wilson, "A New Land-Use Program: The Place of Subsistence Homesteads," *Journal of Land and Public Utility Economics* 10, no. 1 (February 1934): 3; M. L. Wilson, "Decentralization of Industry in the New Deal," *Social Forces* 13, no. 4 (May 1935): 591–92.

9. Conkin, *Tomorrow a New World*, 42–48; Daniel T. Rogers, *Atlantic Crossings: Social Politics in a Progressive Age* (Cambridge, Mass.: Harvard University Press, 1998), 343–44, 347–51.

10. Wilson, "A New Land-Use Program," 10. Despite the program philosophy of not competing with established farmers, some homesteaders did. Walter M. Kollmorgen, "The Subsistence Homesteads near Birmingham," in *A Place on Earth: A Critical Appraisal of Subsistence Homesteads,* ed. Russell Lord and Paul H. Johnstone (Washington, D.C.: Bureau of Agricultural Economics, USDA, 1942), 65–82.

11. Wilson, "Decentralization of Industry," 595–96; Conkin, *Tomorrow a New World*, 23–24, 29.

12. *National Industrial Recovery Act,* Public Law 67, title 2, sec. 208, *U.S. Statutes at Large* 48 (1934): 205–6; "Delegation of Presidential Powers to the Secretary of the Interior Relating to Subsistence Homesteads," 21 July 1933, Executive Order 6209, in *The Public Papers and Addresses of Franklin D. Roosevelt,* ed. Samuel I. Rosenman (New York: Random House, 1938), 2:290–95.

13. Rexford G. Tugwell, "The Resettlement Idea," *Agricultural History* 33, no. 4 (Fall 1959): 159–64; Baldwin, *Poverty and Politics*, 84.

14. Harold M. Ware and Webster Powell, "Planning for Permanent Poverty: What Subsistence Farming Really Stands For," *Harper's Magazine*, April 1935, 25; McDean, "Western Thought in Planning Rural America," 17, 22; Rexford G. Tugwell, *The Democratic Roosevelt: A Biography of Franklin D. Roosevelt* (Garden City, N.Y.: Doubleday, 1957), 158; Lord, *The Wallaces of Iowa*, 410.

15. Conkin, *Tomorrow a New World*, 99; Lord, *The Wallaces of Iowa*, 417.

16. Conkin, *Tomorrow a New World*, 87–89; Baldwin, *Poverty and Politics*, 68–76; Lester M. Salamon, "The Time Dimension in Policy Evaluation: The Case of the New Deal Land-Reform Experiments," *Public Policy* 27, no. 2 (Spring 1979): 142.

17. Conkin, *Tomorrow a New World*, 99–100.

18. Ibid., 104–16.

19. Ibid., 119.

20. Thomas H. Coode and Dennis E. Fabbri, "The New Deal's Arthurdale Project in West Virginia," *West Virginia History* 36, no. 4 (1975): 296.

21. Conkin, *Tomorrow a New World,* 237–55; Harold L. Ickes, *The Secret Diary of Harold L. Ickes: The First Thousand Days, 1933–1936* (New York: Simon and Schuster, 1953), 228.

22. Wesley Stout, "The New Homesteaders," *Saturday Evening Post,* 4 August 1934, 5–7, 61–62, 64–65; Calvert L. Estill, "Blunders at Arthurdale Puts Burden on Miner and Taxpayer," *Washington Post Magazine,* 12 August 1934, 1; Lois Craig and the staff of the Federal Architecture Project, *The Federal Presence: Architecture, Politics, and Symbols in United States Government Building* (Cambridge, Mass.: MIT Press, 1977), 387; Ickes, *Secret Diary,* 207.

23. Conkin, *Tomorrow a New World,* 116–17.

24. Coode and Fabbri, "The New Deal's Arthurdale Project," 303–4; Conkin, *Tomorrow a New World,* 251–55.

25. Robert M. Carricker, "A New Deal Program: The Phoenix Homesteads, 1933–1948" (master's thesis, Arizona State University, 1973); Timothy J. Garvey, "The Duluth Homesteads: A Successful Experiment in Community Housing," *Minnesota History* 46, no. 1 (Spring 1978): 3–16.

26. Olen E. Leonard, "El Monte," in Lord and Johnstone, *A Place on Earth,* 97–106.

27. Dorothy Schwieder, "The Granger Homestead Project," *Palimpsest* 58, no. 5 (1977): 149–61; Conkin, *Tomorrow a New World,* 294–304; Ralph R. Nichols, "Granger Homesteads," in Lord and Johnstone, *A Place on Earth,* 181.

28. Patrick Tracey, "Coming Full Circle," *Historic Preservation* 47, no. 2 (May/June 1995): 64–71, 114; Conkin, *Tomorrow a New World,* 200.

29. Conkin, *Tomorrow a New World,* 120–21; Carricker, "Phoenix Homesteads," 76.

30. "The Resettlement Administration Is Established," Executive Order 7027, 1 May 1935; "Transfer of Land Programs of F.E.R.A. to the Resettlement Administration," Executive Order 7028, 1 May 1935; and "Transfer of Subsistence Homestead Activities to the Resettlement Administration," Executive Order 7041, 15 May 1935, in Rosenman, *Public Papers and Addresses* (1938), 4:143–44, 155–56, 180; Baldwin, *Poverty and Politics,* 60–68; Conkin, *Tomorrow a New World,* 133–43.

31. Conkin, *Tomorrow a New World,* 142–43; Baldwin, *Poverty and Politics,* 92–94; Ickes, *Secret Diary,* 227, 288.

32. Lord, *The Wallaces of Iowa,* 352.

33. Conkin, *Tomorrow a New World,* 149–50; Michael V. Namorato, *Rexford G. Tugwell: A Biography* (New York: Praeger, 1988), 26, 33, 48–49, 51–54; Rexford G. Tugwell, *The Industrial Discipline and the Government Arts* (New York: Columbia University Press, 1933); Thorstein Veblen, *The Theory of Business Enterprise* (New York: Scribner, 1904); Baldwin, *Poverty and Politics,* 93.

34. Baldwin, *Poverty and Politics,* 24–25.

35. *Agricultural Adjustment Act,* Public Law 10, *U.S. Statutes at Large* 48 (1934): 31.

36. Baldwin, *Poverty and Politics,* 25, 29, 39; Greta DeJong, *A Different Day: African-American Struggles for Justice in Rural Louisiana, 1900–1970* (Chapel Hill: University of North Carolina Press, 2002), 96–97; Joseph Gaer, *Toward Farm Security* (Washington, D.C.:

Government Printing Office, 1941), 50; William J. Leuchtenberg, *Franklin D. Roosevelt and the New Deal, 1932–1940* (New York: Harper and Row, 1963), 137.

37. Baldwin, *Poverty and Politics,* 174.

38. Ibid., 76–83.

39. Resettlement Administration, *Greenbelt Towns: A Demonstration in Suburban Planning* (Washington, D.C.: Resettlement Administration, 1936), 3; Conkin, *Tomorrow a New World,* 153.

40. Rogers, *Atlantic Crossings,* 453–54.

41. Conkin, *Tomorrow a New World,* 153–54, 166–67; Baldwin, *Poverty and Politics,* 105; Carol A. Christensen, *The American Garden City and the New Towns Movement* (Ann Arbor, Mich.: UMI Research Press, 1986), 58–59.

42. Brian Q. Cannon, *Remaking the Agrarian Dream: New Deal Rural Resettlement in the Mountain West* (Albuquerque: University of New Mexico Press, 1996), 11, 74, 78, 110, 128–29, 135–36; Marion Clawson, "Resettlement Experience in Nine Resettlement Projects," *Agricultural History* 52, no. 1 (January 1978): 27–33, 69; Baldwin, *Poverty and Politics,* 313–14.

43. Rogers, *Atlantic Crossings,* 330–43.

44. Conkin, *Tomorrow a New World,* 205.

45. Baldwin, *Poverty and Politics,* 207, 203.

46. Thomas R. Clark, "The Limits of State Autonomy: The Medical Cooperatives of the Farm Security Administration, 1935–1946," *Journal of Policy History* 11, no. 3 (1999): 258; Baldwin, *Poverty and Politics,* 209.

47. Arthur M. Schlesinger Jr., *The Coming of the New Deal* (Boston: Houghton Mifflin, 1958), 371–72; Edward C. Banfield, *Government Project* (Glencoe, Ill.: Free Press, 1951); Charles Loomis, *Social Relationships and Institutions in Seven Rural Resettlement Communities,* Social Research Report 18 (Washington, D.C.: Farm Security Administration, 1940); Donald Holley, *Uncle Sam's Farmers: The New Deal Communities in the Lower Mississippi Valley* (Urbana: University of Illinois Press, 1975); Clawson, "Resettlement Experience," 16–17, 50. Banfield went on to become a leading proponent of the argument that poverty was largely a problem of individual failings, most notably in *The Moral Basis of a Backward Society* (Glencoe, Ill.: Free Press, 1958). Cannon, *Remaking the Agrarian Dream,* summarizes this complaint, 89–95.

48. Cannon, *Remaking the Agrarian Dream,* 97, 113; Clawson, "Resettlement Experience," 53; Conkin, *Tomorrow a New World,* 213.

49. Clawson, "Resettlement Experience," 76; Baldwin, *Poverty and Politics,* 313–14; Cannon, *Remaking the Agrarian Dream,* 110, 115–31.

50. Joseph L. Arnold, *The New Deal in the Suburbs: A History of the Greenbelt Town Program, 1935–1954* (Columbus: Ohio State University Press, 1971), 3–16.

51. Arthur W. MacMahon, John D. Millett, and Gladys Ogden, *The Administration of Federal Work Relief* (1941; repr., New York: DeCapo Press, 1971), 31–34, 40–41, 49; Arnold, *New Deal in the Suburbs,* 41.

52. Arnold, *New Deal in the Suburbs,* 29–30, 46–50, 85. Frank Lloyd Wright offered to construct Greenbelt, provided he was given one hundred million dollars and a free hand. Laurence E. Coffin Jr. and Beatriz de Winthuysen Coffin, "Greenbelt: A Maryland 'New Town' Turns 50," *Landscape Architecture* 78, no. 4 (June 1988): 48–49.

53. Arnold, *New Deal in the Suburbs,* 88–89.

54. Ibid., 45–46, 111; Leta Mach, "Constructing the Town of Greenbelt," in *Greenbelt: History of a New Town, 1937–1987,* ed. Mary Lou Williamson (Norfolk, Va.: Donning, 1987), 30.

55. Arnold, *New Deal in the Suburbs,* 61–74, 112, 116–17; Mach, "Constructing the Town of Greenbelt," 33; Daniel Schaffer, "Resettling Industrial America: The Controversy Over FDR's Greenbelt Town Program," *Urbanism Past and Present* 8, no. 1 (Winter/Spring 1983): 18–32.

56. Arnold, *New Deal in the Suburbs,* 90–91, 95–96, 98; Cathy D. Knepper, *Greenbelt, Maryland: A Living Legacy of the New Deal* (Baltimore: Johns Hopkins University Press, 2001), 21.

57. Arnold, *New Deal in the Suburbs,* 115; Mach, "Constructing the Town of Greenbelt," 32–33.

58. Conkin, *Tomorrow a New World,* 311–15; Mach, "Constructing the Town of Greenbelt," 35–36.

59. Mach, "Constructing the Town of Greenbelt," 34; Arnold R. Alanen and Joseph A. Eden, *Main Street Ready-Made: The New Deal Community in Greendale* (Madison: State Historical Society of Wisconsin, 1987), 44; Jane Brown Gillette, "Back to the Future: Utopian Housing Survives in Greenbelt, Maryland," *Historic Preservation* 46, no. 5 (September/October 1994): 83; "Low-Cost Furniture," *House Beautiful,* April 1937, 131–32.

60. Arnold, *New Deal in the Suburbs,* 136–45, 196–98; Cannon, *Remaking the Agrarian Dream,* 20–21. Conservatives were not the only ones bothered by the RA's interest in the social characteristics of applicants for its communities; critics on the left saw fascistic tendencies at work. In fact, a study conducted long after the hysteria had passed found some interesting parallels between the RA's rural efforts and Mussolini's New Town program. See Diane Ghirardo, *Building New Communities: New Deal America and Fascist Italy* (Princeton, N.J.: Princeton University Press, 1989).

61. Conkin, *Tomorrow a New World,* 316–19; Barbara Likowski and Jay McCarl, "Social Construction," in Williamson, *Greenbelt,* 71–80.

62. Arnold, *New Deal in the Suburbs,* 173–77, 180–85; Knepper, *Greenbelt, Maryland: A Living Legacy,* 183.

63. Arnold, *New Deal in the Suburbs,* 229–38; Conkin, *Tomorrow a New World,* 322–25.

64. Conkin, *Tomorrow a New World,* 175–81; Baldwin, *Poverty and Politics,* 187–88; Arnold, *New Deal in the Suburbs,* 196–97.

65. Conkin, *Tomorrow a New World,* 180; Lord, *The Wallaces of Iowa,* 429, 460–62.

66. Baldwin, *Poverty and Politics,* 195–99.

67. Clawson, "Resettlement Experience," 29–31, 34–47; Baldwin, *Poverty and Politics,* 214–17.

68. Steinbeck, *The Grapes of Wrath,* 339; John Steinbeck, *Their Blood Is Strong* (San Francisco: Simon J. Lubin Society, 1938) reprinted in *A Companion to "The Grapes of Wrath,"* ed. Warren French (New York: Viking Press, 1963), 70. The camp that inspired Weedpatch is at Arvin. Three of its original buildings survive and are listed on the National Register of Historic Places. Patricia Leigh Brown, "Oklahomans Try to Save Their California Culture," *New York Times,* 5 February 2002.

69. Walter J. Stein, "A New Deal Experiment with Guided Democracy: The FSA Migrant Camps in California," *Canadian Historical Association Historical Papers* (1970): 141–42.

70. "Farm Security Administration," *Architecture Forum* 74, no. 1 (January 1941): 13; Talbot Hamlin, "Farm Security Architecture: An Appraisal," *Pencil Points* 22 (November 1941): 709; Phoebe Cutler, *The Public Landscape of the New Deal* (New Haven, Conn.: Yale University Press, 1985), 128–31; Craig et al., *The Federal Presence,* 380–84.

71. William Stott, *Documentary Expression and Thirties America* (New York: Oxford University Press, 1973); James Curtis, *Mind's Eye, Mind's Truth: FSA Photography Reconsidered* (Philadelphia, Pa.: Temple University Press, 1989). Another visual artifact of the FSA, much less familiar, is the movie *The City,* directed by Willard van Dyke, with a score by Aaron Copland and commentary by Lewis Mumford, which makes the case for Greenbelt.

72. Bruce Gardner, "The Little Guys Are O.K.," *New York Times,* 7 March 2005.

73. Mike Davis, "How Eden Lost Its Garden," *Perspecta* 30 (1999): 64–75; Christensen, *American Garden City,* 96, 100, 103, 105–25; Herbert Gans, *The Levittowners: Ways of Life and Politics in a New Suburban Community* (New York: Pantheon, 1967), 3–4; Howard Kunstler, "Home from Nowhere," *Atlantic Monthly,* September 1996, 43–66; Timothy Egan, "Drawing the Hard Line on Urban Sprawl," *New York Times,* 13 April 1996.

74. Lester M. Salamon, "The Time Dimension in Policy Evaluation," 129–83, 160–177. For a look at the social life of one of these African American resettlement communities, see John Temple Graves II, "The Big World at Last Reaches Gee's Bend," *New York Times,* 22 August 1937, reprinted in *The New Deal,* ed. Carl N. Degler (Chicago: Quadrangle Books, 1970), 136–44.

75. Cutler, *Public Landscape,* 122.

76. Tugwell, "The Resettlement Idea," 164.

77. Namorato, *Rexford G. Tugwell,* 167.

Chapter 10: Economic Stimulus

1. John Kenneth Galbraith, *The Great Crash, 1929* (Boston: Houghton Mifflin, 1979), 176n9.

2. Robert H. Ferrell, *The Presidency of Calvin Coolidge* (Lawrence: University of Kansas Press, 1998), 167–68.

3. William T. Foster and Waddill Catchings, *The Road to Plenty* (Boston: Houghton Mifflin, 1928), 135; William J. Barber, *From New Era to New Deal: Herbert Hoover, the Economists, and American Economic Policy, 1921–1933* (New York: Cambridge University Press, 1985), 54–58. Many historians have given underconsumption a major role in causing the Depression. Economist Stanley Lebergott quotes several of them in *Consumer Expenditures* (Princeton, N.J.: Princeton University Press, 1996), 17. We can also add Ferrell, *The Presidency of Calvin Coolidge,* 182–85. Lebergott disagrees, however, maintaining that consumption was rising right up to 1929 (*Consumer Expenditures,* 19, table 3.1). At that point, he argues, it fell off drastically, making the difference between a recession and major depression.

4. Foster and Catchings, *The Road to Plenty,* 189.

5. Some economic historians doubt that the division between old and new economics was so sharp. J. Ronnie Davis, "The Last Remake of the New Economics and the Old Economists: Comment," *Southern Economic Journal* 45, no. 3 (January 1979): 919–25, argues that some of the orthodox economists of the twenties favored public works and higher wages. He also documents John Stuart Mill's awareness of underconsumption.

6. Howard J. Sherman, *Business Cycles* (Princeton, N.J.: Princeton University Press, 1991), 192.

7. William T. Foster and Waddill Catchings, *Profits* (Boston: Houghton Mifflin, 1925), 355. By some definitions of the theory of underconsumption, Foster and Catchings may not qualify as true underconsumptionists. Not only were they not greatly concerned with the maldistribution of income, they also do not seem convinced that business slumps were a normal state under capitalism and not passing episodes in general fluctuations. Real underconsumptionists usually emphasize both points. Michael Bleaney, *Underconsumption Theories: A History and Critical Analysis* (New York: International Publishers, 1976), 11, 204.

8. J. Kerwin Williams, *Grants-in-Aid under the Public Works Administration* (1939; repr., New York: AMS Press, 1968), 33; Udo Sautter, *Three Cheers for the Unemployed: Government and Unemployment before the New Deal* (New York: Cambridge University Press, 1991), 314; James Stuart Olson, *Herbert Hoover and the Reconstruction Finance Corporation, 1931–1933* (Ames: University of Iowa Press, 1977), 79; Arthur Gayner, *Public Works in Prosperity and Depression* (New York: National Bureau of Economic Research, 1935), 88.

9. Foster and Catchings, *Road to Plenty*, 195; Barber, *From New Era to New Deal*, 120; Alan Brinkley, *The End of Reform: New Deal Liberalism in Recession and War* (New York: Vintage, 1995), 77.

10. Sautter, *Three Cheers*, 272; Barber, *From New Era to New Deal*, 58.

11. Laurence S. Knappen, *Revenue Bonds and the Investor* (New York: Prentice-Hall, 1939), 8–14; David C. Perry, "Building the City through the Back Door: The Politics of Debt, Law, and Public Infrastructure," in *Building the Public City*, ed. David C. Perry (Thousand Oaks, Calif.: Sage, 1995), 214–18; Gail Radford, "Public Authorities and the Dilemma of New Deal State-Building" (paper presented at the Annual Meeting of the Organization of America Historians, Los Angeles, 2001).

12. Forrest A. Walker, *The Civil Works Administration: An Experiment in Federal Work Relief* (New York: Garland Press, 1979), 72–74; Harry Hopkins, *Spending to Save* (New York: W. W. Norton, 1936), 116–17; Bonnie Fox Schwartz, *The Civil Works Administration, 1933–1934: The Business of Emergency Employment in the New Deal* (Princeton, N.J.: Princeton University Press, 1985), 48–50.

13. *Wall Street Journal*, 5 January 1934; ibid., 27 January 1934.

14. "Business Outlook," *Business Week*, 20 January 1934, 3; ibid., 10 February 1934, 3; ibid., 24 February 1934, 3.

15. Robert D. Leighninger Jr., "Economic Stimulus from the Civil Works Administration to Market Patriotism" (paper presented at the Policy History Conference, St. Louis, Mo., 2002).

16. Brinkley, *End of Reform*, 28; Henry H. Adams, *Harry Hopkins* (New York: Putnam, 1977), 117–19; Theodore Rosenof, *Economics in the Long Run: New Deal Theorists and Their Legacies, 1933–1993* (Chapel Hill: University of North Carolina Press, 1997), 9.

17. Ellis Hawley, *The New Deal and the Problem of Monopoly* (Princeton, N.J.: Princeton University Press, 1966), 390; Brinkley, *End of Reform*, 23, 28–30; Robert Aaron Gordon, *Economic Instability and Growth: The American Record* (New York: Harper and Row, 1974), 69.

18. Brinkley, *End of Reform*, 95–97.

19. Rosenof, *Economics in the Long Run*, 58–63.

20. Brinkley, *End of Reform,* 83–84, 98–99; Rosenof, *Economics in the Long Run,* 9–10.

21. Brinkley, *End of Reform,* 73; Gordon, *Economic Instability,* 59; Rosenof, *Economics in the Long Run,* 49–50; Alvin Hansen, *Full Recovery or Stagnation?* (New York: W. W. Norton, 1938); Kenneth Roose, *The Economics of Recession and Revival* (New Haven, Conn.: Yale University Press, 1954), 5, 9, 173–78, 241; Gordon, *Economic Instability,* 68. There are those who believe that fiscal policy had nothing to do with the recovery. Christina H. Romer, "What Ended the Great Depression?" *Journal of Economic History* 52, no. 4 (December 1992): 757–84, gives all the credit to the influx of gold.

22. Price V. Fishback, William C. Horrace, and Shawn Kantor, "Did New Deal Grant Programs Stimulate Local Economies? A Study of Federal Grants and Retail Sales, 1929–1939," *Journal of Economic History* (March 2005): 36–71.

23. Gordon, *Economic Instability,* 64.

24. Jason Scott Smith, *Building New Deal Liberalism: The Political Economy of Public Works, 1933–1956* (New York: Cambridge University Press, 2005).

25. Herbert Stein, *Presidential Economics: The Making of Economic Policy from Roosevelt to Reagan and Beyond* (New York: Simon and Schuster, 1984), 101.

26. Gordon, *Economic Instability,* 142; Stein, *Presidential Economics,* 109.

27. Stein, *Presidential Economics,* 245–49; David Brooks, "The Zero-Sum Tax Cut," *New York Times,* 1 June 2001.

28. Holcomb B. Noble, "James Tobin, Nobel Laureate in Economics and an Advisor to Kennedy, Is Dead at 84," *New York Times,* 13 March 2002; Stein, *Presidential Economics,* 110. The tax cut may not deserve all the credit, says Stein, because monetary policy was also at work increasing the money supply. In any case, the effects of the tax cut were soon overshadowed by the growing investment in the Vietnam War (ibid., 108–10).

29. Robert Robb, "Liberals' Fiscal Policies Based on Twisted History," *Arizona Republic,* 18 November 2001; Lawrence Lindsey, *The Growth Experiment: How the New Tax Policy Is Transforming the U.S. Economy* (New York: Basic Books, 1990).

30. Herman I. Liebling, "The Myth of the Keynesian Recovery," *Journal of Macroeconomics* 7, no. 2 (Spring 1985): 257–60; Charles B. Garrison, "The Role of Business Investment, Residential Investment, and Tax Incentives in the Economic Expansion of the 1980s," *American Economic Journal* 14, no. 4 (December 1991): 11–18; Robert J. Samuelson, "The Reagan Tax Myth," *Washington Post,* 28 July 1999.

31. Garrison, "Role of Business Investment," 16; Herbert Stein, *Presidential Economics,* 278; Barry Bosworth and Gary Burtless, "Effects of Tax Reform on Labor Supply, Investment, and Savings," *Journal of Economic Perspectives* 6, no. 1 (Winter 1992): 3–25, 23; Henry J. Aaron, review of *The Growth Experiment,* by Lawrence Lindsey, *Journal of Economic Literature* 24 (June 1991): 621–23, 623.

32. Stein, *Presidential Economics,* 290–300.

33. Richard W. Stevenson, "The Battle of the Decades: Reaganomics vs. Clintonomics Is a Central Issue in 2000," *New York Times,* 8 February 2000; Richard W. Stevenson, "Roots of Prosperity Reach Past Clinton Years," *New York Times,* 9 October 2000; Henry Kaufman, "Tax Cuts: Bad for the Market," *Washington Post Weekly Edition,* 16 August 1991.

34. Louis Uchitelle, "Wary Spending by Executives Cools Economy," *New York Times,* 14 May 2001.

35. Paul Krugman, "The Universal Elixir," *New York Times,* 16 May 2001.

36. Liz Kowalczyk, "Patriotic Purchasing: Americans Are Being Urged to Spend, but Analysts Doubt the Strategy Will Have an Impact in the Long Run," *Boston Globe,* 28 September 2001; Patrice Hill, "Tax Rebates Fail to Stir New Spending; Going to Savings, Debt Reduction," *Washington Times,* 2 October 2001; Matthew D. Shapiro and Joel Slemrod, "Consumer Responses to Tax Rebates," *American Economic Review* 93, no. 1 (March 2003): 381–96.

37. Robert B. Reich, "How Did Spending Become Our Patriotic Duty?," *American Prospect,* 23 September 2001.

38. Rachael Beck, "Tax Cuts Do Little to Economy," *Arizona Republic,* 8 November 2004; Paul Krugman, "An Alternative Reality," *New York Times,* 25 November 2001; see also Gordon, *Economic Instability,* 61.

39. Anna Bernasek, "Do Taxes Thwart Growth? Prove It," *New York Times,* 3 April 2005; Joel Slemrod and Jon Bakija, *Taxing Ourselves: A Citizen's Guide to the Debate over Taxes* (Cambridge, Mass.: MIT Press, 2004), 116–20.

40. George Will, "Buy B-2, Cut Corporate Taxes, Build High-Speed Rail System," *Arizona Republic,* 30 September 2001; William Safire, "Let's Double the Tax Cut, End 'Lock-Box' Fiscal Folly," *New York Times,* 11 September 2001.

Chapter 11: Public Jobs

1. *Social Security Act,* Public Law 271, *U.S. Statutes at Large* 49 (1936): 620; Edwin Amenta, *Bold Relief: Institutional Politics and the Origins of Modern American Social Policy* (Princeton, N.J.: Princeton University Press, 1998), 3; Gail Radford, *Modern Housing in America: Policy Struggles in the New Deal Era* (Chicago: University of Chicago Press, 1996). Jerry Cates argues that the further separation of social insurance and public assistance was a conscious policy pursued by Social Security's early administrators in Jerry R. Cates, *Insuring Inequality: Administrative Leadership in Social Security, 1935–1954* (Ann Arbor: University of Michigan Press, 1983).

2. Margaret Weir, *Politics and Jobs: The Boundaries of Employment Policy in the United States* (Princeton, N.J.: Princeton University Press, 1992), 62, 82.

3. Paul Bullock, *Youth Training and Employment: From New Deal to New Federalism* (Los Angeles: Institute of Industrial Relations, University of California, Los Angeles, 1985), 73.

4. Weir, *Politics and Jobs,* 10; James T. Patterson, *America's Struggle against Poverty in the Twentieth Century* (Cambridge, Mass.: Harvard University Press, 2000), 65.

5. Alan Brinkley, *The End of Reform: New Deal Liberalism in Recession and War* (New York: Vintage Books, 1996), 233.

6. "State of the Union Message," 11 January 1944, in *The Public Papers and Addresses of Franklin D. Roosevelt,* ed. Samuel I. Rosenman (New York: Random House, 1950), 13:41–42.

7. *Employment Act of 1946,* Public Law 304, *U.S. Statutes at Large* 60 (1947): 23.

8. Brinkley, *End of Reform,* 260–64; Nancy E. Rose, *Workfare or Fair Work: Women, Welfare, and Government Work Programs* (New Brunswick, N.J.: Rutgers University Press, 1995), 63–66; Weir, *Politics and Jobs,* 45–47. Cass Sunstein's *The Second Bill of Rights: FDR's Unfinished Revolution and Why We Need It More Than Ever* (New York: Basic Books, 2004) tries to revive this idea.

9. Brinkley, *End of Reform,* 234–35; Weir, *Politics and Jobs,* 42, 49.

10. *Servicemen's Readjustment Act of 1944,* Public Law 346, *U.S. Statutes at Large* 58 (1945): 284; Brinkley, *End of Reform,* 258–59; Amenta, *Bold Relief,* 192, 202; Harold Hyman,

American Singularity: The 1787 Northwest Ordinance, the 1861 Homestead and Morrill Acts, and the 1944 G.I. Bill (Athens: University of Georgia Press, 1986), 62–76. Hyman argues that "the G.I. Bill vastly reinforced these enduring New Deal 'civilian' legacies" (ibid., 65).

11. Weir, *Politics and Jobs,* 164–65.

12. Ibid., 56–57.

13. "PWA Has Changed Face of U.S.," *Life,* 1 April 1940, 61–66.

14. Weir, *Politics and Jobs,* 5, 98.

15. Ibid., 62.

16. James Russell Woods, "The Legend and Legacy of FDR and the CCC" (PhD. diss., Syracuse University, 1964), 353–57, 359–77.

17. Woods, "Legend and Legacy," 390; Sar A. Levitan and Benjamin H. Johnston, *The Job Corps: A Social Experiment That Works* (Baltimore, Md.: Johns Hopkins University Press, 1975), 3.

18. *Economic Opportunity Act of 1964,* Public Law 88–452, *U.S. Statutes at Large* 78 (1965): 508; Patterson, *America's Struggle against Poverty,* 129–31.

19. Bullock, *Youth Training and Employment,* 78–84; Grace A. Franklin and Randall B. Ripley, *C.E.T.A.: Politics and Policy, 1973–1982* (Knoxville: University of Tennessee Press, 1984), 9; Rose, *Workfare or Fair Work,* 85; Weir, *Politics and Jobs,* 74.

20. Bullock, *Youth Training and Employment,* 105–6; Levitan and Johnston, *Job Corps,* 4.

21. Bullock, *Youth Training and Employment,* 84–95, 100.

22. Deane McGowen, "People in Sports," *New York Times,* 8 February 1973; Bullock, *Youth Training and Employment,* 103, 142.

23. Bullock, *Youth Training and Employment,* 114.

24. Ibid., 118, 127, 136, 148.

25. Ibid., 121–22.

26. Ibid., 109, 148–49.

27. Ibid., 140–41; Levitan and Johnston, *Job Corps,* 38–54; Patterson, *America's Struggle against Poverty,* 133.

28. Levitan and Johnston, *Job Corps,* 1.

29. Sheena McConnell and Steven Glazerman, *National Job Corps Study: The Benefits and Costs of Job Corps* (Washington, D.C.: Mathematica Research, Inc., 2001).

30. *Comprehensive Employment and Training Act of 1978,* Public Law 95–524, *U.S. Statutes at Large* 92 (1980): 1909.

31. Weir, *Politics and Jobs,* 117; Rose, *Workfare or Fair Work,* 98.

32. Franklin and Ripley, *C.E.T.A.,* 12–22.

33. Weir, *Politics and Jobs,* 118–19; Bullock, *Youth Training and Employment,* 166–67; Franklin and Ripley, *C.E.T.A.,* 45, 64–66, 204–5.

34. William Mirengoff, Lester Rindler, Harry Greenspan, and Scott Seablom, *CETA: Assessment of Public Service Employment Programs* (Washington, D.C.: National Academy of Sciences, 1980), 140–45.

35. Weir, *Politics and Jobs,* 120–28; Franklin and Ripley, *C.E.T.A.,* 45, 199, 204–6; Mirengoff et al., *Public Service Employment,* 3–5; William Mirengoff, Lester Rindler, Harry Greenspan, and Charles Harris, *CETA: Accomplishments, Problems, Solutions* (Kalamazoo, Mich.: W. E. Upjohn Institute for Employment Research, 1982), 27–29.

36. Bullock, *Youth Training and Employment,* 212–21.

37. California Conservation Corps, http://www.ccc.ca.gov/CCCWEB/ABOUT/HISTORY; Bullock, *Youth Training and Employment*, 220–32.

38. National Association of Service and Conservation Corps, http://www.nascc.org /history2.shtml.

39. Allen Freeman, "We Need Love, We Need Support, We Need Skills . . . ," *Historic Preservation* 14, no. 3 (May–June 1993): 26–32, 84–85; L. J. Piatrowski, "These Heroes Wear Hard Hats," *Ford Foundation Report,* Summer–Fall 1997, 57; Maureen McGee, "Nailing Down a Brighter Future," *San Diego Union-Tribune,* 19 January 2002.

40. Bullock, *Youth Training and Employment,* 141, 147–50, 188, 202, 273–74, 282, 335, 339–40; Franklin and Ripley, *C.E.T.A.,* 187–88, 198, 202; McConnell and Glazerman, *National Job Corps Study,* 48.

41. Weir, *Politics and Jobs,* 135–43; Rose, *Workfare or Fair Work,* 120–22.

42. Patterson, *America's Struggle against Poverty,* 223–25; Rose, *Workfare or Fair Work,* 139–41.

43. Donald Howard, *The WPA and Federal Relief Policy* (New York: Russell Sage Foundation, 1943), 136–37, 254–55; Rose, *Workfare or Fair Work,* 16–17.

44. Weir, *Politics and Jobs,* 99; Irwin Garfinkel and John L. Palmer, "Issues, Evidence, and Implications," in *Creating Jobs: Public Employment Programs and Wage Subsidies,* ed. John L. Palmer (Washington, D.C.: Brookings Institution, 1977), 6.

45. Jonathan R. Kesselman, "Work Relief Programs in the Great Depression," in Palmer, *Creating Jobs,* 153–229.

46. E. Wright Bakke, *The Unemployed Worker: A Study of the Task of Making a Living without a Job* (1940; repr., Hamden, Conn.: Archon, 1969), 241–43.

47. Bonnie Fox Schwartz, *The Civil Works Administration, 1933–1934: The Business of Emergency Employment in the New Deal* (Princeton, N.J.: Princeton University Press, 1984), 216–17.

48. Rose, *Workfare or Fair Work,* 15; Bullock, *Youth Training and Employment,* 13.

49. Lois Craig, "Beyond Leaf-Raking: WPA's Lasting Legacy," *City,* October/November 1970, 29.

50. Arnold R. Weber, "Comments," in Palmer, *Creating Jobs,* 239.

51. Rose, *Workfare or Fair Work,* 182–84.

52. Joe Queenan, "The Beer Barrel Polka: Does President Now Risk Losing the Lawrence Welk Vote?" *Washington Post,* 2 February 1992; Skip Thurman, "Governors' Lesson in the Art of the Line-Item Veto," *Christian Science Monitor,* 13 August 1997; George F. Will, "Lawrence Welk and Line Items," *Washington Post,* 23 February 1992.

53. In 1941, as WPA was closing down, Howard Hunter, a WPA official, was asked if there was anything left to do. He replied that he could easily find useful work for eight million people. Howard, *The WPA and Federal Relief Policy,* 131.

54. Louis Uchitelle, "Maybe It's Time for Another New Deal," *New York Times,* 4 November 2004.

Chapter 12: Federalism

1. David C. Perry, introduction to *Building the Public City: The Politics, Governance, and Finance of Public Infrastructure,* ed. David C. Perry (Thousands Oaks, Calif.: Sage, 1995), 6. The term was borrowed from the military. It meant fixed installations like base camps, airstrips, and ports. The origins of "pork" will be explored in chapter 13.

2. All but nine states now tax personal income and/or dividends and interest. David Firestone, "Tennessee's Fiscal Stature Dives after Futile Push for Income Tax," *New York Times,* 23 August 2001.

3. Ronald John Hy and William L. Waugh Jr., *State and Local Tax Policies* (Westport, Conn.: Greenwood Press, 1995), 164, 256; Glenn Beamer, *Creative Politics: Taxes and Public Goods in a Federal System* (Ann Arbor: University of Michigan Press, 1999), 30–31.

4. Fees and surcharges have been appearing in "free" public education in recent decades as funding deteriorates. Students are charged laboratory and shop fees, asked to pay for field trips and extracurricular activities, and expected to supply basic materials like pens, markers, calculators, and paper. Teachers increasingly pay out of their own pockets not only for learning materials but also for paper towels, tissues, and Band-Aids.

5. Wallace E. Oates, *Fiscal Federalism* (New York: Harcourt, Brace, Jovanovich, 1972), 159; David C. Perry, "Building the City through the Back Door: The Politics of Debt, Law, and Public Infrastructure," in Perry, *Building the Public City,* 214–16; James Leigland, "Public Infrastructure and Special Purpose Governments: Who Pays and How?" in Perry, *Building the Public City,* 139, 154.

6. George E. Peterson, Rita Bamberger, Nancy Humphrey, and Kenneth M. Steil, *Guide to Financing the Capital Budget and Maintenance Plan* (Washington, D.C.: Urban Institute Press, 1984), 4; Haywood T. Sanders, "Public Works and Public Dollars: Federal Infrastructure Aid and Local Investment Policy," in Perry, *Building the Public City,* 191; Jeffrey Chapman, "The Impact of Public Fiscal Tools on Private Development Decisions," *Proceedings, 95th Annual Conference on Taxation* (conference held in Orlando, 2002; Washington, D.C.: National Tax Association), 311.

7. Beamer, *Creative Politics,* 38; Leigland, "Public Infrastructure," 165; Alicia H. Munnell and Leah M. Cook, "Financing Capital Expenditures in Massachusetts," *New England Economic Review,* March/April 1991, 64–66.

8. Munnell and Cook, "Financing Capital Expenditures in Massachusetts," 53–55; Leigland, "Public Infrastructure," 142–43.

9. Adam Smith, *An Inquiry into the Nature and Causes of the Wealth of Nations* (1776; repr., Chicago: University of Chicago Press, 1976), 350. Some have argued that markets and private ownership of property are impossible without a legal context that defines them. A sociopolitical context is, in turn, required to support the legal system, and this arrangement requires taxes to support it. Thus, taxes are intrinsic to, not impositions upon, social organization, and progressive taxation is a logical derivative. Since rich people have more to lose if the system collapses, it is reasonable that they pay higher taxes to sustain it. Liam Murphy and Thomas Nagel, *The Myth of Ownership: Taxes and Justice* (New York: Oxford University Press, 2002).

10. Michael J. Graetz, *The Decline (and Fall?) of the Income Tax* (New York: W. W. Norton, 1997), 5, 93–94; Beamer, *Creative Politics,* 40–42, 47; Firestone, "Tennessee's Fiscal Stature Dives"; Robert Tannenwald, "Devolution: The New Federalism–An Overview," *New England Economic Review,* May/June 1998, 7; Paul Krugman, "Our Banana Republics," *New York Times,* 30 July 2002; Gregory D. Saxton, Christopher W. Hoene, and Steven P. Erie, "Fiscal Constraints and the Loss of Home Rule: The Long-Term Impacts of California's Post–Proposition 13 Fiscal Regime," *American Review of Public Administration* 32 (December 2002): 423–54.

11. Timothy Conlan, *From New Federalism to Devolution: 25 Years of Intergovernmental Reform* (Washington, D.C.: The Brookings Institution, 1998), 10–14.

12. Benjamin Kleinberg, *Urban America in Transformation: Perspectives on Urban Policy and Development* (Thousand Oaks, Calif.: Sage, 1995), 95–96.

13. Kleinberg, *Urban America in Transformation,* 96–97; John James Wallis and Wallace E. Oates, "The Impact of the New Deal on American Federalism" in *The Defining Moment: The Great Depression and the American Economy in the Twentieth Century,* ed. Michael D. Bordo, Claudia Goldin, and Eugene N. White (Chicago: University of Chicago Press, 1998), 170.

14. Wallis and Oates, "The Impact of the New Deal on American Federalism," 179.

15. Perry, introduction to *Building the Public City,* 5, table 1.1.

16. Richard E. Thompson, *Revenue Sharing: A New Era in Federalism* (Washington, D.C.: Revenue Sharing Advisory Service, 1973), vi; Wallis and Oates, "The Impact of the New Deal on American Federalism," 171.

17. Wallace E. Oates, introduction to *Financing the New Federalism: Revenue Sharing, Conditional Grants, and Taxation,* ed. Wallace E. Oates (Baltimore, Md.: Johns Hopkins University Press, 1975), 2–3; Thompson, *Revenue Sharing,* 11–26; Walter W. Heller, "A Sympathetic Reappraisal of Revenue Sharing," in *Revenue Sharing and the Cities,* ed. Harvey S. Perloff and Richard P. Nathan (Baltimore, Md.: Johns Hopkins University Press, 1968), 3–38.

18. Heller, "A Sympathetic Reappraisal," 17–18 (author's emphasis).

19. Quoted in Oates, introduction to *Financing the New Federalism,* 4.

20. Thompson, *Revenue Sharing,* 30–31; Jeffrey L. Pressman, "Political Implications of the New Federalism," in Oates, *Financing the New Federalism,* 18–19.

21. Conlan, *From New Federalism,* 24–26; *Comprehensive Health Planning and Public Health Services Amendments of 1966,* Public Law 89–749, *U.S. Statutes at Large* 80 (1967): 1180; *Omnibus Crime Control and Safe Streets Act of 1968,* Public Law 90–351, *U.S. Statutes at Large* 82 (1969): 197.

22. Sheldon D. Pollack, *Refinancing America: The Republican Antitax Agenda* (Albany: State University of New York Press, 2003), 19–29, 57–58; Leigland, "Public Infrastructure," 143.

23. Leigland, "Public Infrastructure," 143–44, 165; Alberta M. Sbragia, *Debt Wish: Entrepreneurial Cities, U.S. Federalism, and Economic Development* (Pittsburgh, Penn.: University of Pittsburgh Press, 1996), 166–67; Chapman, "The Impact of Public Fiscal Tools," 310, 312; Munnell and Cook, "Financing Capital Expenditures in Massachusetts," 59–60.

24. Claire L. Felbinger, "Conditions of Confusion and Conflict: Rethinking the Infrastructure-Economic Development Link," in Perry, *Building the Public City,* 111–16, 129–33.

25. D. A. Aschauer, "Is Public Expenditure Productive?" *Journal of Monetary Economics* 23 (1989): 177–200; Alicia H. Munnell, "Why Has Productivity Growth Declined? Productivity and Public Investment," *New England Economic Review,* January/February 1990, 3–22; Felbinger, "Conditions of Confusion," 122–26.

26. Patrick Choate and Susan Walter, *America in Ruins: The Decaying Infrastructure* (Washington, D.C.: Council of State Planning Agencies, 1981); Sanders, "Public Works and Public Dollars," 181.

27. Felbinger, "Conditions of Confusion," 116–18; David Brunori, *State Tax Policy: A Political Perspective* (Washington, D.C.: Urban Institute Press, 2001), 32.

28. Sanders, "Public Works and Public Dollars," 182–83; Felbinger, "Conditions of Confusion," 116.

29. Sbragia, *Debt Wish,* 189–202.

30. Allen D. Manvel and Robert D. Reischauer, "General Revenue Sharing," in *Setting National Priorities: The 1972 Budget,* ed. Charles L. Schultze, Edward R. Fried, Alice M. Rivlin, and Nancy H. Teeters (Washington, D.C.: The Brookings Institution, 1971), 138–39; Paul Krugman, "Our Wretched States," *New York Times,* 11 January 2002; Louis Uchitelle, "Red Ink in States Beginning to Hurt Economic Recovery," *New York Times,* 28 July 2003; David E. Rosenbaum, "States Balance Budgets with Smoke and Mirrors," *New York Times,* 24 August 2003; T. R. Reid, "In the Pink, but Not Quite Rosy: Higher Taxes and Fees Help States Stay in the Black," *Washington Post Weekly Edition,* 17–23 May 2004, 30.

31. Dennis Cauchon, "States Consider Property-Tax Limits," *USA Today,* 12 April 2004; James Dao, "Virginia Political Shocker: Republicans for High Taxes; State Senators Advocate the Unthinkable," *New York Times,* 28 March 2004; Michael D. Shear and Chris L. Jenkins, "Va. Budget Approved, Ending Marathon; Rise in Spending, Taxes Is Major Change for State," *Washington Post,* 8 May 2004; T. R. Reid, "Read Our Lips: We Need New Taxes," *Washington Post Weekly Edition,* 4–10 April 2005, 13.

32. William R. Barnes and Larry C. Ledebur, *The New Regional Economics: The U.S. Common Market and the Global Economy* (Thousand Oaks, Calif.: Sage, 1998), 21, 40, 92–98, 152. Rex Tugwell saw this coming in the early 1960s. Rexford G. Tugwell, *Reforming the Constitution: An Imperative for Modern America* (Oxford: Clio Press, 1972).

33. Manvel and Reischauer, "General Revenue Sharing," 144; Tannenwald, "Devolution," 11; Thompson, *Revenue Sharing,* vii; Jeffrey L. Pressman, "Political Implications of the New Federalism," in Oates, *Financing the New Federalism,* 15–18, 37; George E. Peterson, ed., *Big-City Politics, Governance, and Fiscal Constraints* (Washington, D.C.: The Urban Institute Press, 1994).

34. J. Eric Oliver, *Democracy in Suburbia* (Princeton, N.J.: Princeton University Press, 2001), 5–6, 187–213.

35. Dale P. Swoboda, "Accuracy and Accountability in Reporting Local Government Budget Activities: Evidence from the Newsroom and from Newsmakers," *Public Budgeting and Finance,* Fall 1995, 81–82, 89; Teresa Mastin, "Media Use and Civic Participation in the African American Population: Exploring Participation among Professional and Nonprofessional," *Journalism and Mass Communication Quarterly* 77, no. 1 (Spring 2000): 115–27; Swoboda, "Accuracy and Accountability," 85–86; David Burnham, *The Role of the Media in Controlling Corruption* (New York: John Jay Press, 1977), 5; John J. Pauly and Melissa Eckert, "The Myth of 'The Local' in American Journalism," *Journalism and Mass Communication Quarterly* 79, no. 2 (Summer 2002): 310–26.

36. Alexander Hamilton, John Jay, and James Madison, *The Federalist* (1787; repr., New York: Modern Library, 1941), 60–61, 339–41.

37. Kleinberg, *Urban America in Transformation,* 104.

38. For just one example, see *Public Housing, Public Disgrace: Hearings before the Employment and Housing Subcommittee of the Committee on Government Operations, House of*

Representatives, 102nd Congress, May 28–July 31, 1992 (Washington, D.C.: Government Printing Office, 1993).

39. Fred A. Bernstein, "In My Backyard, Please: The Infrastructure Beautiful Movement," *New York Times,* 27 February 2005.

40. Gail Radford, "From Municipal Socialism to Public Authorities: Institutional Factors in the Shaping of American Public Enterprise," *Journal of American History* 90, no. 3 (December 2003): 889.

41. Munnell and Cook, "Financing Capital Expenditures in Massachusetts," 72. For examples of reconciling infrastructure with economic development, see Robert Mier, "Economic Development and Infrastructure: Planning in the Context of Progressive Politics," in Perry, *Building the Public City,* 71–102.

42. Philip Dine, "Both Parties Agree School Buildings Need Repairs, but They Can't Agree on How Much to Spend," *St. Louis Post-Dispatch,* 12 September 1999; Pat Flannery, "School Repairs to Cost $1 Billion," *Arizona Republic* (29 April 2001); Eric Pianin, "Not Fit for Company; Shabby National Parks Are a Monument to a Lack of Money for Maintenance and Repair," *Washington Post Weekly Edition,* 13–19 May 2002, 29; Douglas Jehl, "As Cities Move to Privatize Water, Atlanta Steps Back," *New York Times,* 10 February 2003; Andrew C. Revkin, "Federal Study Calls Spending on Water Systems Perilously Inadequate," *New York Times,* 10 April 2002; Sara Thorson, "Most Arizona Bridges OK, but Many Near Retirement," *Arizona Republic,* 8 December 2002; Ledyard King, "Cost to Fix Crumbling Public Works: $1.6 Trillion," *Arizona Republic,* 5 September 2003; Mary Jo Pitzl, "Grand Canyon in a Jam; Lack of Funding Hurts Tourist Experience, Nature," *Arizona Republic,* 19 May 2003.

Chapter 13: The Paradox of Pork

1. William Safire, *Safire's Political Dictionary* (New York: Random House, 1978), 553.

2. William J. Shultz and M. R. Caine, *Financial Development of the United States* (New York: Prentice-Hall, 1937), 134–37; Aaron Wildavsky, *The New Politics of the Budgetary Process* (Glenview, Ill.: Scott, Foresman, 1988), 43–45.

3. J. Kerwin Williams, *Grants-in-Aid under the Public Works Administration* (1939; repr., New York: AMS Press, 1968), 261; Arthur W. MacMahon, John D. Millett, and Gladys Ogden, *The Administration of Federal Work Relief* (Chicago: Public Administration Service, 1941), 296–300. The Memphis city dog pound, built by WPA, was regarded by some as more comfortable than necessary with "curtained windows, shower baths, spacious runways, individual rooms, and [offering] a daily change of bedding." Douglas L. Smith, *The New Deal in the Urban South* (Baton Rouge: Louisiana State University Press, 1988), 106–7. But Smith concludes that "there were few 'boondoggling' dogpounds."

4. C. W. Short, *Survey of the Architecture of Completed Projects of the Public Works Administration, 1939* (Alexandria, Va.: Chadwick-Healey, 1986), microform; the original is in the National Archives, College Park, Maryland, Still Photographs Division, RG 135.

5. Phoebe Cutler, *The Public Landscape of the New Deal* (New Haven, Conn.: Yale University Press, 1985), 152–53.

6. David E. Sanger, "Sometimes, National Security Says It All," *New York Times,* 7 May 2000.

7. Michael Grunwald, "GOP's Ax No Match for Pork Barrel," *Washington Post,* 3 August 1999; Dan Morgan and Juliet Eilperin, "Mississippi Bounty: Lott, Cochran and Others in

Congress Make Sure Federal Money Continues to Roll in to the State," *Washington Post National Weekly Edition,* 15 November 1999, 31; Lizette Alvarez, "Congress on Record Course for 'Pork,' with Alaska in a Class of Its Own," *New York Times,* 19 November 1999; Billy House and Ginger D. Richardson, "Shadegg Refuses Funds for Ariz. Roads; No 'Pork' for Phoenix Priority," *Arizona Republic,* 29 March 2005; Martin and Susan Tolchin, *To the Victor . . . : Political Patronage from the Clubhouse to the White House* (New York: Vintage, 1972), 218.

8. Tim Weiner, "Lobbying for Research Money, Colleges Bypass Review Process," *New York Times,* 24 August 1999; George Brown, quoted in Gary J. Andres, "Pork Barrel Spending— On the Wane?" *P.S.: Political Science and Politics* 28, no. 2 (June 1995): 207.

9. Dan Morgan, "Along for the Rider: Lawmakers Slip Provisions onto Spending Bills to Win Points with Voters," *Washington Post Weekly Edition,* 19–25 August 2002, 15.

10. Tom Webb, "Government Tries to Peddle Golf Courses," *Miami Herald,* 19 August 1990; Daniel P. Moynihan, "Squeezing the Big Apple: Should the East Pay for S&L Green Out West?" *Washington Post,* 19 August 1990; Leslie Wayne, "Bush 'Corporate Welfare' Attack Faces a Strong Challenge by Lott," *New York Times,* 25 June 2001; Leslie Wayne, "Government's Ship Project Is Christened the U.S.S. Pork," *New York Times,* 18 June 2002.

11. William Ashworth, *Under the Influence: Congress, Lobbies, and the American Pork-Barrel System* (New York: Doubleday, 1981); David Mayhew, *Congress: The Electoral Connection* (New Haven, Conn.: Yale University Press, 1974), 57.

12. Anthony Downs, *An Economic Theory of Democracy* (New York: Harper, 1957), 265–73, 27–28, 96, 108, 113; Mancur Olson, *The Logic of Collective Action* (Cambridge, Mass.: Harvard University Press, 1965), 5–52.

13. Barry Hindess, *Choice, Rationality, and Social Theory* (London: Unwin Hyman, 1988), 5, 43, 108–15; J. Eric Oliver, *Democracy in Suburbia* (Princeton, N.J.: Princeton University Press, 2001), 17; Steven Kelman, *Making Public Policy: A Hopeful View of American Government* (New York: Basic Books, 1987), 250–65; Susan Rose-Ackerman, *Rethinking the Progressive Agenda: The Reform of the American Regulatory State* (New York: Free Press, 1992); Jac C. Heckelman, John C. Moorhouse, and Robert M. Whaples, eds., *Public Choice Interpretations of American Economic History* (Boston: Kluwer, 2000).

14. Mayhew, *Congress,* 6, 15–16; Ross-Ackerman, *Rethinking the Progressive Agenda,* 58.

15. Robert M. Stein and Kenneth N. Bickers, *Perpetuating the Pork Barrel: Policy Subsystems and American Democracy* (New York: Cambridge University Press, 1995), 118–36; John Lancaster, "Bringing Home the Bacon: Lawmakers in Tight Races Are Padding the Federal Budget with Funds for Local Projects," *Washington Post Weekly Edition,* 15–21 April 2002, 10; Morris P. Fiorina, *Congress: Keystone of the Washington Establishment* (New Haven, Conn.: Yale University Press, 1977).

16. Juliet Eilperin, "Projects Multiply as House Leaders Seek to Win Votes; VA-HUD Bill Includes 215 Earmarks," *Washington Post,* 29 July 1999; Carl Hulse, "Spending Bill Is Scorned but Is a Sure Vote-Getter," *New York Times,* 14 February 2003; Dan Morgan, "He Brings Home the Bacon; the House Speaker Earmarks Funds for His Birthplace, Bypassing Procedures Others Must Use," *Washington Post Weekly Edition,* 6–12 June 2005, 13.

17. Stein and Bickers, *Perpetuating the Pork Barrel,* 4–6; Wildavsky, *New Politics of Budgetary Process,* 51; Ashworth, *Under the Influence,* 101–45.

18. Stein and Bickers, *Perpetuating the Pork Barrel,* 78–89; Grunwald, "GOP's Ax."

19. Stein and Bickers, *Perpetuating the Pork Barrel*, 47, 140; Wildavsky, *New Politics of the Budgetary Process*, 295; Herbert Kaufman, *Are Government Organizations Immortal?* (Washington, D.C.: Brookings Institution, 1976).

20. Kaufman, *Are Government Organizations Immortal?* 64; Alexis de Tocqueville, *Democracy in America*, ed. J. P. Mayer and Max Lerner (1835; repr., New York: Harper and Row, 1966), 497–99; Kelman, *Making Public Policy*, 263–70; Kenneth P. Ruscio, "Pork and the Public Interest," *American Prospect* 21 (March 1994): 89–95; Samuel H. Beer, "A Political Scientist's View of Fiscal Federalism," in *The Political Economy of Fiscal Federalism*, ed. Wallace E. Oates (Lexington, Mass.: Lexington Books, 1977), 21–46.

21. "The Roads Are Paved with Pork," *New York Times*, 12 May 2005; Citizens Against Government Waste, http://www.cagw.convio.com.

22. Wildavsky, *New Politics of Budgetary Process*, 422–23.

23. Ross-Ackerman, *Rethinking the Progressive Agenda*, 65–69; Wildavsky, *New Politics of the Budgetary Process*, 226–27; 397–401.

24. Daniel S. Greenburg, "Some Pork Is Good for Us," *Washington Post*, 8 August 1999. Kelly Field, "Colleges Find Road to Riches in Transit Bill," *Chronicle of Higher Education*, 2 September 2005, Al.

25. Alice Goldfarb Marquis, *Art Lessons: Learning from the Rise and Fall of Public Arts Funding* (New York: Basic Books, 1995); Kevin V. Mulcahy, "The NEA and the Reauthorization Process: Congress and Arts Policy Issues," in *America's Commitment to Culture: Government and the Arts*, ed. Kevin V. Mulcahy and Margaret Jane Wyszomirski (Boulder, Colo.: Westview Press, 1995), 169–88; Ann M. Galligan, "The Politicization of Peer-Review Panels at the NEA," in *Paying the Piper: Causes and Consequences of Art Patronage*, ed. Judith Huggins Balfe (Urbana: University of Illinois Press, 1993), 254–70.

26. Ashworth, *Under the Influence*, 175.

27. Thomas R. Wolanin, *Presidential Advisory Commissions from Truman to Nixon* (Madison: University of Wisconsin Press, 1975).

28. Associated Press, "McCain, Stevens Rehearse Battle on Congressional Pork," *Arizona Republic*, 19 July 2003.

29. David S. Sorenson, *Shutting Down the Cold War: The Politics of Military Base Closure* (New York: St. Martin's Press, 1998), 31, 38, 46–47; Marsha Lynn Whicker and Nicholas A. Giannatasio, "The Politics of Military Base Closing: A New Theory of Influence," *Public Administration Quarterly* 21 (Summer 1977): 176–208; Wildavsky, *New Politics of the Budgetary Process*, 160.

30. Sorenson, *Shutting Down the Cold War*, 4; Whicker and Giannatasio, "The Politics of Military Base Closure," 181–82.

31. Whicker and Giannatasio, "The Politics of Military Base Closure," 202; Sorenson, *Shutting Down the Cold War*, 203, 242, 228. Some see an ongoing need for the BRAC: O. Ricardo Pimentel, "Luke AFB Shouldn't Be Special Case," *Arizona Republic*, 27 March 2001.

32. Eric Schmitt, "Military Base Closings: The Overview," *New York Times*, 14 May 2005, Al.

Index

Illustrations are indicated in **boldface** page numbers.